Our Love Affair with Dance

Karen McKinlay Kurnaedy

Copyright © 2022 by Karen McKinlay Kurnaedy
All rights reserved.

No part of this publication may be reproduced or transmitted in any form, or by any means, electronic or mechanical, including photocopying, recording or any information browsing, storage, or retrieval system, without written permission, except for the inclusion of brief quotations in a review.

ISBN
978-1-7781114-1-9 (Hardcover)
978-1-7781114-0-2 (Paperback)
978-1-7781114-2-6 (eBook)

Book design by Irwan Kurnaedy

DEDICATION

This book is dedicated to Magda and Gertrud Hanova, whose love for the dance arts was an inspiration to dancers the world over.

Additionally, I dedicate this book to my husband, Irwan Kurnaedy, for his constant support and talented designing skills. This book would not have been shaped into the satisfying, final product it became without his untiring assistance.

CONTENTS

Introduction i

My Haven: The Hanova School of Modern Creative Dance 1

A Vibrant and Transformative Pedagogy 35

You are Never too Old to Dance 83

A Love Affair with Dance Begins 91

Dance as the Highest Calling 121

The Protective Shield of Terpsichore, Wherein Terpsichore Meets Siva . . 195

Following the Voice of the Muse 335

Dancing Into New Horizons 355

Coming Full Circle with Terpsichore 395

Conclusion 411

INTRODUCTION

This book's primary focus centers on the power and spirituality of the dance told through the life stories of two dance artists. This work is further a visual-cultural archive that contains a significant background of modern dance pedagogy. The intention of the book is to celebrate the sublime and nuanced inner and outer experiences achieved through dancing and leave a significant historical record of two dance artist's accomplishments. Foremost in these pages, you will accompany two sisters who faced many challenges throughout their lives but were sustained and inspired by their love of dance.

Dance artists Magda and Gertrud Hahn came to Vancouver in the late 1950s and opened the first modern dance school in the city. Born at the turn of the 20th century, their lives had already spanned two continents in performance and mentorship. In Vancouver, the sisters started teaching their own unique style of modern dance, which was innovative and ground breaking for its time. They soon garnered a large following of students. Over the next four decades in Vancouver, the Hahn sisters influenced hundreds of lives through their teaching and example.

Through the Hahn sisters' deep conviction that dance is a transformative art form, which all people should experience to feel truly alive, the sisters not only trained dancers who went on to professional careers, but most importantly, joyously shared their message with hundreds of dancers who would never be professionals. Nevertheless, these dancers experienced and felt the deep and satisfying merits of creating dance works and dancing as an artistic experience. The Hahn sisters believed that through the art of movement we may experience a profound discovery of ourselves.

The creation of this work is also an invitation to step into the world of the dancer and vicariously experience the passion and motivation for the dance arts. As Magda and Gertrud Hahn were born in pre-World War I Bohemia, their stories are fascinating from many historical and artistic perspectives. The sisters were dance artists during the golden age of the Weimar Republic in Vienna, Berlin, Paris, Dresden, and Karlsbad during the 1920s. They were privileged to dance with many famous schools of modern dance and ballet during this period.

Their story is also one of Jewish survival before and during WWII. In the early 1930s, the sisters were forced to flee the Nazi takeover of their homeland, Czechoslovakia. They fled to India and spent sixteen years in Bombay, where they participated and were witness to the revival of Indian classical dance during the 1930s and 1940s. The sisters continued to again build new lives moving to London, England in 1949. They finally settled in Vancouver, Canada in 1957, where they taught modern physical culture and dance for almost forty years.

In the telling of the Hahn sisters' story I draw on the methodology of arts-based research. Specifically, the narrative method or narrative inquiry, which "attempts to collaboratively access participants' life experiences and engage in a process of storying and re-storying in order to reveal multi-dimensional meanings and present an authentic and compelling rendering of the data" (Leavy, 2009. p. 27). Including fictional scenes, based on true events told to the author by the Hahn sisters, has further produced a book that goes beyond a conventional biography and enables the reader to step into the lives of the Hahn sisters and experience what life might have been like for them from the early 1900s up until 2002.

As well, this work employs the methodology of embodiment research, which strives to illuminate the transcendent and consciousness raising aspects of dance. Dance and the body as areas of research are often underrepresented among the arts as dance is often considered something ephemeral, abstract, and hard to describe. To address this I have paired exceptional dance photographs with poetic passages, which endeavour to call the reader to an understanding and experience of the art of movement.

As I was one of the Hahn sisters' students, this biography is also partially a memoir and an auto ethnographical view of their lives. Auto ethnography utilizes the autobiographical material of the writer/researcher as data to link to an aspect of the subject and in this case the modern dance culture of Vancouver from 1965 until 2002.

The Hahn sisters' lives are further documented and explored by drawing on historical writings, newspaper clippings, programs kept from dance performances, recorded recollections, and an extensive collection of photographs from the sisters' memorabilia. The photographs beautifully capture moments in the sisters' lives and invite the reader to view and ponder glimpses of a particular and never before seen dance history. Above all, this book is a homage to two ground breaking dance artists who understood that dance as an art form is synonymous with life, in that movement,

Introduction

breath, and the body are what power our life force and existence.

While the early part of this book examines the Hahn sisters' contributions as modern dance pioneers in Vancouver, British Columbia and their contributions to Vancouver's dance community over many years, this work also looks back at the sisters' early lives as dancers in Europe and India and uncovers a unique dance history that has largely been obscured or forgotten. The book also links to other important topics connected to world history and the dance arts, which draw the reader to experience not just the sisters' life stories but also a history which delves into topics of feminism, ethnicity, the disruption and strife of war, and the life of women as artists. All of these topics very much retain their relevance for discussion in today's world as they have in the past century.

Through reading the Hahn sisters' story we may reflect on the many positive changes for women that have occurred throughout the 20th century and especially ponder that the stigma and barriers for women becoming artists of all kinds has diminished. But additionally, the Hahn sisters' story reminds us that many of the same conflicts, such as misogyny, racism, and continuous war fare still exist in the world today, and still need brave women to stand up and live the lives they desire without feeling they must conform to constrictive social norms. The woman as artist has been a forerunner, a powerful instigator, and catalyst in challenging traditional ideas of how women should live their lives. By emphasizing and acknowledging the personal histories of women as artists, we can appreciate that these stories are key to understanding the past in a fuller and more intimate way and to inspire others to forge their own individual, artistic paths for today and the future.

The Hanova Dance School which occurred in many locations and times around the world may be largely forgotten, but a record of the Hahn sisters' lives may be seen as one of many important personal narratives to be read in order to understand the history and formation of the dance we enjoy today. The essence of their story, a message that the Hahn sisters constantly championed, is that dance should be for everyone and has a universal, spiritual, and powerful nature seen in all cultures. Further, exploring the stories of people's lives helps us to reflect on ourselves and make connections to others and to the world. Through reading the story of Magda and Gertrud Hahn, we are able to experience a dance history of Vancouver and other past dance communities around the world that the sisters were part of. These communities may have disappeared but are nevertheless too important to be forgotten.

PART 1

1

MY HAVEN: THE HANOVA SCHOOL OF MODERN CREATIVE DANCE

Our Love Affair with Dance

I have a sensuous memory of my mother, sitting with her feet propped up on the open oven door of our wood stove, reading, with the pure sounds of opera playing on the record player behind her. I remember this music seemed to climb right inside me and release a flow of energy and emotion which whorled through my blood stream until I could no longer contain it. As this power spilled forth, I found myself dancing around the room, lost in the beauty of the music and voices, feeling like I was riding something miraculous. When the song ended, my mother looked up from her book, clapped quietly, and said bravo as she smiled at me.

All through my early life, dancing to the music from that record player was my happy pleasure. The sweet sounds seemed to fill me up and sweep me away into images and stories which I felt compelled to discover through moving my body. My mother, my biggest fan, had enrolled me in ballet classes as a four year old but after some time watching the classes she decided that there was actually little dancing happening and a lot more posturing as teapots and windup dolls. I also had some wonderful years as an eight and nine year old, Ukrainian folk dancing, even though our family had a Scottish background. But it wasn't until I was eleven that I found my 'true' dance home.

I vividly remember my first dance lesson at The Hanova School of Modern Studies in Body Sculpture and the Classical Dance. It was late 1965 and the Hahn sisters' studio was on the top floor of a small building in downtown Vancouver, on the corner of Drake and Seymour. After climbing up a steep flight of stairs to the foyer of the studio, the first thing I saw was a wall covered in beautiful photographs of dancers captured in graceful poses. These pictures seemed to immediately speak to me on a deep level of my consciousness. I felt an intense recognition. Some inner longing I had always felt was made clear by the photographs.

In those first moments, standing on the precipice of awakening, I was overcome with the beauty of movement and dancing in a whole new way. I had a clear revelation that if I could embody this dancing and make it a part of me, I would be able to satisfy an inner yearning that I'd had my whole life thus far. This yearning was to dance in a way that addressed my need to express my creativity through my body. Of course, I wasn't able to articulate these feelings then as I can now. I was simply overjoyed in the recognition of discovering the elusive quality that I knew on some profound level I had been missing. The pictures seemed to stir up memories of the gratification I had experienced dancing alone as a little girl with the record player.

My Haven: The Hanova School of Modern Creative Dance

Unknown Hanova dance students on the Bombay beach, early 1940s.

One might wonder how these static photographs could have had such an impact and moved me so deeply? The black and white and sepia toned pictures were decades old and the dancers wore what seemed like odd costumes and workout garments. But there was no doubt in my mind that these photographs held something special. What I was seeing struck me as a brand new way of regarding movement. From the postures and joyous faces of the dancers in the photographs, I discerned that dancing had the potential to be much more than the outer physical experience of the moving body and could contain essential elements of the inner person. The photographs revealed and illuminated a gracious glimpse of the possibilities that dancing held.

From then on, every time I waited for my dance lesson to begin at the Hanova Dance School on Seymour Street, I would sit on the small bed beneath the photographs and gaze at the pictures. I happily appreciated the images and pondered when and where the photographs had been taken. I wondered who all the young dancers were and especially admired the photographs of the Hahn sisters which I could see had been taken somewhere far way, in a distant time.

Our Love Affair with Dance

Magda and Gertrud in a pose from the Viennese Waltz, Bombay 1941.

The secrets of the photographs were eventually revealed to me. As my curiosity grew I slowly gained the courage to ask the sisters questions about the pictures. They shared that some of the pictures were students from the Hahn sisters' dance school in Karlsbad, Czechoslovakia from the 1920s and some were of their students in India during the 1930s and 1940s. My favourites were photographs of the Hahn sisters in Czechoslovakian costume taken in India. I was always struck by the inner light that seemed to shine forth from their faces in these pictures and readily communicated their delight in dancing.

On this initial lesson, standing self-consciously on the landing, drinking in the pictures, I was greeted warmly by Magda Hahn and told I could either observe or participate in the lesson. I decided to participate and joined several girls in the main room. The girls were bent over from the waist, bouncing forward and undulating their spines. As I copied them, in what I thought then to be very strange movements, I also felt I was starting on a wonderful adventure. These 'strange' movements soon became familiar as did yoga, ballet, modern creative dance, and as Gertrud would say with a twinkle in her eye, the 'worship of the Terpsichorean Arts'. The Hanova School of Modern Studies in Body Sculpture and the Classical Dance would change my existence forever. And so my life impacting relationship began that day with Magda and Gertrud Hahn.

My Haven: The Hanova School of Modern Creative Dance

Unknown Hanova dance students on the Bombay beach sands, 1940s.

It was not until many years later that I came to understand the reason the Czechoslovakian sisters had added 'ova' to their last name Hahn. I found out that in Czech and other Slavic languages 'ova' is routinely added to the last names of all females. The Hahn sisters adopted the Hanova surname in India from 1932 onward, which I think was to emphasize their Czechoslovakian heritage. Interestingly, the region they came from in Bohemia consisted of mostly German speakers and German was their first language and so they both spoke English with a cultured German accent.

I began classes with the Hanova sisters by taking one class a week on Saturday mornings. I took public transit so I usually got to the school a little early and had to wait outside for their arrival. They would zip up in their red Austin-Mini, Magda always at the wheel, as Gertrud had never learned to drive. Myself and the other waiting students would respectfully greet them and help them carry their bags or equipment up to the studio. There was an unspoken atmosphere of reverence for the sisters which I quickly adhered to. The Hahn sisters, with very few words, managed to communicate in what seemed to me a strong and firm manner that they would not settle for any behaviour that they deemed was unmannerly or disruptive in their classes. To the young girl, I was, they appeared to be royalty. I somehow knew to be silent and attentive.

Magda, the driver, with the Hanova red Austin Mini, mid 1960s.

I soon learned that the sisters had strong opinions about 'the dance' as they called it and could lecture about their beliefs with authority and conviction. Having grown up in the early 1900s, the sisters seemed to teach their classes with an order and discipline from this bygone era and demanded our full attention. They had a serious presence and I always had a bit of awe mixed in with my appreciation for them. There was never idle chatter between participants during their classes and the sisters expected one's complete effort and concentration throughout the lesson.

In discussing the quite uncompromising and strict demeanour of the Hanova sisters' teaching, I want to convey that this didn't mean their classes were stuffy or oppressive. Over their long reign in Vancouver, the Hanova sisters were popular and in demand as dance teachers. Students seemed to accept the sisters' unwavering focus on the dance and the sometimes stern atmosphere of their dance classes as a European standard and so students stayed in order to reap the many benefits offered.

Gertrud, always the passenger, with the Hanova red Austin Mini, mid 1960s.

I imagine that one of the reasons that the Hahn sisters attracted so many students initially was that the sisters' classes were quite unique and very different from other dance classes offered in Vancouver in the late 1950s and early 1960s. The sisters claimed to be the first modern dance studio in the city, which in itself presented something original to the Vancouver dance scene. They also brought the mysteries of the east in philosophy and practice, which were mostly unknown by mainstream Canadians at this time. Consequently, their classes held something of the exotic as they blended their experiences of yoga, Indian dance, European modern dance, and ballet into a cohesive whole. As well, the sisters added the European movement philosophies of E. Jacques-Dalcroze and Rudolph Laban. These movement philosophies in counterpoint to ballet's focus on uniform steps and set movements instead addressed the inner experiences of the dancer by focusing on the feelings produced when dancing in moments. Pupils were encouraged to express their internal and individual person in the movements they produced while improvising and in so doing satisfy their creative and artistic needs. At the Hanova Dance School improvisation was emphasized as a means of self-discovery and self expression but also as a way of developing new choreographic ideas.

So despite the somewhat authoritarian atmosphere, for me personally, the most endearing quality of the Hanova sisters was the special way they had of making 'you' feel you were a real dance artist and that you were contributing to making the world more beautiful through movement. When you went home you were just an ordinary person again, but at the studio for those brief hours you were part of a creative and inspirational atmosphere. And despite what seemed to me as old world, European discipline, Gertrud and Magda were generous with praise for everyone's achievement and had a knack of drawing out of each student their movement strengths and talents. Plus the rigorous and exacting classes really paid off. Students who took the classes to heart inevitably saw continuous improvement in their flexibility, balance, and ability to create movement that had depth and variety. The Hanova sisters got results.

In 1965, the Hanova School of Modern Studies in Body Sculpture and the Classical Dance was well attended by students of all ages and both sexes. I observed that whole families took classes and were Hanova converts which could include the mother, father, and children.

The Hanova sisters showcased the achievement of their students by renting a theatre once a year or using their studio space to present a recital in which all of their students participated in some capacity. From the inception of the Hanova School in Vancouver in 1957, the sisters consistently presented their work to the public in lecture demonstrations, performances, and television appearances. The sisters believed that presenting dance studies and new choreography to an audience was part of being a dance artist and polishing a work for performance showed discipline and evidence of the growth of their students, despite the students not being professionals.

Each class started with an individual curtsy and greeting towards the sisters. Magda and Gertrud always participated wholeheartedly in the classes and demonstrated movements or exercises with vitality. As a child I never guessed or wondered too much about the sisters' ages. To me they were adults, never old ladies. They seemed timeless. They did not exhibit any signs of old age. They were vibrant and energetic. It wasn't until the 1990s that I learned that the sisters were both over sixty years old when I started with them in the mid 1960's.

After our formal acknowledgement of the sisters with our curtsy, the Hanova classes always started with a loosening up of the body, usually led by Gertrud, which was a gentle shaking and flexing of each body part from head down to toe to music. Then we transitioned to yoga exercises also led by Gertrud. She would sit on a low, raised dais, when demonstrating yoga positions, wearing her signature black leotard and black dance skirt. Supple and very flexible, Gertrud could always bend farther and lie flatter than any of her students in the yoga positions.

With her strong dynamics, Gertrud was inspirational. I always felt it a privilege to watch her in action and try to duplicate that special something she exuded before executing any asana or yoga pose. She would take a breath, lift her torso, and visibly pause before flowing into a position. Gertrud would summon, what seemed to me as a child, some magical, inner force, which imbued each posture with an impressive presence.

The yoga portion of the classes consisted of mastering many asanas to encourage flexibility, balance, good posture, and improved strength. After the warm up and yoga exercises with Gertrud, Magda would lead ballet exercises at the barre. She was less stern than Gertrud and seemed to like children more but nevertheless in no uncertain terms demanded we do our very best. Magda always emoted a great inner joy when leading any movement activities and one could tell from her voice and expression that she adored 'the dance' as the sisters called it. As Magda demonstrated barre work, développé or rond de jambe, I remember she would pull up her dance skirt slightly to reveal her long, elegantly shaped legs so that students could clearly see how to execute the movement. Magda markedly loved teaching ballet technique and it was only as an older student that I found out that both Gertrud and Magda had studied and performed with the Vienna Opera Ballet and Magda with the Paris Opera Ballet in the 1920s.

After our barre routine, we might do ballet technique au milieu (in the middle of the floor) to practice jumps and turns. Each class could be different. But there was usually the basic warm up, yoga, ballet barre, moving across the floor to explore a multitude of ways to travel and jump, kinetic explorations, based on Rudolph Laban's work, learning or creating some kind of choreographic study or dance, and at the end of the class, a group improvisation.

The kinetic studies often focused on specific Hanova inspired movements, which the sisters said were based on the figure of eight they had learned through Indian dance. These were rounded, flowing movements such as the front and side impulse and the tortillé. We might in addition spend time exploring Laban's movement elements which are time, space, effort, and flow, or Dalcroze type rhythms with music or a drum. The Hanova sisters especially stressed 'center control' which was a method of flexing the back out and then tucking under the pelvis to attain good posture and line.

Magda and Gertrud would always collaborate on the choreographic portion of the class. Although the sisters liked to recreate specific pieces and studies from their past, they mostly choreographed new work for each group or individual. This choreography would be worked on for many months and was never rushed. Performance of a finished piece was seen as important but never overshadowed by the idea that the moments dancing in the class were foremost and were adding to a student's present sense of creativity and expression.

The classes usually ended with my favourite part, improvisation, which could be accompanied by a cymbal, a drum, verbal instructions, or music. While improvising, the dancers would freeze at the sound of two distinct drum beats, and then a name would be called out which allowed that one person to dance alone as in an imaginary spot light. We also could be directed to move in various ways. For example, Gertrud might say, "Only move your hands, your head, your eyes." Magda might add, "Everyone turn, whirl, tilt, demonstrate a side impulse, or a bound flow, or lead only with the sternum." Gertrud might interject, "Use strength, or softness, resist gravity, or assist gravity, flow freely across the room, or make a twisted shape or a small shape." This improvising allowed for individuality and expression as each dancer performed the movements in his or her own way.

At rehearsals before a performance, the sisters would gather all of their students together at the studio to run through the programme. I was always more than happy to sit quietly on the sidelines for the hours it took and observe the pieces that the other Hanova students were presenting. I marvelled at the distinct movements and style of each student's presentation. Then at the end of the rehearsal to my delight, all of the students, young and old, were invited to improvise together.

Karen: I stand motionless, waiting for my turn to dance. Others swirl around me, slowly or quickly, gracefully traversing the space, expressing their individuality so beautifully. We are dancers, together, creating a kaleidoscope of shapes, moods, impressions, and gestures. I hear my name called and gratefully release myself from being stationary. I inhale vigorously and simultaneously stretch my rib cage. I shoot my arms over my head, toss back my hair, and expand my diaphragm, opening myself to the energy of the dance. I listen to my inner voice which connects to my limbs and torso and brings forth a rush of movement that has not been planned or formulated. The motions are just suddenly there. I feel the expanse of my body, the height, the width, the extent of my glorious reach. I launch into open spaces, gliding, twisting, and turning between the immobile dancers, creating and weaving a unique pattern of arms and legs that lifts my spirit. I feel a deep sense of belonging, both to the dance and this group of dancers. At the Hanova studio, I allow myself to overflow, express my inner longing, and transcend the mere physical. These are moments of ineffable interconnectivity and communion.

At this time in my life, I knew almost nothing of dance history or movement theory. I eagerly learned about the origins of ballet, modern dance, Indian dance, and about modern dance pioneers such as Mary Wigman, Rudolph Laban, and Isadora Duncan. The Hanova sisters rich and varied dance background all contributed to captivating lessons and conversations.

Over the many years I took classes with the sisters, the details of each class might vary but each lesson would always retain the core structure that stressed yoga to foster flexibility and balance, ballet barre work to impart solid technique, and the dance elements of Rudolph Laban to give students a framework for choreography and an understanding of the components of dance. Laban's, (see Preston, 1963), elements or movement principles are contained in sixteen basic movement themes. They are the awareness of the body, weight and time, space, the flow of the weight of the body in space and time, adaptation to a partner, the awareness of basic effort actions, occupational rhythms, of shape in movement, transitions between the basic effort actions, orientation in space, the combination of shapes and efforts, elevation, the awakening of group feeling, group formations, and the expressive qualities of movement.

But most importantly, the core philosophy at the heart of Laban's teaching, that dance is for everyone in some capacity and that dance can revolutionize society, was echoed and emphasized in the Hanova dance philosophy. The Hanova sisters were clearly influenced by Laban's ideas. First, through Gertrud's study with Mary Wigman, who was Laban's student, and later when they studied with Rudolph Laban and Sigurd Leeder directly in London in the 1950s. The Hanova sisters accepted a student into their school based on the student's enthusiasm and desire to dance, not on the student's ability or star quality. Dance historian McCaw (2011) informs us:

> Laban's specific focus on the human body in terms of its capabilities created a concept in which the individual being is central. ... His conception of dance as a practice for all people meant a shift away from the dancer as a conservatorie-trained and technically skilled practitioner, and instead he sought to foster an engagement of an individual's body, mind, and spirit in the act of dancing. (p. 63)

After the warm up and bar exercises, for a change of pace, my class of preteen, Saturday morning, dance students might write down information Gertrud or Magda shared about a famous artist, poet, composer, or dancer. We had in depth discussions about many subjects. I remember Gertrud and Magda showing us many books about art and dance and we often listened to many pieces of music as the sisters identified the composers.

I felt quite ignorant about my lack of knowledge concerning the arts and remember the Hahn sisters remarking on more than one occasion that they thought the Canadian education system seemed to be leaving out what was most important, an understanding and appreciation for humanities creative and expressive pursuits. I gratefully listened to what the sisters had to say, as I knew I had finally found what I'd been looking for, a circle of kindred spirits, who loved dance and the fine arts as much as I did.

Looking back, I realize how significant this was for me. I was on the verge of transitioning from childhood to teen and finding a place where I could mature, belong, and study something I loved so much as dance, with such unique and I see now, feminist role models, strongly shaped my values and the adult I was to become. I remember every lesson being a special hour which built up my sense of self and fostered my self esteem.

My Haven: The Hanova School of Modern Creative Dance

Karen Wenn (Kurnaedy) at the Hanova Dance School on Seymour Street, demonstrating the yoga position, the tree, 1966.

During classes with the Hanova sisters, I recall being very impressed when they demonstrated or danced set concepts or movements to illustrate what they hoped we would kinaesthetically absorb and later interpret in our own way. It was fascinating to watch them as they transitioned instantaneously from verbal instructions as the teacher, to showing the movement as the artist. The Hanova sisters' movements were never mere motions or gestures. I always felt that the sisters' movements conveyed powerful dynamics that held wonder.

I especially remember Gertrud could readily change a simple pose into a body filled with purpose and strength. Her eyes could suddenly contain mystery and a veiled secret. Her head would tilt to the side and convey majesty. As a young girl, observing and learning these principles of dynamics, I was absolutely engaged. As a Hanova student, I absorbed what really cannot be put into words adequately, that the dance artist has only to call upon their inner muse to manifest this powerful animation.

Through the Hanova sisters, I came to understand that the dancer holds this vital energy in his or her body which stems from the core or center as Isadora Duncan, the mother of modern dance professed. I came to know that this vibrancy dwells within us, waiting to be accessed for our art. The unfolding of this energy in dance seems to be the most important element the dance artist can utilize to make their work come alive, be authentic, and embodied.

At the Vancouver Hanova Dance Studio, the students were not professional dancers nor were most of them ever going to be professional dancers, but the students returned every week seeking and finding inspiration. The Hanova sisters were our guides to unlock our creativity and passion. As students, we were always encouraged to create our own movements and choreography and through these movements find within ourselves a confirmation of our inventiveness, a release of emotion, and a mode of expression.

Choreography and kinetic studies were inspired by Laban movement elements, stories, poetry, music, and the individual and personal interests of students. The Hanova sisters loved choreographing studies which could incorporate geometrical designs, yoga exercises, or ballet technique. Looking back at old programs from the 1960s through to the 1990s, I note the gong and drum were used to accompany dances, poetry was voiced with dances, and music was selected from a wide selection of diverse composers such as Chopin, Tchaikovsky, Debussy, Bach, Schubert, Grieg, Satie, Handel, Gould, Previn, and Shankar.

The Hanova sisters also taught outside of Vancouver and were invited to teach dance at the Okanagan Summer School of the Arts in Penticton several times during the 1960s through to the 1980s. I note from a brochure kept by the sisters from 1967 that they offered six separate classes to various age groups. Their lessons were advertised as "designed to promote health and happiness through creativity and body fitness." The sisters said they enjoyed travelling to the Okanagan during the hot summer months. Magda always drove them in their red Austin Mini and she would often remark that she loved the heat in the Okanagan as it reminded her of India.

My Haven: The Hanova School of Modern Creative Dance

The cover of the Okanagan Summer School of the Arts brochure, 1984, featuring a photograph taken in the 1960s of Hanova dance students.

Magda, with students improvising outdoors. Okanagan Summer School of the Arts Penticton, July 1967.

Magda: Validation. Important validation is provided while the students are moving, turning, posing, and transitioning from one movement to another. Gerti and I shine forth our positive regard to all. The students bask in our approval. The nods of their heads, their smiles, and looks of satisfaction proclaim their engagement in the dance. Our students are manifesting their body learning. We have transmitted our art, from our bodies into their bodies, communicated in silent dance conversations which have disclosed the beauty of movement, to form a mutual declaration of our delight and adoration for the dance arts. I feel reciprocal satisfaction. The mentor basking in the glow of the student's validation. Shared pleasure in creativity, come to fruition. The dancers' bodies interpret and reflect back what they have absorbed. Unspoken, but voiced in their 'presentness'.

What power the teacher holds. Perhaps not always realizing the delicate, fragile ego that may rest in his or her hands. The short and tender impressionable years of youth when one is most open to learning should be cherished by the teacher and pupil. The learner only wishing for acceptance, inclusion, and being part of something that imparts proof that one is progressing in this thing called life. For the student, praise and encouragement are like rain on a parched landscape. The welcome moisture of validation can heal dry and thirsty souls and impart courage, confidence, and aid in the fulfillment of dreams.

Sonja Christjansen in a pose from Seagull, 1960s.

An article from the Penticton Herald highlighted the dance classes and final performance by the students who attended the Hanova dance sessions at the Okanagan Summer School for the Arts in July 1967. I note how dancing bare foot seemed unusual to this reporter.

> SOCKS OUT Socks, however, were out for the Hanova sisters' creative dance group which improvised barefoot on stage. Gertrud Hanova introducing the group, said hard work and discipline are essential for perfection of the modern dance, based on a basic set of movements.
>
> Nine students from the summer school class demonstrated the basic movements, warming up exercises, and improvisations. The more elaborate dances were left to three students from the sisters' Vancouver studio. Barry Austin, Elizabeth Terry, and Astrid Fisher-Credo danced as seagulls, gossiping women, and construction workers.
>
> Miss Hanova said the dances are not mimes, although miming does enter them. They are expressions of the dancer's feelings she said. Under the guidance of the two sisters, who came from Czechoslovakia, dancers learn which movement(s) to use for what expression. Miss Hanova said although most of the summer school students had never taken dance before they are now confident enough to appear on stage. (Before) They were too self-conscious to use their bodies she said.

On December 9, 1967, the Hanova sisters rented the York Theatre in Vancouver for a performance titled Studies in Exercises and The Creative Dance. An article promoting the performance from The Province newspaper, December 7, 1967, highlights the Hanova sisters' dance philosophy and the health benefits achieved from exercising. Excerpts from the article, 'A new philosophy of beauty given', state:

> Through a disciplined approach to body movement the various facets of beauty can be awakened in all women, and can lead ultimately to a totally new vision of life. That's the philosophy of the Hanova sisters, whose lives are devoted to the promotion

of health and happiness through creativity and body fitness.

In this highly mechanized age, the Hanova sisters believe it is of the utmost importance to keep mind and body healthy. "It is wonderful to see people who could hardly bend suddenly realize that they can," said Gertrud. "They have control over their bodies and then they start to dance."

Many students of the Hanova sisters begin as "just physically stiff and mentally tense," but eventually they lose their inhibitions and shyness. "We let them start by loosening up physically and mentally and then we go into the exercises."

Once body control is mastered, Gertrud explained, students feel able to tackle other physical and mental problems because they have disciplined themselves.

HANOVA PRESENTS

Students of three age groups - Seniors, Intermediate and Juniors
in a Performance of

Studies in EXERCISES and THE CREATIVE DANCE
York Theatre, 639 Commercial   Phone: 255-0141

SATURDAY, DECEMBER 9, 1967 – 8:30 p.m.

Included in the Programme will be Dance-Theatre Compositions

'Phantasmagoria'

'Rustic Bohemia'

Tickets available now:
HANOVA STUDIO - 1242 Seymour St., Vancouver 2, B.C.
PHONE: 685-5016
681-8088

Prices: $2.00, $1.50

Programme card from the York Theatre, December 9, 1967.

This programme began with a demonstration of Exercises, then Kinetics, which included a demonstration of Flow, Impulse, and Figure of 8, Basic Movements, Gravity Movements, Improvisations with Percussion, and Three Space Designs. Next on the programme was a dance-theatre composition called Phantasmagoria which consisted of five dances: Moods of Nature, Sundial, Stupid Phantoms, Illusionary Night, and Stone age or? The last piece on the program was Rustic Bohemia inspired by the area in Czechoslovakia where the Hanova sisters were born. I was in several pieces for this programme but especially remember Rustic Bohemia as I found the story and music so beautiful and dynamic.

Gertrud: For Rustic Bohemia we have created a charming and nostalgic dance composition. Nostalgic, in that Magda and I have choreographed this work based on our early memories of our homeland. The dance story centers on the Vltava River, the longest river within Czechoslovakia, which runs southeast along the Bohemian Forest. Selected works by the renowned Czech composers Dvorak and Smetana provide the music. Specifically, The Moldau by Smetana provides the majority of the soundscape and The Moldau is the German name for the Vltava River. Every student in our school was in this production, from the youngest to the oldest.

The dance-theatre composition, Rustic Bohemia, has separate dances which smoothly transition from one to the other. First, Oreads, Maidens of the Valley or water nymphs, make the Vltava River flow. In this opening dance, two dancers create the impression of a river by laying down long, shimmering, blue and green fabric strips to represent the water. Next, peasant girls dance by the river and a nanny takes her charge for a stroll by the shore in a huge, old-fashioned, baby buggy. After this, water nymphs and dryads, which are enchanted trees, protect the water way. Workers harvest the fields beside the river's edge and a goose girl herds her flock nearby. Gossipping women stop to chatter and more peasant girls come to carry water away for washing and cooking. As the music flows to its end, the water dryads emerge once again to protect the river and village as night gently falls.

Magda: This was such a successful evening of dance. Phantasmagoria, an English word defined as "a sequence of real or imaginary images like those seen in a dream" aptly describes this group of dances, which we hope poked fun at certain subjects but also showed the dance to be something ethereal and open to interpretation by the audience.

The last work on the programme, Rustic Bohemia, fulfilled all my expectations. Czechoslovakian composers provided the perfect music for telling this dance story. And it is worth noting that choosing beautiful music does not automatically guarantee a successful dance. The music may inspire an idea, yes, but then if anything is to come of the idea, one must look beyond the music and decide what exactly as the choreographer one wishes to communicate. So essentially the music remains less important at the beginning of the creation. The dance concept must come first. Later, after the ideas have been confirmed, if the music is well chosen and fits the intention, the music will partner the dance, not overpower the project, assisting the dancers to share the story or ideas of the choreographer. As a dance is formulated or unfolds in its choreography, one can only marvel at the mystery of artistic creation.

Forming this work gave me a wistful yearning for the happiness we experienced long ago in our homeland. We deliberately tried not to be sentimental. As the river is part of our heritage, real scenes of life by the river came to our minds. But I did not expect all the feelings that arose. I did not expect the memories that surfaced. It was a long time ago that we lived in Bohemia and yet where one is born and lived one's early life stays with one on many levels. We have never returned to Bohemia, to Karlsbad or Teplitz, and now probably will never go back because of the devastation of the war and the terrible hold communism has on Czechoslovakia.

But this dance is a success because in Rustic Bohemia we created a graceful picture of life long ago that transcends politics and war. We showed the everlasting and deep tranquillity

My Haven: The Hanova School of Modern Creative Dance

of the river and the fertile earth, human drama, emotion, and shared folly. We explored how nature can be a wild and graceful creature, perpetually and permanently present in the land. This dance delves beyond national borders and home lands and celebrates lost and found memories which we can enjoy where ever we are living now.

The following newspaper story captures the tremendous impact the Hanova sisters had on one individual who took classes at their Vancouver dance studio in the 1960s. The story relates how Beverly Crook (Babette) quit her office job to become a full time Indian dancer. This article, published in February of 1968, from the Woman's section of the Province newspaper, highlights the transformative qualities of dance. The Hanova sisters are mentioned in the article as Beverly Crook's inspirational teachers.

A Hanova student in The Province newspaper, February 15, 1968.

Our Love Affair with Dance

The caption reads, "The dream of an office girl—she quits 9 to 5 job to be an Indian dancer". "From competent office girl ...to exotic Indian dancer" by Maggie Wilkinson. An excerpt reads:

> The Indian costume, featuring Punjabi trousers and skirt with a choli top, was copied by Babette from an authentic Indian stage costume belonging to her teachers, Gertrud and Magda Hanova. Babette channels much of the Hanova sisters' philosophy when she states, "Indian dancing seeks to arouse the inner consciousness, it has a spiritual fervour that seems to be lacking in our Western dance art. It is essentially experiencing this oneness with what you are doing," she said. "You dance for yourself and the audience enjoys this through you, because you are able to convey your enjoyment to them. There seems to be a tremendous depth in this dancing and, to me, it contains all forms of art and philosophy. In Indian dancing you are not trying to be anything other than what you are—it is really just being yourself."

Late 1960s brochure for The Hanova School featuring Magda and Gertrud as photographers and Hanova students posing at Stanley Park.

My Haven: The Hanova School of Modern Creative Dance

Hanova students pose on the Stanley Park shore.
From left to right: Judy Philippo, Monica Ragetli, Mary Philippo, Beth Minsky, Karen Wenn (Kurnaedy), Tineke Ragetli, 1968.

Gertrud: The girls from the Saturday class have come to the park to pose amongst the trees, rocks, and ocean water. They spontaneously move into different positions, and then when Magda and I see an interesting configuration, we ask them to freeze and we snap a picture. Directing the dancers to experiment and improvise for these photographs has shaped the final compositions into something original but reminiscent in some ways of the Weimar era when nature and the dance were very much partners. The end result is an aesthetic co-creation between the photographer, the dancers, and the landscape.

We are so fortunate that we came to live in Vancouver. It is a place where the arts and the elements may conjoin in a glorious fusion. Vancouver is a place blessed with a climate that allows year round enjoyment of the mountains, parks, ocean, and forests. In taking these photographs, we are creating lasting images of the beauty of the body united with the natural formations surrounding the city.

Beth Minsky and Judy Philippo jumping on the Stanley Park sea wall, 1968.

Judy Philippo and Karen Wenn (Kurnaedy), Stanley Park, 1968.

My Haven: The Hanova School of Modern Creative Dance

Karen Wenn (Kurnaedy), Stanley Park seaside, 1968.

Posing in the Pacific Ocean, Stanley Park, 1968.
Note. From left to right: Judy Philippo, Beth Minsky, Karen Wenn (Kurnaedy), Monica Ragetli, Mary Philippo, Tineke Ragetli.

Hanova students posing on the beach rocks. Stanley Park, 1968.
Note. From left to right: Monica Ragetli, Karen Wenn (Kurnaedy), Beth Minsky, Judy Philippo, Mary Philippo, Tineke Ragetli.

My Haven: The Hanova School of Modern Creative Dance

On the Stanley Park sea wall, 1968. The fish jump demonstrated by Judy Philippo, Tineke Ragetli, Mary Philippo, and Beth Minsky.

Hanova students pose with grass and rocks. Stanley Park, 1968. Note. Monica Ragetli, Tineke Ragetli, Judy Philippo, Beth Minsky, Karen Wenn (Kurnaedy), and Mary Philippo.

Our Love Affair with Dance

Hanova students at Stanley Park, 1968.
From left to right: Mary Philippo, Beth Minsky, Karen Wenn (Kurnaedy), Tineke Ragetli, Judy Philippo, Monica Ragetli. Gertrud Hanova in the foreground.

Hanova students pose on the ocean rocks, Stanley Park, 1968.
From left to right: Judy Philippo, Mary Philippo, Monica Ragetli, Karen Wenn (Kurnaedy), Tineke Ragetli, Beth Minsky.

My Haven: The Hanova School of Modern Creative Dance

Hanova students pose on the beach rocks, 1968.
From left to right: Karen Wenn (Kurnaedy), Beth Minsky,
Mary Philippo, Judy Philippo, Monica Ragetli, Tineke Ragetli.

Magda: We feel we are capturing some striking images. Without words the students flow into position, eager to embrace the environmental spaces. Only later after the film has been developed, do we really see what we have caught with our lens. Miraculously, we have recorded some remarkable artistic representations of the body set in nature. Moments of impressive expression, which richly represent the dance philosophy of the Hanova School.

These photographs of the dancing body have their own aesthetic and symbolic value as an art form. I am particularly struck by how natural formations in the landscape come alive and are seen in new ways when partnered with the posing and artfully positioned body. The dancers almost seem to become part of the scenery as they merge with the elements.

Our Love Affair with Dance

Photograph and Advertisement for The Physiological and Psychological Effect of Modern Studies in Exercises and The Creative Dance from The West Ender newspaper, November 19, 1969.

Pupil of The Hanova School of Creative Dance rehearses for the interesting program of Education and Entertainment which will be presented at 8:00 p.m., Saturday, November 29 at the Metro Theatre, 1370 South West Marine Drive, groups of various ages will demonstrate exercises including Yoga, Kinetics, and the Creative Dance with the aim of achieving physical and mental well-being.

Magda: Our next production, this November, will be at the Metro Theatre. Almost all of the dance presentations and kinaesthetic studies are new creations for this year's students. For this performance, we have focused on the physiological and psychological effect of modern studies in exercises and the creative dance in which we stress the many benefits to be gained through dancing for all aspects of a person. We have also focused on pairing poetry with movement for this programme. Students have chosen poems that were inspirational for them and we have co-choreographed movements which complement the spoken words. These dances are imaginative and inventive, with unexpected outcomes.

My Haven: The Hanova School of Modern Creative Dance

This programme on November 19, 1969 at the Metro Theatre presented Exercises and Kinetics which included Peripheral and Zenith, Coordination and Balance, Sketch, and Improvisations. The dance compositions included From Foreign Lands and People, Seagull, Enigma, Marigold, The Tree, The Coin, Temple Dance, The Peacock, Country Style, 1920, Legend, Creation, Infant Prodigies, 3 in Unison, Rhymes, Pranks, and Generations Meet. This was an extensive and diverse program with over twenty presentations which highlighted each dance students strengths and interests.

Karen Wenn (Kurnaedy) posing from The Coin, 1969.

Trudy Philippo in Seagull.
Music by Frederic Chopin. Etude Op. 10 No. 1 in C major.

Gertrud: Seagull is a special dance to keep in our repertoire. This piece was first conceived as part of a full production called "Oh, Sailor" in 1965. The choreography is an expression and impression of a seagull and was inspired from our watching the seagulls that love to swoop down to our window sill looking for food. Building on our observations, we added movements from the Indian dance and Dalcroze exercises. The sound of seagulls squawking was recorded and plays at the beginning of the piece as the dancer enters with a halting, skittery gait on raised toe. As the dancer stops mid stage, moving her head and neck from side to side, the music of Chopin's melodious Etude begins. The dancer now takes flight as her arms open to become wings. She follows the glorious piano music, soaring through space, airborne and uplifted, gliding, floating, and hovering. The piece ends with the seagull settling into a final calm and peaceful nesting stance. Two minutes of beauty...

My Haven: The Hanova School of Modern Creative Dance

As a Hanova student, I will always remember the 1960s ended with this special performance of diverse dances at the Metro Theatre. In 1969, I was fifteen and despite the many sometimes negative influences of the 'swinging sixties' on my early teenage years, I still retained my high regard and ebullience in dancing at the Hanova School. I had somehow learned to compartmentalize the ups and downs going on in my life and would put them aside when I climbed the dance studio stairs. I therefore came to my lessons single-mindedly and determined to dance wholeheartedly and enjoy the creative atmosphere of choreography and improvisation. The Hanova Dance School seemed like a separate world where there were no problems or worries. My only task while there was to be present, receptive, and to focus on the joy and wonder of dancing.

Magda loved capturing dance images, late 1960s.

Our Love Affair with Dance

2

A VIBRANT AND TRANSFORMATIVE PEDAGOGY

In the 1970s, the Hanova sisters' dance school continued to flourish. The classes were still unwaveringly Hanova in nature in that they retained the sisters' solid core of exercises, barre work, kinetics, and improvisation. The dance pieces in the 1970s were again unique and infused with the Hanova sisters' early dance experiences reminiscent of the 1920s Weimar German body culture, which stressed a beauty, flow, and naturalness of movement. But the Hanova style of modern dance cannot be so simply labelled or defined as European in view of the fact that the sisters spent sixteen years in India, where they studied Indian dance and culture. The Hanova system, as the sisters called their brand of modern dance, was a rich blend of all their dance experiences from the east and the west. I note that many of the most memorable pieces choreographed by the sisters in the 1970s were quite different from one another, and for example, could be based on Laban movement elements, Indian dance, or ballet. Choreography was created for the individual student's personal movement qualities, the student's choice of subject matter, or the student's need for a deep expression of emotion. Accordingly, dances in the 1970s diversely expressed grief, female strength, spirituality, a pondering of the human condition, or the wonders of nature.

The Hanova sisters' choreography deliberately did not stress what they deemed the prettiness of ballet but instead focused on each dancer's need to tell their own story. For that reason, the choreography was distinctive, original, and sometimes appeared idiosyncratic, in that it could seem peculiar or dated by the 1970s standards of modern dance. But the choreography was always a reflection of the individual dancer's character and these dancers were foremost dancing what they needed, which was to fulfill themselves in the art form. The Hanova performances were consequently an interesting mixture of choreographed ideas, which might convey a story or theme with emotion, humour, or strong dynamics. Each dance was an individual expression of who each dancer was. Performances in the 1970s were striking, passionate, and personal, focusing on a student's need to express through the dance arts. The Hanova sisters continued to stick to what they believed in and ignored trends or copying others in the dance world.

From The Province June 1970. 'Pied pipers of the dance …where they go students follow' by Nikki Moir.

This article promoted the Hanova sisters' Summer Dance Intensive which was held in Kelowna in July 1970 and mentions that 10 Vancouver students are following the sisters to Kelowna for the dance studies. I was one of the students who attended. Gweneth Lloyd, founding director and choreographer of the Winnipeg Ballet, loaned the Hanova sisters her studio in Kelowna for the sessions. The dancers from Vancouver roomed at the home of Ann Briggs, a friend of the sisters and fellow lover of the dance arts.

The article also discusses the curriculum of the Hanova sisters' Vancouver school and the benefits gained through dancing for their pupils.

> Their Vancouver students go in age from 5 to 75. Both male and female. In fact they have at least one family where the daughter started, mother followed, then they persuaded dad. The latter, a reluctant dragon, found he liked it. It made him feel better. Indeed when he had his last check-up with his doctor, he was pronounced in better shape than ever.

A Vibrant and Transformative Pedagogy

Hanova Summer Dance Intensive, Kelowna, July 1970. Karen Wenn (Kurnaedy), Helene Fuldauer, and her young daughter improvise outdoors.

Gertrud: Our Kelowna Dance Intensive has been a great success. I note the girls from Vancouver showed, as we say in German, die Verbesserung, a betterment or refinement through the full day lessons. And most importantly, I witnessed a transition, for some, to a new level of execution in which they were able to externalize their inward experiences as authentic bodily expression in the choreography.

Magda: I was so happy to have the full two weeks, whole days, to work with the Vancouver girls. After our morning extensive barre work and exercises, the students in the intermediate/

advanced class showed immediate improvement in strength, flexibility, and correct alignment. The afternoon concentration on choreography, which was presented at the end of the session in a well attended public performance, was not the whole focus for me. Rather, to see the students come away at the end of the two weeks with a sense of what it might have been like to dance as we did in Europe, wholly dedicated, encircled by their youth, and all that is dancing, that was my reward!

Posing in front of the Canadian School of Ballet in Kelowna, 1970. From left to right: Gertrud Hanova, Beth Minsky, Karen Wenn (Kurnaedy), Mary Philippo, Judy Philippo. Sitting: an unknown dancer, Lisa Briggs, Sara Ratner.

Hanova dance students taking their bows after a studio performance at the Seymour Street Hanova Dance School, 1970. Gertrud (far right), Magda (middle).

As I moved into my older teens, my commitment to dance grew. I went from one class a week with the Hanova sisters to three. I continued with the large, Saturday morning, group class of students my age, joined the Hanova production group, and also took private lessons. The Hanova sisters generously gave me a scholarship each year to help pay for my extra lessons.

Before showing any choreographed work at a performance, the sisters always made a point of educating their audience about their system of modern dance and would share a prepared statement explaining their philosophy. Here is a short excerpt I found in a program from 1977 which is a good example of what was generally shared, usually by Gertrud, at Hanova performances, especially in the 1970s.

> Modern Dance is a creative Art form basically arising from the need to express through movements the emotion and ideas that are the experience of every human being. Our students are non-professionals but have to undergo much the same training as professionals, only in a very much lesser degree. It lies within our nature to approach everything with an enquiring attitude. To us, each class and each student contributes to the opening of new vistas. We believe true guidance can only be given by fully perceiving the personality of the student and

the problems that emerge. Technique is essential, but it should never become greater than oneself. The unity of the physical and spiritual has been our guide throughout our teaching.

Programme for the Hanova School of Modern Studies in Exercises and the Creative Dance Studio Performance, June 1971.

This studio performance in June of 1971 featured students demonstrating exercises and kinetics or qualities of movement which included Swings, We Move Through Space and Time, Dimensions, and The Geometrical. Dance compositions included Pompom, Pan and the Maidens, Hope, West Meets East, Solveig, Spring, The Bird, Celestial Infinity, Design in Colour and Rhythm, 1920–1971, and lastly Guided Improvisations in Freedom.

Gertrud: Our studio performance this year is exceptional and extensive. Each student has risen to a new level in their performance and endeavoured to portray the work at their very best. Magda very much enjoyed choreographing two studies for the larger groups, Dimensions and The Geometrical, which both explore Laban's concepts of space, direction, and design.

I so enjoyed working with Astrid on Solveig. The evocative music and story of Greig's Solveig's Song from his Peer Gynt Suite provided the theme on which we based this dance. Astrid was superb as she danced the part of the long forgotten and abandoned Solveig. In this piece, Solveig has spent her life waiting for Peer to return from his wanderings and marry her as he promised. Now an old woman, Solveig reflects on her foolishness and that Peer was undeserving of her. Peer finally does return but dies in her arms and she realizes life should be lived in the moment not spent waiting. A poignant lesson for us all.

Hope, was also a very emotive piece, danced by Trudy Philippo and her daughters, Judy and Mary. The family dynamic provided a truly moving performance. The older girls tried something quite new with Cornelius, Astrid's son, in Celestial Infinity, by using a modern synthesized piece by Bach. Here the students managed to create a continuous ebb and flow that was strong and majestic and had the unconfined figure of eight as the choreographic underlying theme.

In addition to their annual or biannual studio or theatre performances, the Hanova sisters' were consistently invited to present at the Unitarian Church in Vancouver from the early 1970s through to the late 1980s.

Unitarian Universalists believe that each person is free to search for their own personal truth on issues, such as the existence, nature, and meaning of life, deities, creation, and afterlife. Unitarian Universalists can come from any religious background, and hold beliefs and adhere to morals from a variety of cultures or religions. *"Unitarian universalists,"* (17 August 2019). https://en.wikipedia.org/wiki/Unitarian_Universalism.

Looking at the many programs from the Hanova Unitarian Church presentations, I reflect that the dances often expressed spiritual but not religious themes which enriched the messages of the church services. For example, Celestial Infinity with music by Switched on Bach in June of 1971, Vivacious Calm: Blessed Spirit, music by Gluck in 1971, and Hope in April of 1972 with music by Tchaikovsky. The Hanova sisters openly shared that they did not have any religious affiliations (except as they would say with a smile to worship Terpsichore, the Muse of the Dance).

**The Unitarian Church of Vancouver programme cover.
June 20, 1971.**

On June 20, 1971, the Hanova School presented a lecture demonstration of exercises and dance at the Unitarian Church. The performance included five dances: We Move On in Space and Time with music by Cameron McCosh, West Meets East with music by Schoenberg, Vivacious Calm: Blessed Spirit with music by Gluck, Celestial Infinity with music by Switched on Bach, and Hope with music by Tchaikovsky. Hope was again performed in 1972, as the center piece of a sermon called 'What does Hope mean?'

A Vibrant and Transformative Pedagogy

A Lecture Demonstration at the Unitarian Church, 1971.
Mary Philippo demonstrates a yoga position.
Back row from left to right: Tineke Ragetli, Judy Philippo, Beth Minsky,
Cornelius Fischer-Credo, Sarah Ratner, Karen Wenn (Kurnaedy).

Gertrud poses for a photograph at
a Lecture Demonstration at the Unitarian Church, 1971.

Hanova students demonstrate yoga exercises in a Lecture Demonstration at the Unitarian Church, 1971.

Gertrud: The exercises are such an essential part of the whole enterprise of dancing. To master the body is no easy task. The uninformed public does not realize when viewing a dance performance, how much work has gone into the preparation and control of the body before any choreography has been attempted. The yoga exercises and ballet barre are therefore the building blocks of the dance. Perhaps showing the exercises is not the highlight of the whole presentation for everyone but something important to consider, especially for the ignorant and untrained spectator. That is why Magda and I always make a point of including an explanation of our methods and training. We want our audience to know how one may make progress in the dance arts and achieve a level, which allows for confident performance. Without mastery of the body, the dancing can be limited, still something to appreciate and enjoy, but more circumscribed in expression, the depth and extension of bodily grace, and the ability to interpret the movements to the highest quality of the art of dancing. Daily exercises will additionally sustain flexibility, strength, fitness, and well being.

A Vibrant and Transformative Pedagogy

Unitarian Church Performance, 1971.
Sarah Ratner, Beth Minsky, and Karen Wenn (Kurnaedy) in the Hanova repertoire piece Hope. Music: Tchaikovsky: Concerto in D major for violin.

Magda: My heart immediately stirs as I hear the beginning strains of the moving Tchaikovsky violin concerto we have chosen to accompany our dance called Hope. The three dancers stand focused at the back of the stage. First, the middle dancer flows forward, to center front. She draws a slow figure of eight with her hips and sweeps her right arm into a flowing side impulse and then with a flourish and precisely with the music, she circles her arms fully extended backwards and forwards and holds her hands in a gesture of invocation. The dancer to her right then glissades towards the center and sweeps forward. She slowly extends her right leg into a side arabesque. Her arms are held straight up in a gesture of supplication to the heavens. Then she bends her leg and infinitely slowly, rotates on her foot until she has made a full turn. She ends with her hands in the same precise gesture of petition as the first dancer. Now, the third dancer glides to her left and surges forward. With arms first extended skyward, she bends slowly back and touches the floor. She then raises her right leg, pauses, and pushes off to propel herself to standing, where she briefly balances holding her left foot almost to her head. She circles her arms backwards and brings her hands forward to join the two other dancers in the same gesture of appeal. Then as one, the three dancers flow together into a close line and sweep their right arms up, supplicating the gods, to grace their offering with 'hope' and blessing.

Celestial Infinity performed by Beth Minsky, Cornelius Fischer-Credo, Karen Wenn (Kurnaedy), and Sara Ratner at the Unitarian Church, 1971.

Gertrud: The dance piece Celestial Infinity is set to the music of J. S. Bach's Brandenburg Concerto No. 2. We have chosen a very new version which has been played on a new electronic device called a Moog synthesizer. This sound is very modern but still stays true to the original piece. This flowing dance aims to capture the moving infinity of the heavens and illustrates the never ending vastness of space and humanities small part in the scheme of the universe. The message is, "We need to look beyond our small lives to understand our place amongst the stars." We invited Cornelius to be in this dance.

He is Astrid's son and has been dancing with us only recently. Magda and I are very impressed with how quickly he has mastered the ballet and modern dance movements and built up his muscles and posture to execute each movement with top proficiency. He will soon go on to dance with an established company in Eastern Canada.

On April 16, 1972, the Hanova School of Creative Dance presented The Peasant Cantata at the Unitarian Church with music by Johann Sebastian Bach. This production had live music performed by the church orchestra and was also accompanied by the church vocal group.

The Peasant Cantata performed at The Unitarian Church, April 16, 1972. Front: Tom Pierce, Judy Philippo, Karen Wenn (Kurnaedy). Middle: Tineke Ragetli, Mary Philippo, Ingrid Dinter, and Astrid Fischer-Credo. Back row: Trudy Philippo and Raila Katona.

Magda: This performance, with so many performers, seemed to effortlessly come together. The vocal group was polished and the musicians were well-rehearsed. The Hanova students, although amateurs, performed very well. It was evident in the dancers' expressions that they were enjoying the experience of dancing with live music and voice. The audience was extremely gracious in their thanks and praise.

Karen Wenn (Kurnaedy) in a solo from The Peasant Cantata, April 1972.

Dancer and musician, Tom Pierce, first studied dance with the Hanova sisters in the early 1970s. He quickly went on to many successful, artistic endeavours, which include studying with Maurice Bejart and Delores Laga in Brussels, Belgium, dancing professionally with The Montreal Ballet Jazz, Ys Ballet of Canada, Cabarets Lido and Moulin Rouge, and touring Europe and South America as a dancer. He also was the co-founder of the Ballets Jazz de Paris. Tom later became a professional musician and theatre technician. He presently lives in Paris, France and is a conductor, arranger, and professionally plays the soprano sax and bassoon.

ORDER OF SERVICE   Sunday, April 16, 1972

✗ CANTATA #212 (The Peasant Cantata) .. J.S. Bach

<u>Collection</u>   The ushers will be at the church doors with baskets for your contributions as you arrive or leave.

* * * * *

<u>Members of the Vocal Group</u>, under the direction of Dennis Tupman

Sopranos:
    Ruth Tupman*
    Lillian Hart
    Christel Schneider*
    Pat Cassie
    Mary Thomson
    Jean Barber
    June James*
    Joan Murrell
    Joan Oakey
    Gwyn Houghton
    Eva Spencer
    Joyce Moore*

Altos:
    Margaret Hewett
    Dorothy Gaiesky
    Anita LoSasso*
    Lesia Voth
    June Burman
    Catherine Cowan
    Gail McDermid
    Joyce Warner
    Joan Carter

Tenors:
    Ted Furnes*
    Vojislav Vasic*
    Marion Bertram
    Jim Oakey
    Bryan Spencer

Bass:
    Don James
    Derek Darling*
    Ted Anderson
    John Turner

* soloist

✗ <u>Hanova School of Creative Dance Members</u>
    choreography by Gertrud and Magda Hanova

Ingrid Dinter
Astrid Fischer-Credo
Reila Katona
Tom Pearce

Judy Philippo
Mary Philippo
Trudy Philippo
Tineke Ragetli
Karen Wenn

<u>Orchestra</u>
Flute- Jane Cassie
Violins - Corinne Field
         Pat Armstrong
         Sarah Bennett
         Cam Trowsdale
Violas - Angela Schneider
        David Gaudry

Cellos - Noel Armstrong
        Barb Broening
        Charles Inkman

Harpsichord - Ken Bertram

Inside the programme from The Peasant Cantata performed at the Unitarian Church, April 16, 1972, listing the performers from the vocal group, the dancers, and orchestra members.

In 1972, the Hanova Production Group, consisting of Judy Philippo, Mary Philippo, and Karen Wenn (Kurnaedy) consistently performed throughout the year. Performances included several dates at the Unitarian Church, the Vancouver Art Gallery on June 2, 1972 in a programme called 'Romantic Images', and at the Bentall Centre performing for a university women's organization. The Art Gallery performance included: With Music in My Heart performed by Karen Wenn (Kurnaedy), Freedom In Movement performed by Judy Philippo and Mary Philippo, Confession performed by Karen Wenn (Kurnaedy), and a new version of Hope performed by Judy Philippo, Mary Philippo, and Karen Wenn (Kurnaedy).

Hope performed by Mary Philippo, Judy Philippo, and Karen Wenn (Kurnaedy) at the Vancouver Art Gallery, June 1972.

Hope performed by Mary Philippo, Karen Wenn (Kurnaedy), and Judy Philippo at the Vancouver Art Gallery, June 1972.

Magda: We have recently had another successful presentation with Hope as one of the dances. The girls have rendered an exquisite and emotive version. After the performance, ladies came up to me with tears in their eyes to thank us and said they were very moved. The dance can certainly evoke deep emotion. The movements for Hope are ballet based but we added many Hanova kinetics such as the 'side and forward impulse' and the 'figure of eight'. Of course the wonderful music contributed to the success of the piece. Tchaikovsky's Concerto in D major for violin has such a triumphant and uplifting theme. I enjoy reworking the choreography when different dancers from the school take on an established piece from our repertoire. The dance then becomes unique again and the movements are interpreted in each dancer's own way.

Confession performed by Karen Wenn (Kurnaedy). Music by Grieg Piano Concerto No. 1. Poem by Herman Hesse. Vancouver Art Gallery, June 1972.

Confession performed by Karen Wenn (Kurnaedy). Music by Grieg Piano Concerto No. 1. Poem by Herman Hesse. Vancouver Art Gallery, June 1972.

Gertrud: Confession was choreographed with Karen in her private classes. This dance was a very dynamic piece because of the powerful gestures, music, and actions. The beginning of the dance opens with Karen dramatically jumping and twisting forward and then bending far back in sync with the opening, strong piano chords. The music later becomes flowing and Karen travels passionately, running, turning, and leaping, swept up in the ecstasy of the dance. She found the following poem as inspiration.

Sweet semblance, to your games behold me
Willingly surrendered; others have purposes,
Aims, for me it is enough to live!
All that ever moved my senses seems to me
A reflection of the Infinite and One that
I ever felt vitally.
To read such hieroglyphics will always
Recompense me for life, for the Eternal,
Essence I know to dwell within me.
(Herman Hesse, 2008)

Mary Philippo, Judy Philippo, and Karen Wenn (Kurnaedy) perform Improvisation. Vancouver Art Gallery, June 1972.

The West Ender newspaper, March 15, 1973, advertises a temporary change of address for the Hanova School and includes a photograph of Hanova dance students captioned with 'Students of the Hanova School enjoy modern studies in creative dance at English Bay'.

A Vibrant and Transformative Pedagogy

An unknown Hanova student poses in the studio, 1973.

In 1973, the Hanova sisters held a summer intensive at their studio from July 9th to July 21st. They usually taught in the Okanagan or travelled in Europe during the summer months. This year the sisters stayed in Vancouver to offer two different courses. Course A: to all aspiring dancers, be they on the stage, teachers, or students and Course B: to all who want to be in good physical and mental condition. The courses included exercises and dance technique, Eukinetics (practical studies in the energies which govern the expressive content of movement), Choreutics (harmony of movement relating to spatial design), and Improvisation and Choreography. Gertrud mentioned that their summer courses were always well attended as many of the sisters' regular students enrolled in these classes as they felt the two months of the summer break were too long to wait to enjoy 'the dance'.

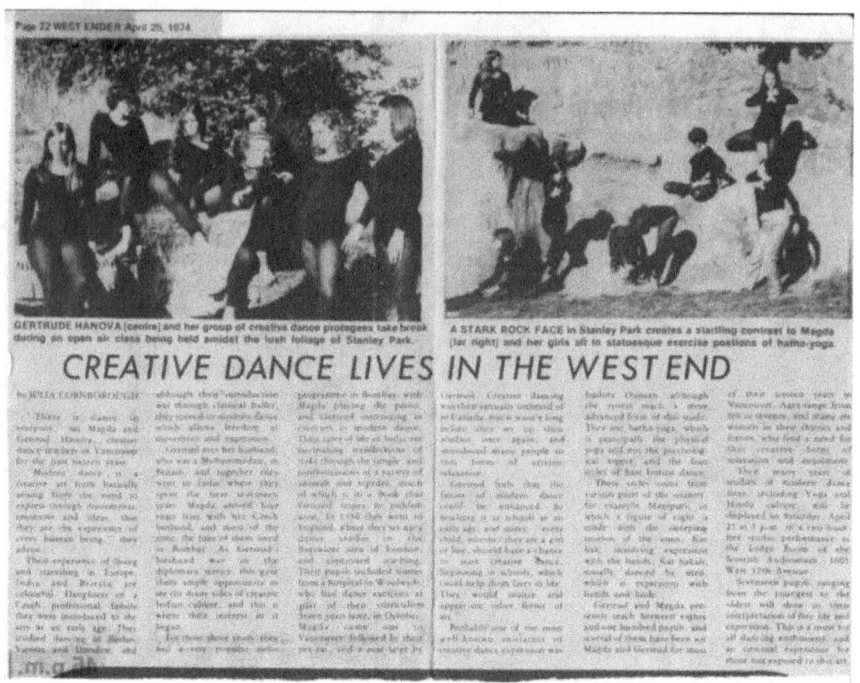

An article captioned Creative Dance Lives in the West End in the West Ender newspaper, April 25, 1974, by Julia Cornborough.

This article from the West Ender newspaper profiles the Hanova sisters' lives, details their philosophy of dance, and discusses their Vancouver dance school's upcoming performance.

> "There is dance in everyone," say Magda and Gertrud Hanova, creative dance teachers in Vancouver for the past sixteen years. Gertrud and Magda presently teach between eighty and one hundred pupils, and several of them have been with Magda and Gertrud for most of their sixteen years in Vancouver. Ages range from ten to seventy, and many are in their thirties and forties, who find a need for this creative form of relaxation and enjoyment.
>
> Their many years of studies of modern dance form, including Yoga and Hindu culture, will be displayed on Saturday, April 27 at 3 p.m. in a two hour, free studio performance at the Lodge Room of the Scottish Auditorium, 1605 West 12th Avenue."

A Vibrant and Transformative Pedagogy

In early 1974, the Hanova sisters moved their dance studio from downtown Vancouver to the Scottish Auditorium, located on 10th Avenue and Fir Street. The Scottish Auditorium had ample space for classes, rehearsals, and a stage on the top floor for performances. To celebrate their move, the sisters had a studio performance using the upstairs theatre of their new dance home.

Helene Fuldauer in the new studio on 10th and Fir, 1974.

Following the exercises, a usual Hanova performance would include various demonstrations of kinetics, choreographed in short studies. I note that from this 1974 performance the kinetics featured were: Andante, Arm Movements: the eight arm movements and their adaptations, Etude, Composition, and Study in Co-ordination. After the kinetics, each group of students presented their latest piece or pieces, as well as solo performances by students who took private classes. Dance creations presented in this year's performance were Impressions, Aphorism, The Peacock, My Crickets, Lady of the Court, Tango, La Ville Inconnue, Dance Poem, Nebulae, The Seasons, Sunspots, From Raw-Materials to Aesthetic Forms, The Tramp, They are Cuckoo, and Max and Moritz. And last but not least, a mass improvisation by all students. As usual, the improvisations were spontaneous and mixed the young and older dancers in new and interesting configurations. I especially enjoyed performances as we got to meet and mingle with all the other Hanova students.

Gertrud: Time passes so quickly. And here I find myself in my seventh decade. As they say, "youth is wasted on the young." When we are young we do not realize how precious our days can be or how fleeting. When I look back at our early lives, I remember fondly those days of freely dancing on stage, glorying in creation with such abandon and exuberance.

The abrupt transition from performing to no longer performing occurred when Magda and I moved back to Europe. We knew that we had left our celebrity and the solid regard we had built for our art in Bombay. But shortly after arriving in London, we couldn't help noting how young all the dancers were. We saw that the middle-aged dancer was absent and realized that our days on stage were now over, as we had returned to a culture that worshipped the 'youth'. Our reunion with Europe was an end of some things and a beginning for others.

A melancholy and sometimes pensive despondency arises when I think on this. But emphatically, the aging dancer has a revered place at our school in Canada. We have thrown out the rule book on the dos and don'ts of when to stop performing and profess that one should continue to dance, in fact, forever.

A Vibrant and Transformative Pedagogy

**Muna Tseng in From Raw-Materials to Aesthetic Forms.
Scottish Auditorium. April 27, 1974.**

Dancer Muna Tseng studied with the Hanova sisters for several years before moving to New York in 1978 to become a professional dancer with Jean Erdman. She later formed her own company, Muna Tseng Dance Projects. Over the years, Muna kept in touch with the Hanova sisters and visited them when she was in Vancouver showing them her choreography. Muna has also taught as adjunct faculty at New York University in the Playwrights Horizon Program (1996) and the Atlantic Theater Program (2002–2004). She was also an adjunct professor at Rutgers University from 1980–1983 and was the founder and directed the Caumsett Summer Dance Residency program at Queens College from 1984–1987. She also regularly teaches residency workshops in Tallinn, Estonia at Pollitalu Arts Centre, as well as in Bordeaux, France.

**Study in Co-ordination, Scottish Auditorium Theatre, 1974.
From left to right, Helga Strassman, Sue Rowe-Evans, Muna Tseng,
Karen Wenn (Kurnaedy), Raila Katona, Birthe Kulich, Hilary Craigen,
and Louise Martin (not shown in the photograph).**

Gertrud: We have choreographed so many outstanding and personal dances, which are showcased in this performance, such as Louise in the forceful Tango, Astrid in the stately Lady of the Court, and Helene passionately dancing to Edith Piaf's La Ville Inconnue. Helene's piece was especially magnificent and moving. She captured the mood precisely with her expressive facial features and heartfelt gestures. Piaf's haunting voice provided a unique soundscape. We vicariously experienced the despondency of lost love through watching Helene's fervent and sincere interpretation of this song.

Magda: We always try to guide our students in the private classes to choose their own themes or subjects. Helene, being from France, has chosen one of her favourite songs, a 'torch ballad' about love, loss, and sorrow called La Ville Inconnue sung by Edith Piaf. Her choice was ideal to explore her unique movement capabilities and expressions. Helene was able to embody and articulate the deep heartache of the song and to reveal its essence without being maudlin or overly dramatic.

La Ville Inconnue (Loneliness in a Big City) danced by Helene Fuldauer. Music by Edith Piaf, 1974.

La Ville Inconnue (Loneliness in a Big City) danced by Helene Fuldauer. Music by Edith Piaf, 1974.

A Vibrant and Transformative Pedagogy

Magda demonstrating at the barre. Scottish Auditorium studio, 1974.

Magda: In order to fully explore the dance in all of its facets, the body must be made ready through a careful regime of practice and training. And so I continue to stress ballet exercises in each lesson as an important foundation for the technique it imparts. The ballet exercises strengthen the feet, ankles, and limbs and elicit the height and stamina for the jumps and turns. Through the ballet exercises the dancer also learns body control, improved balance, and to add a flow and grace to their movements. The dancer is consequently made ready to move, improvise, and create with a strong instrument.

Our Love Affair with Dance

Studio work at the Scottish Auditorium.
Muna Tseng, Karen Wenn (Kurnaedy), Birthe Kulich, 1974.

Gertrud: I leave teaching the barre to Magda as she will never stop adoring the ballet. I enjoy leading the exercises but most of all I love the creation of new choreography. I never tire of working with students in producing new work. We are often so engaged in the process that an hour lesson flies by and seems barely enough time to develop the idea or to capture the essence of the piece. Each phrase of the new dance has to be slowly teased out. We rehearse what we have conceived and then the next part of the dance starts to materialize. But alas too soon our hour is up. I so look forward to the next time we will meet. What will come out of what transpired in the last lesson? How will it continue to unfold or develop? This is always exciting! Creation has a flow and rhythm all its own. The sequence of steps, jumps, pauses, dynamics, expression, timing, flow, transitions, and the combinations of partners,

A Vibrant and Transformative Pedagogy

groups, or solo work have unlimited choices. The music adds colour, time, and rhythm. For me, the most important element in conception is the idea, story, or theme. What does the choreographer want to convey to an audience that has meaning and will intrigue and pull them into the dance? Not necessarily entertain. But impart something of the human condition so that everyone in the audience may receive something from the performance. Authentic choreography comes from allowing the spirit of the dance to take over, unfolding from the heart and soul. Never forcing a movement to be in accord. It is like a puzzle, each movement must fit together seamlessly. The whole is complete when? Well, perhaps like a piece of writing, there are drafts and one may always improve a piece. But at some time one must declare the piece ready for performance. This is essential! To share the work with an audience is to see it come alive!

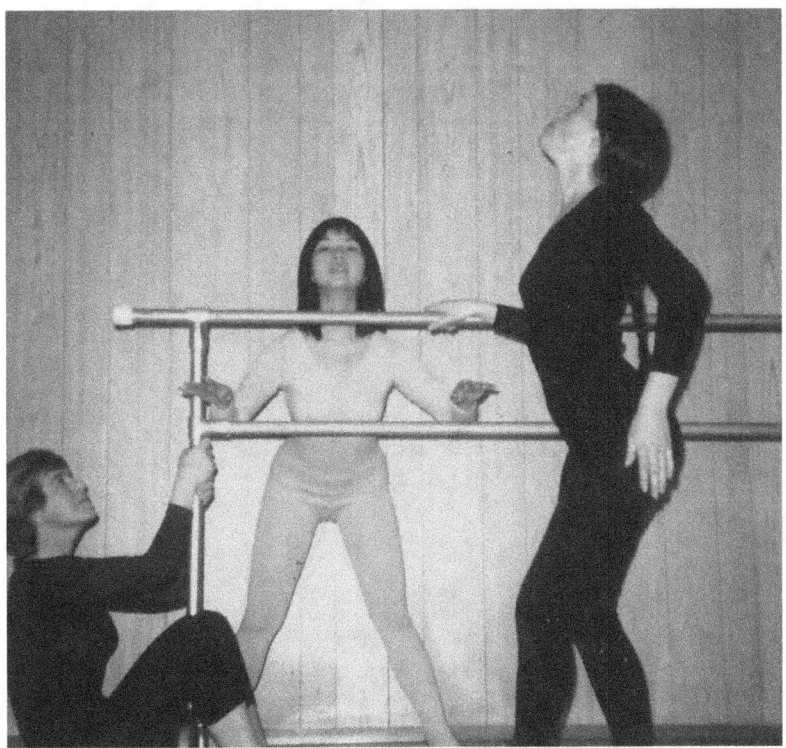

At the barre Birthe Kulich, Muna Tseng, Karen Wenn (Kurnaedy), 1974.

Heather Pinch at the Hanova Studio, Scottish Auditorium, 1975.

An unknown student at the Hanova Studio, Scottish Auditorium, 1975.

Helene Fuldauer, Hanova School, Scottish Auditorium, 1975.

Our Love Affair with Dance

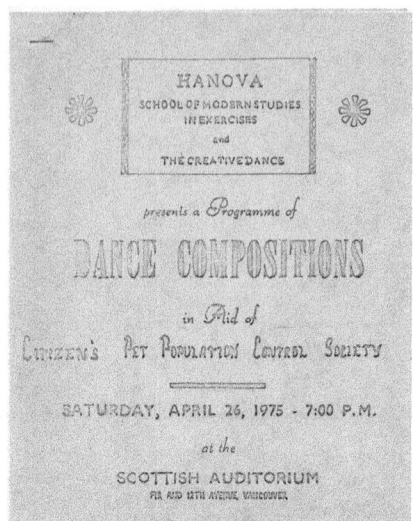

Programme cover for Hanova School of Modern Studies in Exercises and the Creative Dance presents a Programme of Dance Compositions in Aid of Citizen's Pet Population Control Society, April 26, 1975, at the Scottish Auditorium.

Rehearsal for the upcoming performance at the Scottish Auditorium, April 1975. Three unknown children, with left to right, Tineke Ragetli, Louise Martin, Jeanne Elworthy, Teresa Slomen, Karen Wenn (Kurnaedy), Hilary Craigen, and Sue Rowe-Evans.

The extensive 1975 Hanova studio performance, featured first a number of exercise sequences, which were: To Achieve Co-ordination, Composition, Sequential Exercises, and Seagull. On the second part of the bill were short kinetic compositions, which this year were all set to poems and songs, which included: Light, Roses, Awareness, Patience, Surprise, and Happiness.

After a brief intermission, a short film was shown of a dance performed and choreographed by Monica and Tineke Ragetli called Destiny, concerning their days of youth and the death of their mother. The last part of the bill featured dances, also set to poems, which were: The Garden, A Jest, Puja, The Ghost, Memories, Cycle of Nature, The Miser, Positive and Negative, and Jazz. The interests of individual dance students always inspired solo dances. In this case, each student had found their own poem and theme that they wished to explore and convey through dance. The last item on the programme was as always Improvisation by all the performers.

Karen Wenn (Kurnaedy) in The Garden, 1975.

Gertrud: The Garden is composed of a blend of Indian dance styles that illuminate a poem by the revered Indian poet Rabindranath Tagore. Over our many years in Vancouver, we have consistently taught Indian dance to interested students and since Karen has recently returned from a trip to India, she had a keen desire to experience the eastern movements. The choreography for this dance seemed to magically evolve as the words of the poem conjured up mudras and steps that Magda and I have long kept in our memories of the Indian dance.

Thou hast taken every moment of my life in thine own hands. Hidden in the heart of things thou art nourishing seeds into sprouts, buds into blossoms, and ripening flowers into fruitfulness. I was tired and sleeping on my idle bed and imagined all work had ceased. In the morning I woke up and found my garden full with wonders of flowers.

(Tagore, 2019, p. 1)

The creation of this dance evoked sweet and sometimes bitter reminiscence of times long gone. Times of lost friends and lost husbands. Times of carefree dancing and performing. In recalling movements for this dance I am reminded of an India which could boldly take over all of one's senses. My recollections are vividly visual and auditory, certainly sensual and kinaesthetic but ironically savoured most strongly with the olfactory. When I smell a certain combination of spices, I am again walking in an Indian market, where one is inundated with a pungent bouquet, a melange of the aromatic with distinct and individual fragrances coming through at odd moments, such as the gentle herbs of coriander and cumin, the bitterness of yellow turmeric, the tantalizing, zesty ginger and the hotness of chili peppers. These aromas bring back moments of my time in India, moments which were indeed sometimes zesty, gentle, or bitter but are remembered and blended together now much as a curry, a constant swirl of scented memories spilling forth as this Indian dance unfolds.

A Vibrant and Transformative Pedagogy

Puja (Worship), performed by Louise Martin in the Manipuri style, 1975. This dance was recreated for Louise from the Hanova repertoire of Indian dances from the 1940s in Bombay.

She, Rati, immortal Goddess, throws her veil
Over low valley, rising ground, and hill:
But soon with bright effulgence dissipate
The darkness she produces; soon advancing
She calls Usha, her sister morning to return,
And then each darksome shadow melts away.
O Goddess, grant me the brightest,
Best of treasures,
A judging mind, prosperity abiding,
Riches abundant, lasting health of body,
The grace of eloquence
And days propitious.

- Hindu prayer

Our Love Affair with Dance

Memories, music by Frederic Chopin, Nocturne Op. 15: No. 2. Karen Wenn (Kurnaedy) at the Scottish Auditorium, 1975.

Memories
The night is very calm and still
No trace of breeze comes o'er the hill;
No sound comes drifting on the air
To break the silence anywhere;
The night is still and very calm
With quiet like a healing balm,
As not a leaf stirs on the trees;
As nothing stirs—save memories.

- E.H. Hodson

Magda: Memories… Gerti and I have many. Mine are not shadowed by any regret or disappointment. I have lived mostly in the moment and perceive life as a gift. No life is perfect or without some sorrow. But I have been handed so many glorious opportunities and have taken them up with optimism and joy. As Chopin elevated his art, creating musical poetry, so Gerti and I have endeavoured to elevate the art of the dance to new heights for our students and the public. Life can be a poem, lyrical, imaginative, flamboyant, and pure in its message. Challenges come and go, that is the exciting part. How we interpret and illuminate these challenges, that is where self-confidence and the support of our loved ones come in.

Memories performed by Karen Wenn (Kurnaedy), Hanova Scottish Auditorium Studio, 1975.

Gertrud: A long life has memories filled to the brim. I have so many wonderful memories of guiding dance students to fulfill their potential. As a mentor, one must share one's expertise but also stand back at times and encourage the student in developing their own style and personal movement qualities. Creating new work together is indispensable for growth to occur, the life blood for pupils and teachers. Making each piece deeply personal and original is done with collaboration and by allowing the student to find their own way. Guiding the student through the evolution of the choreography and providing encouragement will produce a work that is the student's own but still reflects the Hanova style and philosophy. The creation is hence satisfying and artistically fulfilling for the student and the instructors.

Cycle of Nature performed at the Scottish Auditorium Theatre, 1975. Susan McFadayen, Sonja Christjansen, Jeanne Elworthy, Hilary Craigen, Louise Martin, Sue Rowe-Evans, Heather Pinch.

Cycle of Nature
Even the severed branch grows again,
and the sunken moon returns;
Wise men who ponder this
are not troubled in adversity.

- Bhaktrhari

A Vibrant and Transformative Pedagogy

A photograph from the Improvisation at the end of the April 26, 1975 performance at the Scottish Auditorium. Kathleen Pinch, Karen Wenn (Kurnaedy), Raila Katona, Heather Pinch. Photo credit: Martin Hahn.

Magda: Once again this year we have had a wonderful group of dedicated dancers with which to create and compose new dances. Students have come and gone but we have retained a core of loyal followers, who have stuck with us through the years. Over time, I have seen this nucleus of students grow as dance artists and appreciate their uniqueness and individuality.

75

The dancers at our school are experiencing the art of dancing on a level that is deeply personal but shared beautifully at performances and in improvisations. As the dances' nature is ephemeral, I have had the privilege of witnessing these moments and storing them as edifying memories, which bolster my relationship with Terpsichore as my Muse.

Hanova Summer Dance Intensive, 1976, held at the Scottish Auditorium. Hilary Craigen and two unknown dance students pose outdoors.

Gertrud: We have become close with our longtime students and empathize with their ups and downs in life. I know from my own experiences that people's lives are seldom without problems. Our students are no exception. In the studio, through the dance, we strive to dispel any stress, negativity, or depression with dancing and exercises. Dancing can lift the mood through releasing tension in the body and changing our thoughts from darkness to light. Simply lifting the arms, stretching up with all one has, then bending back and thanking all that is for life, can alter the mood effectively. Speaking from my own experience, physical gestures can inspire the body to generate positive and relaxed emotions and banish negativity to another realm.

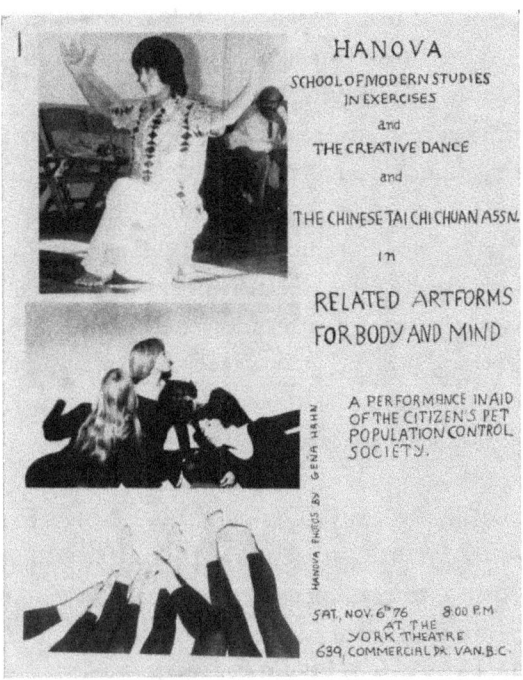

Programme cover for the Hanova Dance School and The Chinese Tai Chi Chuan Assn. in Related Art Forms For Body and Mind, November 6, 1976 at the York Theatre.

Always open to new partnerships, the Hanova sisters collaborated on this production with The Chinese Tai Chi Association which also held classes at the Scottish Auditorium. The description of Tai Chi in the programme notes by the Chinese Association aptly compliment the Hanova philosophy of exercise and creative movement.

Tai Chi Chuan is one of the oldest Chinese art forms; meditation, discipline and exercise for health. Our method involves breathing techniques, meditative postures, individual patterns of movements, partnered forms and weapon forms. Meditation is stillness, relaxation in movements, balance and harmony of Ying and Yang, for body and mind in all aspects.

The November 1976 performance started with Creative Exercises, Sequential Exercises, Swings to show the 'flow' of movement, a sequence called At the Barre and a new variation of Seagull. Kinetics included Dimensions: an awareness of space, Andante: transference of body weight, Geometrical: exploring floor design, and Shuang Chia Tai Chi Chuan, an ancient Chinese art form emphasizing balance, rhythm, and relaxation in movements, performed by David Wu and group.

Dance Creations were 3 Impressions, The Sea-Nymph Legend, Danced Philosophy: a group dance concerning the relationship of individuals striving to interpret the thoughts of Anatole France, and La Ville Inconnue.

The following paragraphs are taken from A Talk on the Modern Creative Dance given by Gertrud before a Hanova performance in the 1970s, and I note that Gertrud made similar statements before presentations throughout the 1980s and 1990s. Over the years, Gertrud and Magda did not change their basic philosophy about the necessity for freedom of expression and individuality to be included in dance instruction and choreography.

> For most people the word 'Dance' finds a concrete meaning in the Ballet—a romantic presentation of a fairy-like story, costumes, and atmosphere, executed in a strictly designed pattern, to a rigid technique. But since the beginning of the present century, the Dance has begun to change both its form and presentation. Isadora Duncan was the first to discard the traditional style of the stage dance and bring back the art of Terpsichore in dance movements closer to nature, born of impulse, yet founded on the natural movements of the body. The modern creative dance was thus born and has continued to evolve to this day and to go through many stages of development.
>
> At the Hanova school our style of modern dance reflects our early training in Europe in the ballet and modern dance and further with our many years in residence in India learning the Indian dance arts and yoga. We have blended our dance experiences from both cultures, which has produced our unique Hanova style. After giving our students a firm foundation of Hanova fundamentals, exercises, technique, and movement principles, we then encourage our students to develop their own individual movement style and expression, exploring

the dance on their own terms to fulfill their needs as dancers, choreographers, and artists. The capacity of the dance is then a lifelong enjoyment and pursuit.

On the rooftop of the Hanova penthouse, Margaret Hebold, Sonja Christiansen, and Sue Rowe-Evans, in a pose from an unknown work, May 1978.

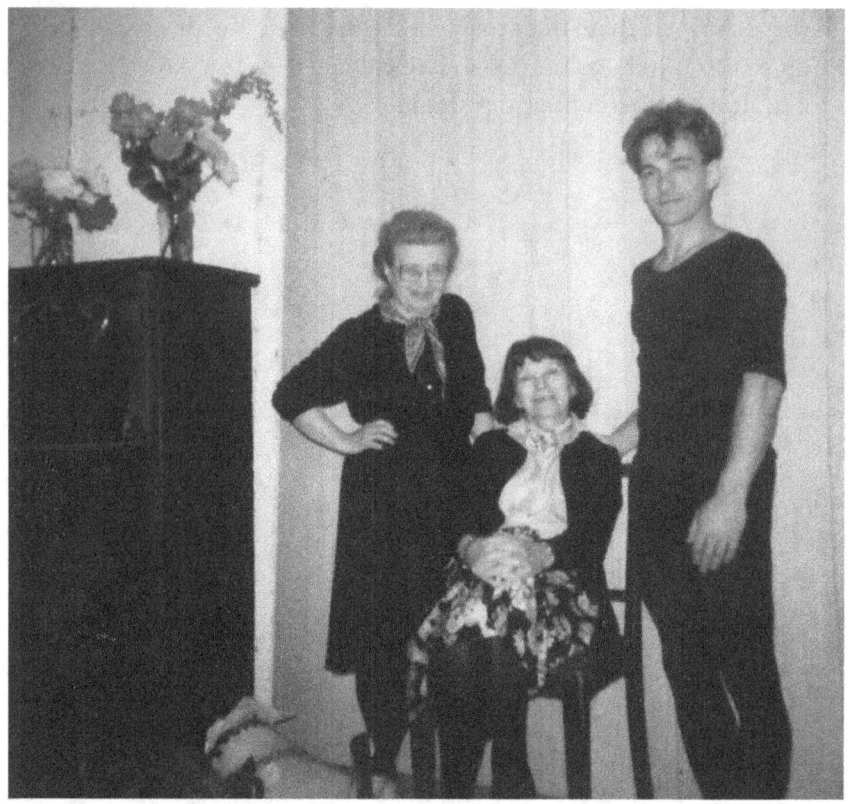

Gertrud, Magda, and Cornelius Fischer-Credo, who was visiting at the Scottish Auditorium Hanova Studio, 1979.

After starting dance lessons in the early 1970s with the Hanova sisters, Cornelius Fischer-Credo quickly went on to become a professional dancer. Cornelius has had an extensive international career in dance, both as a choreographer and performer. He has choreographed over 30 original works for Dancecorps, a company he co-directed since 1988. His company, Astrid, named after his mother, presented its inaugural production in the fall of 1999. He has also choreographed works for Toronto's Dancemakers, the National Ballet of Canada, Ballet British Columbia and Group de la Place Royale in Ottawa. He has been an instructor of modern dance for over 15 years teaching primarily within professional dance communities, locally and internationally. He currently lives in Vancouver, BC and is a certified instructor at the Vancouver Gyrotonic and Gyrokineis studio. Cornelius' mother Astrid, was a long time student and friend of the Hanova sisters.

Cornelius Fischer-Credo and Astrid Fischer-Credo in a photograph from an improvisation at the Scottish Auditorium Studio, 1979.

Astrid Fischer-Credo and Birthe Kulich in an unknown work at the Scottish Auditorium Hanova Studio, 1979.

Margaret Hebold in Study at the Barre at the Scottish Auditorium Studio, 1979.

By the end of the 1970s, the Hanova sisters still had a significant following and continued to choreograph and create dance works with their students. They never considered retiring. Many of their students were growing older along with them. But with Magda and Gertrud as models of physical health and creativity, their older students were inspired to keep dancing and taking classes, despite being in their seventies and eighties.

3

YOU ARE NEVER TOO OLD TO DANCE

Over the next two decades in the 1980s and 1990s, the Hanova School of Dance continued to have a loyal following of dancers. In fact, many Hanova students in the 1980s and 1990s had started with the sisters in the 1960s. The Hanova School uninterruptedly persisted in touching lives and had a sustained and profound effect on the dance community. Now in their eighties in the 1980s, the Hanova sisters modeled that one is never too old to dance, one is never too old to be creative and inventive with choreography, and one is never too old to enjoy all that the dance has to offer.

"Namaste". Hanova students at the Scottish Auditorium Studio, early 1980s.

I continued to study and perform with the Hanova sisters until 1975, although I had taken a long break travelling throughout Europe, India, and Nepal for a year and a half in 1973 and part of 1974. When I returned, I danced briefly at the University of British Columbia with a Graham-trained teacher to try something different. I remember at this time I thought the Hanova style seemed a bit old fashioned. Popular new dance companies were touring, such as Alwin Nikolais, Twyla Tharp, and Alvin Ailey Dance, all of which I saw when they came to Vancouver. These modern dance companies were experimenting and creating new forms of contemporary dance, costumes, and music, which were innovative and exciting. But I eventually came back to the Hanova School and they were very understanding about this. In dancing with them I felt I fulfilled something that was not fulfilled anywhere else. I realize this 'something' was how they fostered our individuality and encouraged students to connect to their personal creativity through dance.

However, in 1975 I moved to Kelowna, British Columbia and so had to give up dancing with the sisters. Over the next few years I married, had three sons, and taught the Hanova dance system through the local community center. I kept in touch with the Hanova sisters during the 1980s via letters. From a letter I received dated January 27, 1980, the sisters shared news of other students I had known, who had also moved away or were now married and having children. Magda mentioned that the previous summer they had travelled to Europe for two months. She said they visited 5 countries and went to 32 different places while walking 5–10 hours a day. They also saw several dance groups in Amsterdam which she said were not to their taste. Magda ended her letter by saying, "We enjoyed our holidays in Europe but were very happy to be back in Canada again and very happy that Vancouver is our home. We still love to teach and choreograph, still have a number of students who started with us 21 years ago and are still at the Scottish Auditorium." Gertrud added her greetings and wished me well with my second baby.

In 1986 I moved to Edmonton, Alberta and began studying at the University of Alberta. I completed a Bachelor of Education degree in 1990. After I graduated in 1990, I moved back to British Columbia and found employment as a public school teacher. I joyfully resumed dance lessons with the Hanova sisters and they soon had me performing in their productions again.

While I was away, throughout the early 1980s, the Hanova sisters continued to teach at the Scottish Auditorium and then in 1985 they moved to The Creative Space on 27th Avenue and Dunbar Street in Vancouver.

Magda, Astrid Fischer-Credo, and Gertrud at the Scottish Auditorium, early 1980s. Astrid was one of their many, longtime students.

Hanova students pose outside The Creative Space, Dunbar and 27th, 1985. On the back of the photograph it says: "In front of the new Studio: Audrey, Marjory, Ruth, Patricia, Ethel, Lorna, Hanna, Kay, Lailey, Jo."

**Summer 1986 on the Hanova Penthouse roof.
Magda is serving guests in the background.**

Magda: We are part of a large community of dancers in Vancouver, many of whom we have known for many years now. Gerti and I enjoy our gatherings on our rooftop abode in the summer months. We commune and share our thoughts on the art of dancing, mingling and enjoying our fellowship. There is joy in being with other believers. We have a unifying bond in our knowing that the dance has an important purpose for humanity. The dance enables an expression of the inner self through the body and thus satisfies this compelling, kinaesthetic need of the dancer's creative nature. The world becomes a better place when humankind is able to realize their dream of life in some form outside themselves, expressed as art. The dance is part of life—the very essence, as all people have the capacity to move artfully in their bodies. Our students come from many backgrounds, but regardless, all have come to further understand the joy of movement and creation in our studio. We are co-jointly manifesting in the physical our ideas and emotions to discover ourselves through the dance.

You are Never too Old to Dance

Dancing on the Hanova Penthouse roof, Chilco Street, West End, Vancouver. With dancers Astrid Fischer-Credo, Margaret Severn, and Ruth, late 1980s.

Gertrud: Our good friend and neighbour, Margaret Severn, has recently had a film about her life released called Dance Masks: The World of Margaret Severn directed by Peter Lipskis. Margaret was an internationally acclaimed ballet dancer. She toured the vaudeville circuit in the 1920s and was on Broadway in New York. She is most famous for making and using a dozen Benda masks as part of her act in the Greenwich Village Follies of 1921.

Magda, July 23, 1988.

Left: Gertrud directing choreography with musical assistance from Tineke Ragetli, on the Chilco Street Penthouse rooftop, 1989.
Right: Magda in the Hanova West End apartment with a portrait of herself in the background, November 1989.

Gertrud in the Hanova West End apartment, November 1989.

When I returned to British Columbia in 1990 from Alberta, my relationship with the Hanova sisters changed. We became much closer and besides dance lessons I spent more time with them having lunch or attending dance performances. The sisters remained actively interested in the performing arts in their later years and enjoyed going to the theatre to see what other dancers were producing. I especially remember we saw modern dance companies such as Paul Taylor and Martha Graham which they enjoyed very much. They also made sure to attend any Indian dance and we saw the Jai Govinda Indian Dance School of Vancouver several times.

In the period from 1990 until 1992, we had a very productive time choreographing new work but also recreating older material from their past repertoire. The sisters still had many students and continued to have an annual studio performance and lecture demonstration.

And now I was a thirty something divorced adult and mother of three. The Hanova sisters and I had established a much deeper connection inside and outside of classes. Through life's bumps and missteps I had acquired a more mature life perspective and realized there was much more to the Hahn sister's life stories then the one dimensional facts I had learned about them in my childhood and teen age years. I had also attended university and had broadened my concepts of world history and dance history, which renewed my interest in finding out more specific details about where the sisters had previously lived and who they had studied with.

As this more life experienced adult, while regularly visiting at the Hanova penthouse, I continued with my youthful fascination of looking at the Hanova sisters' photo albums, which featured an array of breathtaking photographs from different periods of their lives. I was now emboldened to ask questions that my previously younger self would never have dared to ask. The awe and reverence I felt for the sisters as a child and teen were now mixed with friendship but still held a cautious familiarity. Awe can be defined as 'a feeling of reverential respect mixed with fear or wonder'. This aptly describes how I would describe my feelings for the Hanova sisters. The sisters deeply inspired their students but seemed to have a mystery and reserve that was hard to penetrate at times. They were a solid unit of two, inseparable, and always in agreement with each other. I had witnessed students who disagreed with them leave the school and understood this as a reflection of the Hanova sister's uncompromising attitude.

As I spent more time with the sisters in the early 1990s, my awe or fear was somewhat waylaid and I now relaxed in their presence enough to start asking more in depth questions about their past lives. I wanted to know more about their birth place and how they had begun their lifelong love affair with the art of dancing? What were their parents like? Who had they married? What had happened to them during the two World Wars they had survived? And I was most curious about the famous dance schools they had studied and performed with, both in Europe and India, and how these experiences had enabled them to formulate their unique Hanova dance philosophy and system.

All of these questions fascinated me. Conceivably, I was trying to put my own life back together through finding out how they had survived and thrived through life's unexpected events and dilemmas. I saw that they were becoming elderly, but they still had energy and a deep interest in many things. Perhaps I wanted to know their secret of successfully living a life to its full capacity so as not to feel old before my time.

In the early 1990s, Magda and Gertrud, more than ever, were role models for me. They were happily divorced, working in the dance arts which they loved, and living lives which were fulfilling and stimulating. They inspired me.

Looking though the sisters' extensive collection of photo albums together continued to be deeply enchanting. I had an epiphany that all of this rich, visual history of dance should not be lost. I somehow knew the time had arrived to begin unravelling the puzzle of their intriguing lives in a more comprehensive way. I realized that my many questions could only be answered by longer and more thoughtful conversations about their past. And so as I became closer to them, I summoned up the nerve to persist in my inquiries and suggested keeping some record of their extraordinary experiences. The sisters were open to this and happily allowed me to duplicate pictures, take notes, and make recordings of their memories. I began to see myself as their biographer and they seemed to be delighted by the idea of some kind of book which would safeguard and preserve their precious photographs, programmes, newspaper reviews, and lifelong achievement.

PART 2

4

A LOVE AFFAIR WITH DANCE BEGINS

Magda Hahn, their maternal Aunt, Gertrud Hahn, 1909.

Over our many discussions, I discovered that the Hahn sisters had grown up in what we can look back at now as a crossroads in time of immense change in the world. Changes that some heralded as a new modern age. Changes that shook and destroyed borders, political systems, social morays, and most importantly for the Hahn sisters, changes that now made it more acceptable and respectable for women to pursue the arts as their livelihood.

I learned that Gertrud and Magda Hahn were born in Bischof-Teinitz, Bohemia, Gertrud in 1903 and Magda in 1905. The area was part of the Austro-Hungarian Empire until its defeat at the end of WWI, when Bohemia was incorporated into the newly formed country of Czechoslovakia. Bischof-Teinitz is now called Horsovsky Tyn and is a small town near the German border in the Czech Republic. In 1938 the town and region were infamously annexed into Nazi Germany as part of the Sudetenland, as until 1945 the area was inhabited by a large German speaking population. Accordingly, the Hahn sisters' first language was German. They spoke of having a Jewish heritage but always included the fact that they were not religious in any traditional sense.

Out of the ordinary for this time, Magda's and Gertrud's parents were both professionals, their mother a dentist/doctor, their father a medical doctor. From an early age, the sisters said they were encouraged by their family to appreciate all of the arts. The Hahn parents had a great interest in music, their mother played the violin and piano, and their father the cello. The sisters shared with me that it was not unusual in the Hahn household to have several musical evenings or chamber concerts a week and the sisters both took piano lessons. The sisters also noted that they were equally mischievous and during the evening concerts, instead of sleeping, they could not resist slipping out of their beds to secretly listen and dance to the music in front of the concert room's closed doors. And so they developed a deep love for music and dance at a very early age.

From my conversations with Magda and Gertrud about their early life, the sisters said, "Our mother was extremely avant-garde and very much interested in the dance and both of our parents greatly encouraged us to try all of the arts, which included music, sculpture, painting, and design. But the dance was what we loved the most."

The sisters told me that when they were still quite small, probably three and five, their mother hired a dance master to come to their village from a nearby larger town called Pilsen. With these private lessons, their talent for dance was expanded and became more structured. They first performed at four and six in local festivals, such dances as the minuet and the schottische, a polka like partnered dance, which originated in Bohemia. In our discussions, the sisters emphasized that their parents helped them to recognize the importance of physical training, with a sound knowledge of basic anatomy, and the importance of nourishing the body with good food and exercise.

**Gustav and Jelly Hahn with their children,
Magda age 4 and Gertrud age 6, Bischof-Teinitz 1909.**

Gerti and Magda: Six year old Gerti awoke to the sound of a distant piano. She threw off her heavy, goose feather comforter and lay completely still on her back, soaking in the music. Slowly she stretched her arms and legs straight into the air and started to move her limbs in swaying motions in time to the music. She had entered her own private reverie of joy, a zone of happiness and buoyancy. Moving to music made her feel as if she was filled with bubbles or the gas that street corner sellers used to fill those balloons that could float. Suddenly, in the midst of her morning devotion, there was a quick rap on her door and it was thrust open. The piano music became much more pronounced. Her nursemaid poked her head around the entrance way and called out in a cheerful voice before going on to her other duties, "It is morning, Gerti, put on your clothes." Gerti did not react to her greeting and with a continued and total concentration on the air above her head, kept moving to the music, seemingly oblivious to her nursemaid's interruption. But as the last note of the music died, she slowly lowered her limbs and sat up. She languidly removed her nightgown and started to get dressed with a slow and satisfied smile on her face.

Meanwhile her younger sister Magda, in the bedroom next door, had been up and dressed for some time. She was also listening to the piano, as well as busily and energetically rearranging her dolls in time with the music. With a doll grasped in each hand, Magda created dances for the dolls in the air. She made the dolls leap and twirl or bow or curtsy to each other before she decided where the dolls' new spot would be on her window seat. As the music finished, Magda stopped repositioning her precious ladies and gave all of her little dancers a final pat on the head, before she made sure each one had its skirt arrayed neatly. Then she skipped with great liveliness out of the room.

The young Hahn sisters loved to dance and took every opportunity to move in dance like ways. They would dance walk, dance run, dance skip, dance turn and leap, to get where ever they needed to go, regardless if there was music or only an inner music, which seemed to accompany them wherever they went. Saturday was their favourite day, as this was the day their parents had hired a dance instructor to come from a larger town nearby to teach them formal dances. So far, they had learned to waltz, minuet, and gavotte, much to their delight and pleasure.

These dances were fun and filled with rhythm but the sisters' favourite dancing activity to date had been when their Auntie, Mutti's sister, came to visit and shared what she knew of the technique of a famous American dancer, who had toured Europe, called Isadora Duncan. Isadora, their Auntie told them, was all the rage in artistic circles and danced in a new, free manner without stockings or dance slippers. She dressed in flowing draperies which revealed her bare legs and arms and this their Auntie said scandalized many people, but of course not them because they were free thinkers and believed in each person, especially women, seeking their true artistic selves to the highest. Gerti thought she wasn't quite sure what their Auntie meant by this, but she certainly intended to find out. Their Auntie also said she had seen Isadora's brother on the street in Paris. He was wearing a toga and sandals, which was how an ancient Greek man had dressed. Isadora Duncan had even started a dance school in Gruenwald which was near Berlin. Oh, how Gerti wished they could go there and dance. But sadly, Mutti said they were too young right now.

Early American modern dancers, who toured Europe, such as the famous Isadora Duncan, Lois Fuller, and Ruth St. Denis, undoubtedly influenced continental views on the newly popular modern dance in the early 1900s. These dancers' innovation and refreshing styles of movement filtered down to the Hahn sisters through conversations and demonstrations with their aunt and mother, who both had a special interest in this new dance form. To give some context to the enormous influence that Duncan had worldwide and on the Hahn sisters in forming their beliefs about dance, I include a brief synopsis of Duncan's philosophy of movement.

Isadora Duncan (1878–1927), by some called the mother of modern dance, is credited by many as being the first dancer to 'rediscover' the body and return to natural expressive gestures. Up until the early nineteen hundreds, the ballet had dominated western concert dance for nearly four hundred years and employed formalized steps and story lines, which did not stray from an established formula. However, just prior to and at the turn of the 20th century, with the advent of many changes in the world, new ideas started to influence the arts. New styles of dance, currently known as contemporary or modern dance, began emerging. Dance now became much more a form for artistic expression, "not interested in spectacle but in the communication of emotional experiences—intuitive perceptions, elusive truths—which cannot be communicated in reasoned terms or reduced to mere statement of fact" (Martin, 1963, p. 138).

> Dance critic and writer Martin (1963) aptly describes the dance art of Duncan:
>
> It was her deepest desire to discard all artifices, all invention, all traditional methods and established vocabularies such as the ballet employed, and to get to the source of man's (sic) expressiveness, using only the natural movements of the body without exaggeration or surface ornamentation, and allowing them to produce themselves only under inner compulsion. (p. 138)

In Duncan's (1928) autobiography, My Life, Duncan outlines her early endeavours to uncover the source or wellspring from which her movement arose.

> I spent long days and nights in the studio seeking that dance which might be the divine expression of the human spirit through the medium of the body's movement. For hours I would stand quite still, my two hands folded between my breasts, covering the solar plexus. My mother often became alarmed to see me remain for such long intervals quite motionless as if in a trance—but I was seeking and finally discovered the central spring of all movement, the crater of motor power, the unity from which all diversities of movements are born, the mirror of vision for the creation of the dance—it was from this discovery that was born the theory on which I founded my school. (p. 84)

In her book Gestures of Genius, dance historian Vigier (1994) recounts how Duncan studied ancient Greek vases to rediscover what she considered a pure and natural form of movement. The vases intrigued Duncan because they depicted poses and gestures of the entire body swept up in the ecstasy of dancing. Vigier (1994) further explains:

> In the Duncan lexicon, this gesture represents a perfect dance movement, where the natural movement of the body emanates from the spirit, marking a moment in which the body can no longer contain the exuberance of the spirit and finally lets itself be carried by an impulse it can no longer resist. It is not the gesture itself, but the power and truth of the spirit behind the gesture which so inspired Duncan in her work. (p. 41)

Vigier (1994) credits Duncan with returning dance to a place of personal expression and fulfillment. Vigier (1994) informs us that Duncan "… removed the external eye from the dancer's consciousness—her students never practiced before mirrors—and returned the impulse of movement to the centre of the body where the dancer assumed responsibility for the evolution of its form" (p. 46). "… Duncan's theories of harmonizing the spiritual and the physical through dance" (Partsch-Bergsohn, 1994, p. 6) has sustained its power and continues to inspire dancers who recognize the truth of her message.

In 1903, Duncan pronounced, "The dance of the future will have to become a high religious art as it was with the Greeks. For art which is not religious is not art, it is mere merchandise"… "The dancer will not belong to a nation but to all humanity. She will dance not in the form of nymph, nor fairy, nor coquette, but in the form of woman in her greatest and purest expression. She will realize the mission of woman's body and the holiness of all its parts" (Duncan, 1928, p.175).

But perhaps one of the most striking demonstrations of Duncan's fame was that Duncan showed the world that a woman could lead a free and artistic life not beholden to any social conventions. Her independent example spread amongst artistic circles and inspired many women to become dancers and to adopt or copy her style of expression.

However, to fully understand the nature of the Hahn sisters' early dance education, it is pertinent to also look at the work of European movement innovators such as Francois Delsarte (1811–1871), Emile Jacques-Dalcroze

(1865–1950), and Rudolph Laban (1879–1958), who provided the foundations for most European systems of movement education and modern dance. Delsarte inspired Isadora Duncan, Ruth St. Denis and Ted Shawn. Dalcroze, Laban, and F. Matthias Alexander also studied Delsarte's teachings before developing their own theories.

Francois Delsarte (1811–1871) was a French musician and singing teacher. He is famous for developing the Science of Applied Aesthetics, which consisted of a study of voice, breath, movement dynamics, and the expressive elements of the body. His work became popular worldwide in 1885 when Genevieve Stebbins, a Delsarte follower, published a book titled The Delsarte System of Expression, outlining his methods to emotionally connect authentically to movement for stage performers.

Emile Jacques-Dalcroze (1865–1950) was a Swiss composer and musician, best known for developing Eurhythmics, also known as rhythmic gymnastics. His movement work concentrated on the body as the original instrument and involved natural movement such as walking and skipping to learn to beat time to music. His fundamental philosophy was that "rhythm both embodies the spiritual and spiritualizes the body" (Partsch-Bergsohn, 1994, p. 6). "Dalcroze's methodical Eurhythmic Art attracted many young females who, following the spirit of the times, craved exposure to the arts and inner harmony through self-expression" (Partsch-Bergsohn, 1994, p. 6).

Rudolph Laban (1879–1958) was an Austro-Hungarian dance artist, choreographer, and movement theoretician. His theories and beliefs about dance have had a lasting and formative effect on modern dance and movement education all over the world. He is considered one of most important dance teachers of the twentieth century.

To further illuminate the Hahn sisters' early dance education and to emphasize the influence Dalcroze's beliefs and philosophy had on the Hahn sisters' creation of their own dance identities, I include dance historian Karl Toepfer's (1997) account of Dalcroze's contributions to the formation of German body culture and in shaping public education in Germany and Czechoslovakia, before and after the First World War.

Toepfer (1997) imparts:

> He suffused the emerging cult of the body with an aura of radiance, linked the discovery of bodily rhythms almost entirely with the experience of joy, and dispelled the anxieties, pho-

bias, and psychic shadows that until that time made the body a supreme sign of irrationality. (p. 16) ... The aim of rhythmic gymnastics was to create a heightened condition of individual freedom as well as a stronger sense of social unity... The expression of individuality required the disclosure of a "unique rhythm". ...it embraced all bodies, regardless of talent, aptitude, or intelligence. p. 18)

In addition Toepfer (1997) shares that, "In 1913 the powerful Sokol (Falcon) Organization of physical educators and bureaucrats ...began to absorb Dalcrozian ideas into a large-scale plan to create a strong body culture in Czechoslovakia... it treated body culture as an international network of ideas that produced an embodiment of power and identity" (p. 123). Gertrud mentioned the Sokol Organization many times in our conversations about the sisters' early dance training, but I could never find any references to this organization until I discovered Toepfer's (1997) book Empire of Ecstasy: Nudity and Movement in German Body Culture 1910–1935. Toepfer's book (1997) is an extensive look at the formation of body culture in the Weimar period and I was gratified to find Toepfer's (1997) reference to the Sokol Organization. As reported by Toepfer (1997), in 1929, in partnership with the Czech government, the Sokol Organization also produced a huge book which set out a state sanctioned method for the rhythmic gymnastic education of females, as the female body was thought at this time to need different exercises than the male body. Toepfer (1997) states, "The book presented a vast treatise on rhythmic gymnastic practice, replete with more than four hundred exercises, each one described in detail regarding musical rhythm, bodily movement, and function through the use of stick figures, drawings, musical notations, and more abstract diagrams, charts and tables" (p. 124).

The work of the Sokol Organization is of significance to the Hahn sisters' dance education, as they would have been eight and ten in 1913 and were trained with Dalcrozian ideals and methods in the dance schools and the public schools they attended. When discussing Dalcroze with the Hahn sisters, they shared that the Dalcroze system starts with an awareness of bodily rhythms and especially of the heartbeat and breathing. This awareness is transferred to an awareness of a drum beat and then piano rhythms. Looking back at the Hahn sisters' choreography and lessons, the sisters employed much of the Dalcroze system in that they always started classes

Our Love Affair with Dance

with shaking the limbs, and swinging and stretching to music. The sisters also loved to create exercise and kinetic studies to set rhythms. In a collection of Dalcroze's lectures published in his book, Eurhythmics-Art Education (1930), it is clear that besides adopting Dalcroze's physical methods, the Hahn sisters also adopted much of Dalcroze's philosophy concerning the dance being an holistic endeavour.

> For the human race to be regarded as having definitely reached its goal, it is not sufficient that bodily technique should be taught, in magisterial fashion, by specialists aiming at an impeccable muscular virtuosity. It must likewise be possible for the individual's motor powers—when their collaboration is necessary—to be placed in immediate contact with the cerebral and the emotional faculties, for the soul and body to be in mutual and intimate communion, the soul idealizing and purifying the body, while the body endows the soul with the strengthening realities of its own energy… (Jacques-Dalcroze, 1930, p. vii)

(iii) Walking   (iv) Running
FIG. 18. – Exercises in Relaxation – *contd.*

Jacques-Dalcroze, 1930, p. 32)

"For all who consider the body in motion as a direct interpreter of human emotions, the main thing is to disdain no method of enriching this body's technical means of expression" (Jacques-Dalcroze, 1930, p. 33).

A Love Affair with Dance Begins

Karlsbad 1914–1921

The times were turbulent and uncertain in Europe during the Hahn sisters' childhood. The First World War broke out on July 28, 1914. At the start of the war, the Hahn family moved from Bischof-Teinitz to Karlsbad, a spa city situated in western Bohemia, now known as Karlovy Vary in the Czech Republic, approximately 130 km (81 mi) west of Prague. Gertrud said that both of the Hahn parents were involved with war work as doctors. The Hahn sisters happily remarked that the larger town afforded the sisters more opportunities for dance lessons and the study of music and art. They could now attend a dance school that taught ballet and Dalcroze Eurhythmics. Magda and Gertrud shared that as young girls, they both taught younger pupils at the school. The sisters mentioned that they were in many local performances during the war time and the proceeds were donated to war relief.

School girls Magda and Gertrud, 1914 (nine and eleven years old), Karlsbad.

Gerti: We have moved to Karlsbad and Magda and I are attending a new school, which is much bigger than our old one and has wonderful rhythmic gymnastic classes. The war has come to Bohemia and although I don't truly understand why the men are fighting, I am glad we have relocated because now we can also attend a real dance school that offers so many classes. I would spend every day there if I could.

I didn't realize how much I didn't know about dancing, in particular, the ballet. This dance has its own language, its own specific rhythms, and exact rules of movement, which I have found are something one cannot easily perform without practice. One must observe the dance master or mistress closely and try to emulate what they show us, feeling the steps and postures in one's body to know one has correctly executed the movements. It is apparent that this is not so easy for everyone in the classes. But I feel like the dance I am learning at the new dance school was already in me, just waiting to emerge. The dance mistress asked Magda and I where we had previously taken dance lessons. We said we have only had lessons from a dance master from Pilsen. She found this hard to believe. But of course she doesn't realize all the time we have spent dancing together, perhaps untrained, but nevertheless, passionately and with the spirit of Isadora very much alive in us.

I know our dancing to be part of us, inseparable from who we are. It seems it has always been this way from the time we were very small. And happily now with every new lesson, Magda and I are discovering more and more about our dancing selves, which goes beyond pleasing an audience or our dance master. This is hard to explain, but I know we dance for ourselves, not just in the studio, but anywhere, to explore the marvellous sensations and energies that dancing produces. These feelings may seem fleeting but are very real nonetheless. With every step, jump, or gesture we can renew these exciting perceptions and find the sublime. Our parents have encouraged us to enjoy all the arts, but the dance has become our highest calling.

A Love Affair with Dance Begins

Magda in Bronze Angel costume, Karlsbad 1914.

Magda: The time was late afternoon, just before supper, and nine year old Magda was in her bedroom diligently practicing ballet foot and arm positions, using her dresser as a barre. Since their family had moved to Karlsbad, Magda was especially thrilled to be learning ballet and had made this dance her exclusive focus and sole passion.

She presently had her feet apart in second position with her arms gracefully raised to the sides of her body. She consciously kept her back very straight, her shoulders down, and her head held as if an invisible string was pulling it skyward. She pretended the floor was winter ice and she could gracefully glide and slip her feet over the surface with little effort.

Her concentration on her movement was intense and she easily transitioned from arm and foot positions to plies and relevés, bending the knees and raising up on the toes while keeping her feet and arms in the correct positions. She thought of her recent performance with her dance school and had to laugh inwardly because her costume had been so ingenious that no one had recognized her. All thanks to her Mutti and her marvellous way with makeup and material. She had been transformed. The audience had thought she was a boy until they looked at the program and saw Magda Hahn as the Bronze Angel. In the ensemble of students performing in the dance play, she had joyfully taken the part of this beautiful creature that had magical abilities and could fly. Oh, she wished that she really could fly! Dancing often gave her a semblance of perhaps what it might feel like to soar and skim over the ground. While jumping and leaping, she often felt like she was going to take to the air and defy gravity.

Magda now started to move her feet to trace circles on the floor which she remembered were called 'rond de jambe'. Ballet terms, she had recently learned, were exclusively in the French language, which encouraged her to be more diligent with her French language studies. Magda thought every movement in ballet flowed so brilliantly from one to the next. She could hardly wait until her next lesson on Saturday. Her older sister Gerti was already in the advanced class and performing with the teenage girls even though she was still eleven. Magda hoped that she would soon be good enough to join Gerti's class so that they could dance together in dance school performances.

A Love Affair with Dance Begins

Magda, Karlsbad 1914.

Gerti: Meanwhile, Gerti was in her bedroom listening to the not too distant, soothing sounds of her parents rehearsing with their fellow musicians for their next concert. Stretched out on her bed on her stomach, a school book ignored by her side, Gerti was deep in thought. She was preoccupied with pondering her part in the latest performance of her dance school. She had a compulsion to go over each step in her mind as she remembered the choreography in minute detail. She did feel proud of herself. She knew she had performed quite well with her group of fellow students as part of a program, which had demonstrated Dalcroze rhythmic gymnastics and ballet waltzes. The dancers had received much applause and took several curtain calls.

But why was she feeling slightly dissatisfied with this well received and acclaimed performance? After some more thinking, she decided that there was nothing wrong with the programme or performance, but perhaps she wanted to do more than perform rhythmic exercises or synchronized movements with other girls. She often felt the dances she made up in the privacy of her bedroom, while listening to her parents music rehearsals, were good and she only needed a little more time to develop this choreography with stronger ideas.

Gerti also had the realization that she wanted to be a solo dancer like Isadora or to perform with her sister Magda. She couldn't help but notice that Magda, in the short time that they both had been taking ballet lessons, had taken to the ballet like a duck to water, or really a swan to water. Here she chuckled to herself at this idea. Gerti had seen that Magda's talent really stood out at the dance school and that everyone had noticed how accomplished Magda was for her age. Gerti openly and happily admired Magda's blossoming, long, elegant limbs and her smile that radiated out to an audience to show the inner pleasure she was feeling while performing. She loved her sister very much and was not jealous of her. To the contrary, she was delighted that they both shared such a strong love of dancing. This love for dancing, above all else, seemed to have created a bond for them that went deeper than the usual sisterly affection. While dancing together Gerti reflected, the sisters had developed an unconscious manner of complimenting each other's artistic and bodily expression. With these thoughts buzzing around her brain, Gerti quickly got up off her bed to join Magda, who she knew was next door in her bedroom, diligently practicing her ballet steps. She imagined that if she wanted to keep up with Magda, she better put in some more practice.

A Love Affair with Dance Begins

Gerti, Mutti, and Magda. On the back of the photograph, 'Summer 1914'.

A photograph of Magda's and Gertrud's mother, Jelly Hahn. Karlsbad, dated 1921.

Magda: Our Mutti. She always smells nice, wears pretty clothes, and her long chestnut hair is always pinned up perfectly. She always talks quietly and firmly to Gerti and I, looking right into our eyes. I think she is checking to see if we understand what she has said. Mutti is also very talented. She can play the piano and violin very well and is a dentist/doctor.

Mutti said that being a dentist is unusual for a woman. She has mentioned that she received a lot of opposition from the men at medical school and was told many times that she should be at home, cooking and cleaning or tending to children. Our mother has stressed that we must set our sights high and not listen to people who like to say things to girls to dishearten them or deter them from their true calling.

Mutti is making sure that Gerti and I are 'well rounded'. I had to ask her what she meant by this term 'well rounded'. I knew

A Love Affair with Dance Begins

that it certainly did not mean we should be soft and fat. She explained, as only she could, with a slow and happy-sad smile that to succeed in life, especially as a woman, one must have many interests and cultivate all of one's talents to have a happy future. So we play many games of strategy together, like chess and checkers, as Mutti says we must develop our powers of deduction and reason. We also take language lessons, discuss many books on different topics, such as anatomy and new scientific discoveries, and read novels. Mutti says novels let us know how others live and think. We also take piano lessons, go to museums, and take art lessons, and our favourite, of course, we take many dance classes. And by the way, our Papa loves that Mutti is a 'free thinker'. He said, "I would not change a hair on her head."

Gustav Hahn in his Austro-Hungarian Empire WWI uniform. Written on the back of the photo "In Prague 1914, before travelling to Krakau, Poland".

Magda: Our Vater (Papa). Our Papa is a doctor. He said he met Mutti at the university medical school and knew right away he better propose and marry her quickly before any of the other young doctors saw how special she was. Mutti always laughs at this part and says he was not only the handsomest young man at the medical university but also the smartest. After all, he thought she was the most beautiful of all the students, even if she was one of the very few females on campus. Then she gets serious and says, actually, your Papa valued me for my thinking processes and always told me I had every right to be at medical school. That is why I married him and also, here she is laughing again, because he can play the cello. We really needed a fourth for our string quartet.

We miss our Papa when he has to travel to help men who have been hurt in the war. He says not to worry because he is privileged not to be fighting and instead must try to put men back together, who have been injured. I love my Papa because he likes to laugh and tell us stories. He smokes a pipe and has an itchy moustache. He says Gerti and I are the most graceful and beautiful dancers he has ever seen.

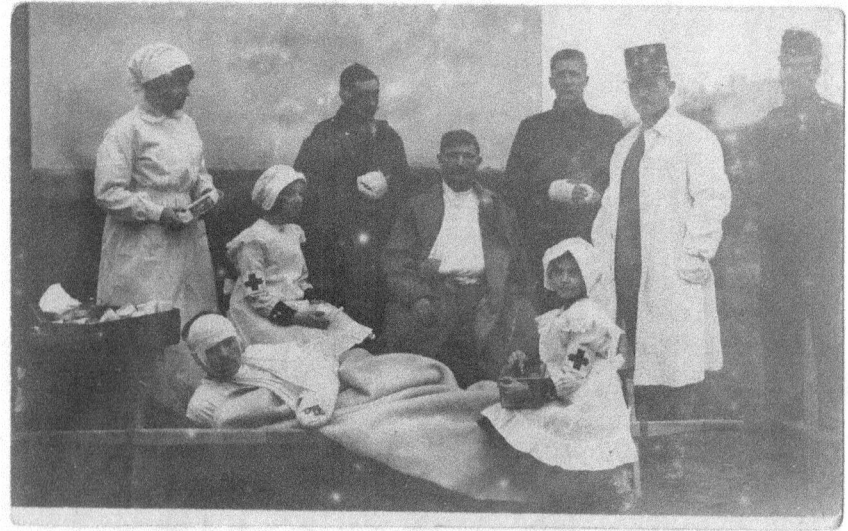

A WW I photo in which Gertrud and Magda sit beside a fallen soldier with their doctor parents, 1914.

A Love Affair with Dance Begins

The First World War ended on November 11, 1918. This led to Germany and Russia losing territory and the Austro-Hungarian and Ottoman Empires ceased to exist. The large German speaking population of Bohemia was incorporated into the new state of Czechoslovakia against their will in accordance with the Treaty of Saint Germain. The German speaking majority of Bohemia protested to no avail.

Jelly and Gustav Hahn, Karlsbad 1918. Written on the back of the postcard/photograph mailed to Zahnatelier Hahn Drei Lilieu (Hahn Dental Studio Three Lilies). "Once again quite a poor picture of me but many heartfelt greetings from us two." Laibach. (now Ljubljana, Slovenia)

The Hahn family decided to stay in Karlsbad after the war. And although German was their first language, the Hahn sisters now always identified themselves as Czechoslovakian. In 1918, the winning army placed many economic and cultural sanctions on the German speaking population of the area and began a systematic purge of German culture which led to much resentment and set the stage for the future claim by the Nazi regime

Our Love Affair with Dance

that Bohemia should be part of Germany. However, the Hahn parents seem to have prospered after the war and enjoyed their professional lives. The Hahn sisters became immersed in the life of their dance school in Karlsbad and said that they were always eager to perform.

> 1919, A war-torn Europe. The conquered people sought to overcome their physical defeat by finding new intellectual values, new forms, new expressions. Out of destruction and uproar, out of the struggle for one's existence, grew the awareness that man was inextricably entangled in political issues that reflected the economic and social revolution of modern man. (Holm, 1951, 1992, p. 24)

After the upheaval of the war, Germany and the newly formed Czechoslovakia reinvented and renewed their culture, society, and political ambitions. The Hahn sisters were privileged to grow up during the creativity of this period which is referred to as Weimar culture. Weimar culture was named after the newly formed Weimar German Republic. This golden age of modernity was a flourishing of the arts and sciences in Germany and Austria after the First World War and up to Hitler's taking power in Germany in 1933. In particular, Berlin and Vienna were sites of fertile, artistic innovation in all of the arts and especially for dance.

According to historian Toepfer (1997), who I mentioned extensively details the dance and body culture of this period in his book Empire of Ecstasy: Nudity and Movement in German Body Culture 1910–1935:

> German culture between 1910 and 1930 cultivated an attitude toward the body unprecedented in its modernity, intensity, and complexity. This attitude motivated the formation of body culture. (p. 6) The uniquely Germanic construction of the modern body involved two large categories of performance: nudity and physical movement, particularly ideas about movement introduced by the most turbulent dance culture in history. (p. 7)

It is important to note, as reported by Toepfer (1997), that the term 'Germanic body culture' "extended beyond the national borders of Germany" (p. 8).

Moreover, many people who contributed significantly to the body culture in Germany did not originally come from Germany. The body culture was "German" insofar as distinct personalities regarded Germany as somehow decisive in shaping their ideas and careers, but it did not exist only and entirely in Germany. (Toepfer, 1997, p. 8)

The young Hahn sisters embraced the philosophy of the new body culture and being from a middle class home with professional parents, who loved the arts, the sisters said they were supported in all of their endeavours to dance. Magda and Gertrud shared that their parents encouraged them to travel and experience life and try different methods and schools of dance. Toepfer (1997), when discussing the emergence of Germanic body culture, makes mention that the rise of body culture was largely due to the achievement of young women. Toepfer (1997) imparts that:

These women believed that unprecedented assertions of freedom and power for their sex depended on revised perceptions of the female body and its expressive capabilities. The desire for a modern identity in a modern body entailed a desire for unprecedented expressions of ecstatic experience resulting from a collapse of difference between inner and outer forms of being and metaphysics, even among the most rational advocates of the body culture. (p. 11)

The Hahn sisters touched on that before WWI, in their perspective, women in Europe had been prevented and discouraged from becoming artists of any kind and deemed successful only as housewives and mothers. Most middle or upper class women did not work outside the home or aspire to an artistic lifestyle as it was not considered respectable. With the acceptance and popularity of the new body culture, the doors of an artistic life as a dancer were suddenly thrown open and became viable for women, who still wished to retain their good reputation. Magda and Gertrud both stated that the only profession they had ever aspired to was dancing.

The sisters related in several conversations about their early life that they were fortunate that their parents had a 'modern' attitude and fully supported their decisions to focus on being dancers. The sisters asserted they were never pressured to marry or to have children. I remember the Hahn

Our Love Affair with Dance

sisters mentioning many times that marriage and children were not important to them. They both did eventually marry and divorce but never had any children with apparently no regrets. In fact, I remember Gertrud mentioning several times that she always sought ways to avoid pregnancy. The sisters clearly felt that 'the dance' provided all that they needed from life.

An early Gerti Hahn programme from a public performance in Karlsbad, July 5, 1918. I note that Frl. Gerti Hahn was a major performer and organizer.

Translated as:

> Lecture with Demonstration/Rhythmic Gymnastic Exercises Saturday July 5th, 1918 Under friendly cooperation from Fraulein Gerti Hahn (15 years) and then several other student dancers' names are listed.

Gerti was on the bill in the following dances: Part 11.

a) Tanzlied von Jacques-Dalcroze (A Dance Story of Jacques-Dalcroze).

d) A Dance (in the outdoor style) by Gerti Hahn. Music by Adolph Adam (Danced by Gerti Hahn).

e) The Song of the Grain by Gerti Hahn (plastic rehearsal). (Plastic in Dalcroze terms means dance with a meaningful continuity and flow between each movement, not a sequence of poses. Gertrud said a plastic rehearsal was also a term to indicate improvisation was included.)

The lecture demonstration model, which showed exercises and dance kinetics as a way to educate one's audience about 'the dance' before any set choreography was presented, was to become a Hahn sisters' staple for all of their future performances.

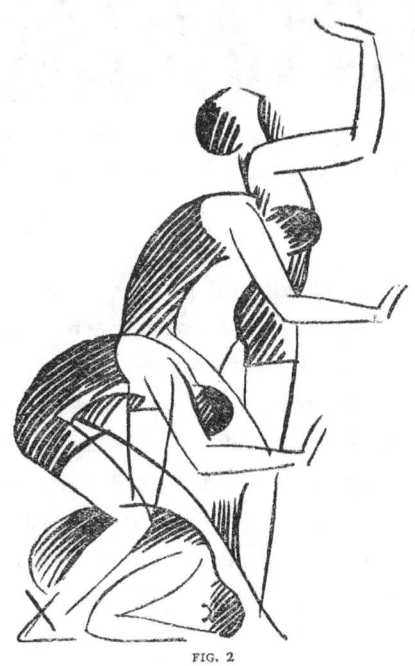

The Technique of Moving Plastic. (Jacques-Dalcroze, 1930, p. 17)

"By what special means can we attempt to restore living or moving plastic, both individual and collective? What new habits of motion are to be created? What fresh combinations are to be sought? What physical means can be placed at the disposal of such technique as will ensure the life and beauty of body movements?" (Jacques-Dalcroze, 1930, p.18).

Congratulatory flowers from Gerti's family and friends for her performance in Karlsbad, July 5, 1918.

Gerti: I am truly pleased with myself today after dancing so well. Not only did I have a successful performance, but I additionally triumphed by presenting some of my own choreography. This has reaffirmed my conviction that the dance is to be my path in life. I also chose what I think is absolutely wonderful music for my performance of A Dance in the Outdoor Style. I adore the works of the Frenchman Adolphe Adam. He is the composer of so many famous songs, ballets, and operas, including Giselle and Le Corsaire.

I know some people think I took a big risk by improvising some of my steps. But really, my dances are not entirely un-

A Love Affair with Dance Begins

planned. Herr Ernst, the stage manager and director, predicted I would fall on my face. He said I should feel shame to attempt to dance for an audience without proper set choreography. (He can be so stuffy). Fortunately, I did not fall on my face. And as famous dancers like Duncan profess, the choreography just opened up before me, the stage a blank slate to be filled in the moment. I was inspired by the Terpsichorean Muse herself. This was heavenly. My body took over as soon as I heard the music. I didn't over think what I was going to do. I simply danced. The audience was enraptured. So many well-wishers and bouquets afterwards! I am thrilled by this success, but more importantly, now I know I will be a dancer forever.

A program from February 20, 1919 with Gerti as one of the performers.

Translated from German, the programme reads:

> Goodbye to the Roho A Benefit for the Children's Kitchen. Note: On the bill, Number 12. Naschkatzchen (Sweet Kitty) (music by Adam, Si j'etais roi translated as If I was king) Frl. Gerda Hahn (I note the misspelling of Gertrud's name)

The piece of music, Si j'etais roi, written in 1852 by Adolphe Adam, was quite a bold choice for the young, teenage Gerti to dance as a solo. She had to have had a lot of confidence in herself and her ability as a dancer. Si j'etais roi is from a light opera and starts with orchestral fanfare before quieting into mellow French horns and harp, then again a swirling of tones like a storm unfurling in its glory, before returning to calmness and a mixture of light waltz like melodies and marches.

Many congratulatory flowers for sixteen year old Gerti, Karlsbad 1919.

Gerti: Again I have triumphed, in that I repeated my past success on stage with the Adam piece. I do not feel smug. On the contrary, I have worked very hard for this. My moments performing were fleeting but will stay with me as a memorable beginning. A beginning of my time to shine forth with my vision for what dance can be. With this performance in particular, I have learned how one must fight and conspire to get on a bill. Other performers are not always welcoming. The other dancers seemed afraid of being upstaged or looking insignificant when positioned before or after my piece. I must confess I have used my parents' good names and contributions to our town to win favour. (Papa being friends with the theatre owner certainly did help.) I seem to be passing from my naive and innocent girlhood to that of a woman. A woman that sees that all is not flowers and sweetness while garnering life's success but sweat, perseverance, and a will to be the best. Ich drucke die Daumen. (I keep my fingers crossed.)

Fifteen year old Magda with the family German Shepherd, 1920.

Magda: I have often pondered what makes one a great dancer, as this is what I aspire to be. Yes, one needs to have a solid technique, to be sure. But there is more. One undoubtedly requires the ability to perform under pressure and make the dance fresh and alive, even though one has performed it a thousand times. But when one examines the truly great dancer, and what separates this dancer from the corps, this dancer has a special magnetic attraction, a charisma that is projected to the audience and inspires devotion because of the purity and authenticity of their motions. The audience can feel this dancer's allure. It is palpable and real. How this is achieved is still a mystery to me. Evoking this ineffable something is what I aim for.

I know that this resonation with one's audience must be present in every part of the body and especially in the expression on one's face. This charismatic force, visible and invisible, in the muscles and tendons, the bones and heart, in each and every gesture the dancer makes, seems to be conveyed by the true artist to an audience through their own individual magic. The art of moving plastic requires bringing the inside, out.

5

DANCE AS THE HIGHEST CALLING

Karlsbad and Europe 1921–1932

Gertrud and Magda reflected that they were enthusiastic and prolific performers in their teens in Karlsbad. I note a review and press clipping Gertrud kept from August 5, 1921 from The Daily German Newspaper. She was eighteen at this time.

A review in The Daily German Newspaper of
Gerti Hahn's performance, August 5, 1921.

A rough translation is:

> She is a young and pretty artist. Gerti Hahn has a perfect dancing art. How she moves is very gracious and elegant. Her grace and elegance come together to make the art of her dancing perfect. A great carrier of art. And she got many ovations.

Gertrud, being two years older than Magda and very much the leader of the two sisters at this time, was the first to leave Karlsbad to travel in Europe and study dance away from her family. Gertrud initially studied at the Vienna Opera with the prima ballerina, Cerri, in 1921, when she was eighteen. Cacilie Cerri (1872–1931) was an Italian ballerina, who established herself as the prima ballerina of the Hofoper (Opera) and subsequently the Staatsoper (State Opera) in Vienna, between 1907 and 1921. With the success of Ausdruckstanz (Expressionist Dance), Cerri also began to have solo dance evenings with her students as well as teaching at the Vienna Opera.

In our conversations about Gertrud's experiences studying dance in Europe during the 1920s, Gertrud shared that her time at the Vienna Opera Ballet was challenging at first. She related that rather than being the young and talented dancer that everyone seemed to have heard of in Karlsbad, she now found herself one of many accomplished teenage girls trying to be noticed and deemed worthy for the corps de ballet. She added that the young, female dance students at the Vienna Opera were called 'rats' and when leaving the Opera House after classes had to navigate many male admirers hanging around outside the stage door. Gertrud commented that the girls, with their dance slippers slung over their shoulders, were told to keep their eyes down on the ground and not to talk to the men as they left the premises. At the Vienna Opera, Gertrud said she danced in ballets which incorporated the minuet, marche, and waltz.

She added that she shared accommodation with several other dance students in very tiny rooms and they went out for most meals. Gertrud also remarked that she loved Vienna right away and was never homesick, except for missing Magda. She said she worked very hard in the classes and made many long time friends, which she stayed in touch with and would meet again at the various ballet and modern dance schools she studied at during the 1920s. Gertrud added that this first experience away from home was for her a dream come true.

Dance as the Highest Calling

Cacilie Cerri Jugend-Ballett Poster, June 19, 1922.

Gertrud kept a large poster from 1922. From the poster we learn that she danced at the Academy Theater in Vienna with Cacilie Cerri's Youth Ballet. Gerti was one of sixteen young guest dancers to perform on this bill. She was nineteen years old.

It reads in a translation from German:

> Akademie Theatre
> Monday the 19 of June, 1922
> 8 o'clock in the evening
> Cacelie Cerri
> Youth Ballet
> Adele Krausenecker, Solo dancer of the State Opera,
> As a Guest Gerti Hahn (amongst the names of other young dancers)

123

Our Love Affair with Dance

Gerti in Vienna, 1922.

Gerti: I am finally out of Karlsbad and in Vienna, dancing! It feels marvellous to be so anonymous and not be the daughter of the well known, town doctors when I walk down the street. No one knows me here. I am free to reinvent myself.

But to tell the truth, I really have no time to think about making any changes to my person. I am far too busy with the ballet. As students at the Vienna Opera Ballet, we are dancing and rehearsing from early morning until afternoon. It is hard work, but I am amazed at how the extra hours have built up my muscles and stamina even further. Richard Strauss, the famous composer, much to my parents delight, has been the director of the Staatsoper (State Opera) in Vienna since 1919.

After classes, my roommates and I quickly eat some supper somewhere and try to get cheap tickets to the theater. If there is nothing available, we go to the pictures or find a dance club. Here in Vienna there is a coffee house culture. Most people in Vienna live in small, cramped flats and use the coffee houses as extended living rooms. Writers, poets, and painters have their favourite coffee houses. Since our lodgings are also very tiny, if we girls want to meet up with anyone, we often gather at a dance café that has live musicians playing American jazz. The fox trot is all the rage right now. My days and nights are thus filled to the brim.

Gerti's First Solo Performance in Karlsbad. September 8, 1922.

This newspaper clipping advertises Gerti Hahn's upcoming performance (Einmaliger Tanz-Abend) 'A Unique Dance Evening'. I note again that the program is in German not Czech as the Karlsbad area of Czechoslovakia at this time was mostly German speaking. Gertrud chose music by Strauss, Mozart, Chopin, and Dvorak amongst others.

Gerti received many flowers from well-wishers after her first solo performance in Karlsbad, September 9, 1922.

Gerti: I have taken a little holiday to visit my parents and Magda in Karlsbad and am thoroughly enjoying being 'someone' again. This is a homecoming but also a chance to show my town my improved talent as a dancer. This time the performance was all my own. There was one exception, as I was very happy to have Magda join me for our special favourite, the waltz by Strauss. How can I describe choreographing a whole program alone? It was exhilarating and intimidating. But I know I am more than ready now. The audience wanted to see their favourite dances, the waltz, the marche, and the minuet. So I gave them their favourites with my special added themes. For example, I was a village swallow waltzing to Strauss, dancing pure ballet to Chopin, and my favourite, Miriam, danced to Alte Weisen (Old Tunes) with a tambourine. This is the story from the Old Testament of Miriam, the prophetess leading the women out of Egypt. I had cheers, tears, and three standing ovations for this dance. Then I performed a lively Marche to leave the audience with an upbeat feeling. The conductor told me he had never seen anyone turn so quickly.

In late 1922, seventeen year old Magda, who loved the ballet and also craved a broader horizon for herself as a dancer, joined Gertrud in Vienna. She also studied and performed at the Vienna Opera with Cerri.

Magda, 1922.

Magda at seventeen, 1922.

Magda: Finally, I am out in the world dancing in Vienna, and with Gerti. Oh, my experiences so far are wonderful. I am learning so much. I realize now that dancing in Karlsbad, I was a big fish in a small pond. What did I know? Nothing about how the real dance world works. I am now immersed in very structured and competitive classes at the Vienna Opera. I am trying to hold my own. Some girls are friendly, some are definitely not. Everything is based on how one looks, how one can remember the sequences and choreography, and how well one can work for hours on end without showing fatigue or complaining.

Notes to self from ballet classes: Things I have been told are good: My port de bras has grace, I have good expression, and I have strong suspension and height in my jumps. Things I am definitely improving in: alignment, turnout, cleaner footwork, and balance. Things I need to really perfect, pointe work, pointe work, pointe work!

In 1923, inconsolably, Gertrud and Magda's mother died unexpectedly, which brought the sisters back to Karlsbad. In 1924, Gertrud opened her own dance school in Karlsbad and taught Dalcroze rhythmic gymnastics, ballet, and modern dance. She related that she attracted many students and choreographed and danced in numerous performances she organized. From conversations with the Hahn sisters about their dance experiences in the 1920s, they said while they periodically took time to study dance at popular schools in other parts of Europe, they kept the Hahn Dance Academy operating in Karlsbad by employing trusted teachers.

Gertrud's and Magda's mother Jelly Hahn, 1922.

Gerti: There is a gaping hole in our lives now that Mutti has left us. For the time being we will stay in Karlsbad, close to our Papa as he is very sad. I have opened a dance school to keep our passion for dance alive, although we dearly miss our classes in Vienna. But family is everything. Magda and I are utilizing all that we have learned at the Opera Ballet to form a school that we can be proud of. I have many plans for future choreography.

We mourn our dear Mutti deeply. I will keep her memory as part of myself and always remember the special childhood she gave us. And I will never forget that she encouraged us as girls, to not be afraid to follow our own path, to always seek to grow in our art, and especially to never give up exalting our Muse. How do we get over this great loss? Papa says we must dance, dance out our grief, and above all support one another as a family…

Gertrud's and Magda's mother, in her dental surgery.

A translation from German on the picture/postcard reads: "With acceptance, one person does everything well."

> **Magda:** Our dear Mutti has gone. She was so young and vital. Too young to leave us. It does not seem fair. Her passing is a great tragedy for our family. Gerti, Papa, and I are stunned. We sit and stare at her clothes, her hairbrush, her beautiful jewelry, and try to realize she will never touch them again. What are we to do? Grief does not go away on a time table. I feel this loss will be with us forever.
>
> I will go on by remembering my mother as someone who wanted Gerti and I to lead big lives. Lives which had a deeper meaning. She often said, "Capability lies in the mind and spirit as well as the body, believing yourself able is the beginning." For us, the deeper meaning lies in the dance and so we will carry on with life, remembering Mutti as our inspiration.

As mentioned, the First World War had brought about immense changes socially, politically, and economically worldwide. After the war, the new stability brought a sustained economic prosperity to Western Europe, particularly to Berlin, Paris, and to the area where the sisters lived in Karlsbad.

> The United States gained dominance in world finance. Thus, when Weimar Republic Germany could no longer afford to pay World War I reparations to the United Kingdom, France, and other Allies, the Americans came up with the Dawes Plan. Wall Street invested heavily in Germany, which repaid its reparations to nations that, in turn, used the dollars to pay off debts to Washington. By the middle of the decade, prosperity was widespread. "The Roaring Twenties", 9 September 2019, en.wikipedia.org/wiki/Roaring_Twenties.

As other young women of this period, the Hahn sisters embraced the 1920s as a new era of independence and self-determination. Socio-cultural norms, attitudes, and practices were undergoing huge revisions and the definition of womanhood was in flux.

The decade 1920 to 1930 was a ground breaking epoch for technology, which drastically changed life for the better for women. These years saw the introduction of electric appliances, such as the washing machine, vacuum cleaner, refrigerator, and electric stove. Automobiles, telephones, motion pictures, and radio were now accessible. Radio became a staple in most homes and this broadcasting medium introduced audiences to a new mass culture of advertising, music, popular singers, and radio stars. In 1925, electrical recording became available for commercially issued gramophone records. People now travelled by plane. Musical tastes changed to jazz and dances such as the Charleston and the Black Bottom became popular worldwide. The 'flapper' became a symbol of women's liberation and of her freedom to choose her role in society. Women's voting rights in representative and direct democracies were expanded in most major European countries.

Gertrud, early 1920s.

In the 1920s, new magazines that appealed to young, German speaking women became popular with their sensuous images and advertisements... The glossy pages of Die Dame and Das Blatt der Hausfrau displayed the "Neue Frauen," "New Girl". She was young and fashionable, financially independent. The magazines kept her up to date on styles, clothes, designers, arts, sports, and modern technology. "The Roaring Twenties", 9 September 2019, en.wikipedia.org/wiki/Roaring_Twenties.

Magda, early 1920s.
"After the Great War, a new female silhouette emerged. Bobbed hair and shorter skirts became the style of the day."

Immortalized in movies and magazine covers, young women's fashions of the 1920s set both a trend and social statement, a breaking-off from the rigid Victorian way of life. These young, rebellious, middle-class women, labeled 'flappers' by older generations, did away with the corset and donned slinky knee length dresses, which exposed their legs and arms. "The Roaring Twenties", 9 September 2019, en.wikipedia.org/wiki/Roaring_Twenties.

Magda Hahn, Gustav Hahn, Gertrud Hahn, 1925.

Gerti: I am in a state of in between. I crave a change. I am feeling like I want to escape Karlsbad, where everyone we know must still stop to talk and offer condolences about Mutti. I actually didn't realize how many kindnesses she had performed anonymously, never seeking public credit or even monetary reward. People hold her in such high esteem. I am told over and over that she had a reputation for great generosity and concern for the health of our community. These do not seem to be just platitudes offered for the one who has passed away but very genuine expressions of loss by each person that has spoken to me. How could I have been so oblivious to these details of my own mother's life? I feel ashamed. She was my Mutti, a very caring and wise mother, but I have been so wrapped up in myself and my goals to dance. I regret not paying her more attention. I was off in Vienna creating a career for myself, not realizing her poor health.

Magda agrees we shall always mourn Mutti's early death but has repeatedly added that I should feel no guilt, for we were both doing what Mutti wanted us to do, which was leading productive and artistic lives dancing. Magda, my only true confidant, is right. Life is not to be wasted on regret or remorse. I want to travel again and leave Karlsbad, even for just a little while. This small town can be so stifling.

Magda: Our life goes on. Mutti's dying has left its mark on all of us. Papa is not the same. He retains a visible appreciation for the small everyday things that make life worth living, but the Papa we knew has disappeared. He hides it well. He still goes to his clinic, helping so many people in our community, especially veterans of the Great War. He still makes small jokes and tells Gerti and I how much he loves us. But he has gone somewhere we cannot follow. I hate to admit that losing the love of one's life is not something I can readily relate to or understand. I have admirers but no one special that could ever replace my true love, which is dancing. This could sound odd to people not in love with the dance. After all, most young women, even in this modern age, seem to be looking for husbands and yearning after babies or new outfits. Gerti and I stand out in our community because we have no interest in 'settling down'. We are free spirits in the dance and make no apology for this. But for Papa, we will, for the time being, stay in Karlsbad.

Gerti Hahn, 1920s.

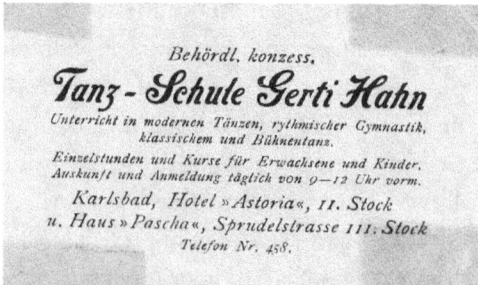

Gerti's business card promoting her Karlsbad dance school. Translated as: Agency certified, Gerti Hahn Dance School. Classes in Modern Dance, Rhythmic Gymnastics, Classical and Stage Dance. Single courses and courses for adults and children.

Dance as the Highest Calling

Magda in a studio pose, mid 1920s.

Magda: I am coming to understand the great secret of the inner mechanisms that enable the dance to metaphorically leap off the stage and connect to an audience. Dalcroze explains this well.

The sensations afforded by the natural rhythms of our bodies strengthen our instinct for rhythm and rhythmic consciousness. It is through this instinct and this consciousness, blended with the aesthetic sense, that we experience complete artistic emotions. For an artist, emotion is not only the outcome of nervous, physical, and instinctive vibrations; it should spring from the mysterious laboratory where physical sensations become transformed by higher energies and wills. Undoubtedly, the artist is generally born such, one whose organism often functions apart from consciousness. (Jacques-Dalcroze, 1925, p. 183)

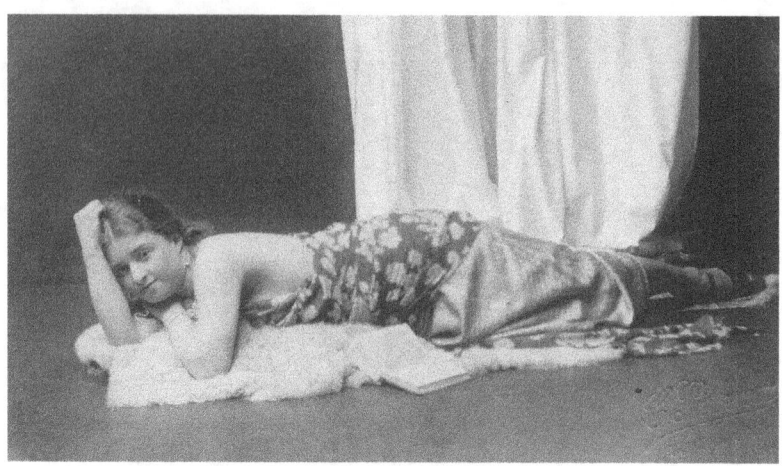

Gerti in a studio pose, mid 1920s.

Gerti: Magda and I have been reading some recent essays by Dalcroze and his views on Eurhythmics and Art. His words provoke an inner debate and make me challenge my long held views on the dance. Dalcroze states:

Does an impression of bodily grace imply a perfect impression of beauty? Not always, for perfect beauty of movement cannot dispense with rhythm. Now, a graceful movement which seems beautiful, repeated again and again in time though without rhythm, inevitably produces an impression of monotony. There is no beauty that does not evoke an idea of the renewal and continuation of life. Examine certain traditional figures of the classic Italian ballet. Could anything be less moving than the spectacle of fifty danseuses obstinately bent upon inclining the head in one direction and raising the leg in the other? If a succession of movements is to be beautiful, the duration and intensity of the rhythms must vary, the imagination must come into play in order to create contrasts and alternations. We should feel the presence of a guiding mind which, profiting by momentary impulses, prevents movements from becoming automatic. The introduction of spontaneous rhythmic movements into a succession of ordered movements inevitably calls forth emotion. (Jacques-Dalcroze, 1925, p. 185)

Dance as the Highest Calling

All of what Dalcroze says calls into question whether I should continue to pursue the ballet or turn to the modern dance or even some other style of dance. Europe has exploded in new and intriguing forms of body expression. I am thus encouraged to seek something more original and that has a deeper meaning. Magda, of course, will be continuing to study the ballet, as she cannot get enough of it, although I notice that Ausdruckstanz (Expressionist Dance) is influencing the style of ballet we are seeing now.

Magda at the Hahn Karlsbad Dance School, mid 1920s.

Magda: A gentle rising on toe, becomes a balance, a new way to feeling, a provision, a glimpse into the ephemeral depths of myself. The feeling is as if lightning is lashing my insides. I tremble with passion or is it nerves? But I give nothing away in my stance, instead I take a small breath and hold my pose. I inhale slowly in and out and am sustained. I float. I am as a statue.

Then a whisper of movement stirs in my arms as I circle them over my head. My limbs become a halo for my vision. With grace I lower my stance and glide forward, silently, across the floor, embracing the very air I move through. I am a breeze flowing lightly, beautifully, in motion, created by my own breath and muscle. I turn, feeling the gorgeousness of space, sweeping my vision into a swirl and whirl, so that I come to know that motion is my true state of being.

I am unravelling the mysteries of my body, searching for my inner truth in the creation of my movement.

Gerti poses at the Hahn Karlsbad Dance Studio, mid 1920s.

Gerti: They say that life should be taken as it comes so I am choosing not to think of unhappy things but concentrate on what is good and enjoy what I have. I am finally fulfilling all of my dreams. I am teaching, creating, and living as a dancer. I am digging into the depths of the performing art I love so much. I absolutely adore being on stage! I ponder what it is that takes me over as I enter into the space to perform? Some force that is so powerful, magnificent, and mystical. I am clay in the hands of this force and cannot deny its charm or calling. But even as this is so wonderful, I must confess to my own insecurity. Why was I chosen? Why did the Muse of the Dance select me to receive this great prize? I thank the spinning, moving, dancing universe, that dance knew my name before I was born and welcomed me as a sister into this world. Toi toi toi!

(The expression 'Toi toi toi' is German and used in the performing arts to wish an artist success in an imminent performance. It is similar to "break a leg" and reflects a superstition that wishing someone "good luck" is in fact bad luck. Gertrud often said this expression to her students before a performance.)

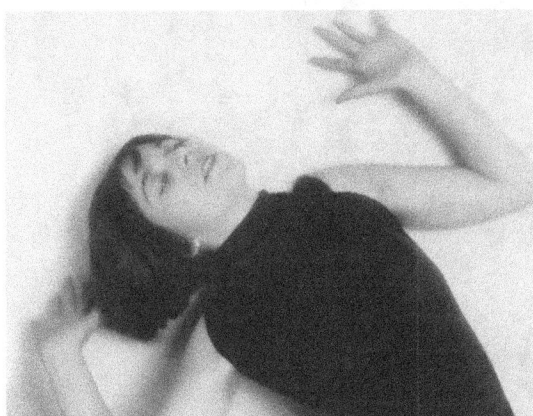 

Magda in two studio portraits, mid 1920s.

Magda: For me, the mystical essence of the dance will never stop being uncovered. I especially love teaching the children at our dance school. I watch the young pupils unfold in their art.

The pleased expressions on their faces to have mastered a gesture, a movement, a sequence of steps. I observe that the very young are quite special beings in that they don't feel anything is impossible yet.

Gerti leaves the little one's teaching to me as she says they are not to her interest. But I see new shapes, spaces, and excitement in everything these children do. They are so unformed, eager, and trusting. In sharing the dance with them I am exhilarated. How can I explain this to people who know nothing of dancing? One is imparting and encouraging a hidden joy to reveal itself and leading the student to find their own particular abilities. The pupils are discovering their physical bodies as well as their inner thoughts and emotions. Each pupil is so unique. I watch their beauty arrive in brief moments. A simple walk, a turn, a jump, is captivating for them.

Magda in a studio dance portrait, mid 1920s.

Dance as the Highest Calling

Gerti in a pose from a character dance piece, mid 1920s.

Gerti: I love exploring the possibilities of the dance. One may take on so many different roles. There is a mystery and excitement in assuming a new persona. I particularly love being the strong woman who seems to save the world from dying of ennui as I deliver a round of fantastic turns and then plunge into quick heels and toes faster than the audience can follow. My calling is the dance and the dance keeps calling me to ever new experiences. I hope to go to Wigman to study at some later date and my friend Liesl keeps asking me to come to Paris. I will. I must. There is so much to learn and try. Papa seems better now but understandably will not ever get over losing Mutti. I hesitate to leave him and Karlsbad, but I know Mutti would want Magda and I to travel again and grow in the dance.

Gerti with two unknown performers in a photograph from an unknown stage production in Karlsbad, 1924.

Gerti: I am expanding my repertoire on the stage to include acting. Magda says I do very well but I think she is just saying this because she is my sister. The play I am in is a period piece. Quite frivolous but surprisingly well attended and we got passable reviews. It is a love story and I am the heroine, whom two boys fight over. Really, how droll. Although if this were my real life, I might be more interested. Here I am twenty-one years old and I have to admit I have not really been in love with anyone yet. Where is my handsome prince? But alas I am not the type to be swept off my feet, unless I am dancing! It is not as if I haven't been asked to walk out or to share a coffee. It is just that nobody seems to measure up to what I need in a partner. And no, it is not vanity. I am solely focused on dancing and any future companion must support my vision and allow me to fulfill my destiny.

Young unknown Karlsbad Hahn dance students, 1925.

Magda: At the Hahn Dance School, I rely on the expertise of the masters of movement, and in particular, the writings of Jacques-Dalcroze, as his words inspire the necessity of allowing children to express themselves individually.

Exercises in athletics or drill aim at a purely material object, whereas we endeavour to produce a common outward expression of individual emotions. Here rhythm is the link between mind and senses, and this to such a degree that each pupil speedily rejects the current opinion which looks upon the body as inferior to the mind. He quickly comes to regard his body as an instrument of incomparable delicacy, susceptible of the noblest and the most artistic expression. (Jacques-Dalcroze, 1925, pp. 110–111)

Magda: We continue to enjoy our teaching and performing at our Karlsbad dance school. Gerti is very driven to be the best and to show the world how wonderful the dance is for everyone. She has worked extremely hard and taken on the many roles of choreographer, writer, stage manager, producer, and inspiring dancer to make our next production a successful venture. The Modern Picture Book is a spectacular presentation that everyone in our town, young and old, should see. I feel confident in the dances and parts I play. Gerti has made sure everyone looks glamorous. She has really gone all out for costumes and scenery. The whole cast has rehearsed once, so far, with the orchestra and I am impressed at how it all is coming together. I am thrilled with how marvellous this show is going to be!

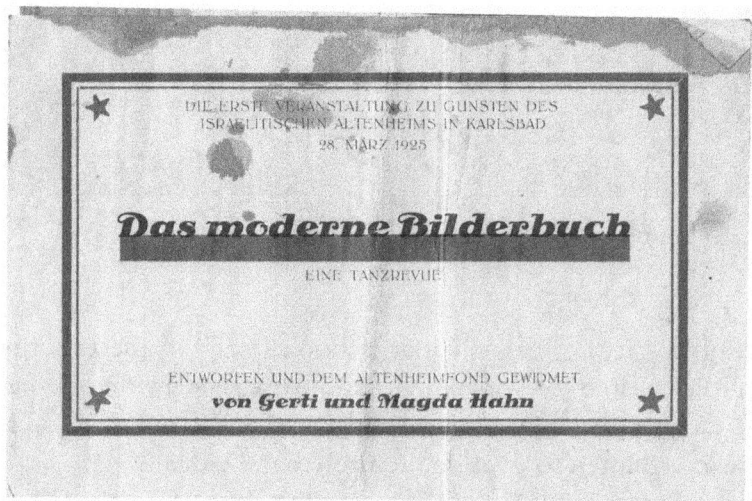

The programme cover for Das moderne Bilderbuch/ Eine Tanzrevue 28 Marz 1925. Entworfen Und Dem Altenheimfond Gewidmet von Gerti und Magda Hahn.

Translated from German as:

The Modern Picture Book/A Dance Review/ March 28, 1925. Designed and dedicated to the Old People's Fund. From Gerti and Magda Hahn.

Dance as the Highest Calling

From the following photograph, The Modern Picture Book appears to have been a very lavish production, featuring the entire Karlsbad Hahn Dance School. There were over one hundred performers. In the first section, the dances were under the title Rural Idyll, with over eighty performers. Magda was billed as the Water Carrier. In the second section, the dances were under the title Zirkus (Circus). Gerti was billed as Tanzerin (Dancer) and Magda was billed as Harlekin (Harlequin). The third section of the evening was called Oriental Scene, with a story line about rival slave owners. Gerti was billed as Ashraff, the main slave owner. Magda was Itu, Lieblingssklavin (her favourite slave). The fourth section on the bill was called Second Picture Series and consisted of various dances which included: Menuett, Nationaltanz (national dance), Marchen (fairy tale), Holzpuppen (wooden puppet), and Magda and Gerti in Wildwest.

A Hahn Karlsbad Dance School production, March 28, 1925, Das moderne Bilderbuch/Eine Tanzrevue.

In this photograph, the main cast of The Modern Picture Book poses with the orchestra. Gerti is wearing a white, full skirted dress, with her arms wide open (center right), and Magda is at her side with a cane as Harlequin. Gerti was the star of the production and the driving force behind the organization and choreography of the show, which the programme outlines as extensive and diverse in the dances and entertainments.

Gerti: I have exceeded my own expectations with this production. Although, the truth be told, I could not have managed everything without the hard work and help of Magda, all of our dance students, and friends, who contributed to the success of this show. It was actually quite glorious. And perhaps I came across as the diva, as I was always in the spotlight! But really, while my enjoyment did come from performing, I did not let it all go to my head. To the contrary, the pleasure I received came mainly from watching the other performers. I cannot say it enough, they were all brilliant.

I must admit I was the director and the 'brains' behind it all. But how can one measure the success of a show? The box office receipts were satisfying and the audience was most appreciative. But I look deeper. We had a great spirit of camaraderie develop amongst the cast and musicians. I think everyone involved has come away with a feeling of being a true artist. What more can one ask of life?

Magda and Gerti posing for A Modern Picture Book/An Oriental Scene.

Dance as the Highest Calling

Magda and Gerti, center, Magda reclining, Gerti standing next to an unknown male performer, from the Karlsbad performance of A Modern Picture Book/An Oriental Scene, 1925.

Magda: Well, I enjoyed being Gerti's favourite slave in this production and this will provide endless humour for us for some time to come. Really, Gerti's imagination and creative powers were in top form for all the story lines and choreography she created for this opulent, and sometimes dazzling, and always outstanding show. The 'Modern' Picture Book, indeed! The production was impressive, dramatic, and memorable. A wonderful evening to keep in my store of exceptional memories of our dance performances.

Everyone at the dance school and their friends and family were actually in awe of what this show accomplished. We put Karlsbad on the map, so to speak, in that we showed the surrounding communities the wealth of talent right here on their doorsteps. One review mentioned that there is really no need to go to a big city to see a first class dance production, as the Hahn Dance School had it all. What a fine compliment! I know Gerti is pleased.

After a smaller performance in Karlsbad, 1926, the dancers and musicians pose for a photograph. I note the band's name is in English and called the Big Fix. Gerti and Magda are both sitting far right, beside some photographs.

Gerti: Well, that show was exhausting but also exhilarating. We definitely impressed the crowd and our musicians were lively and well-rehearsed. We are so fortunate that we were able to get the theatre for the night we wanted. Again, thanks to Papa who knows the theatre owner. I have once again unabashedly resorted to using Papa's influence to gain theatre space to ensure we present as a polished and professional dance group. This must include a decent stage and orchestra pit, dressing rooms, and rehearsal space. The audiences' perceptions of us must be of the highest standard. We must do our best and be our best in this competitive world.

Ah so, after airing my thoughts and grievances, I must again remind myself to remember why we are dancing. It is not to have the best theatre or the most appreciative audience. After all, one may dance anywhere with no one present, and this dancing can be meaningful. We dance to bow down to the Muse and have reverence for the ability and inner art we possess. We dance to be thankful for the feeling and flow of that magical something of which only the called can lay claim to knowing of what I speak. To dance and move is our reason for being and these essential experiences lead us to harmonious living.

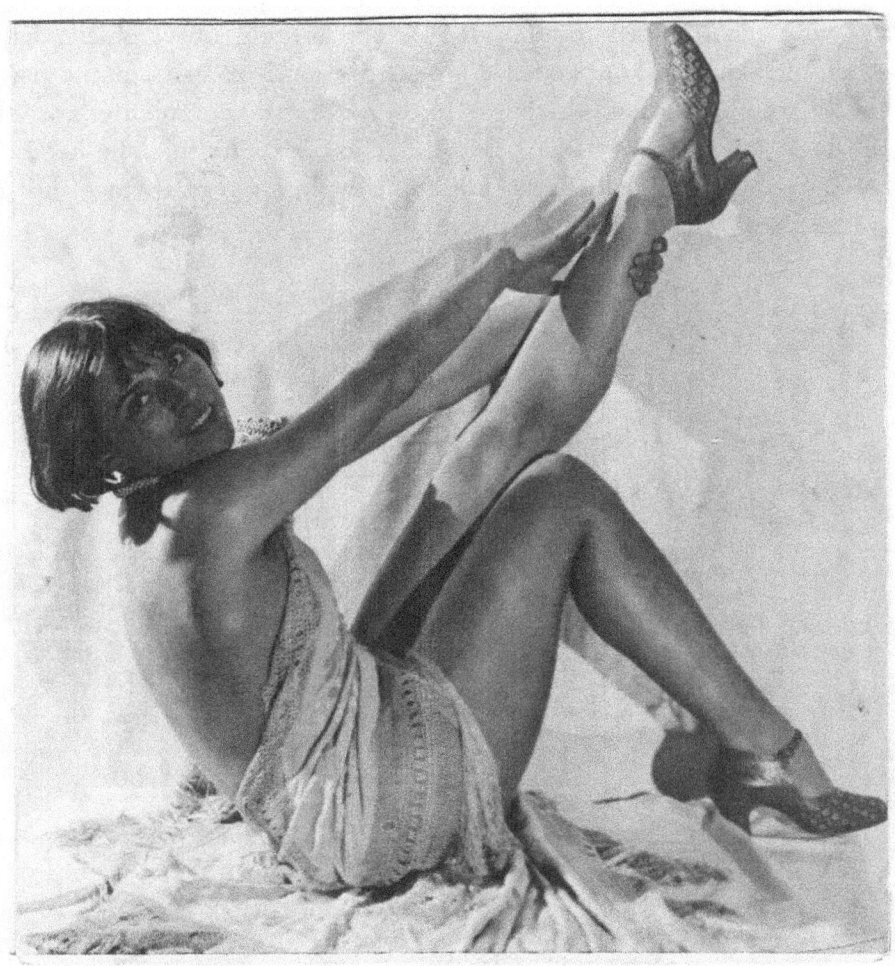

Magda, mid 1920s.

In 1926, Magda, who continued to love the ballet, left Karlsbad again to study in Berlin with Max Terpis (1889–1958), who led the Berlin State Opera as ballet master for six years from 1924 to 1930. Terpis had studied briefly with the famous modern dancer Mary Wigman and excelled at choreographing group movement. He was known for building "individual movements out of classical concepts supplemented by a distinctly modern enthusiasm for swinging motions" (Toepfer, 1997, p. 297). In a 1993 interview, Gertrud mentioned that Magda additionally went to art school while in Berlin and studied drawing and painting.

In 1927, Magda next studied with Ellen Tels-Rabanek (1885–1944) in Paris, who according to Toepfer (1997) "had an influential modern dance school and company,"… and … "pursued a kind of pantomimic dance derived from Delsartian principles" (p. 179). Gertrud commented that she saw Magda perform with the Ellen Tels company. She said she liked the choreography very much for its innovative exploration of themes and she also liked the beautiful brocade costumes.

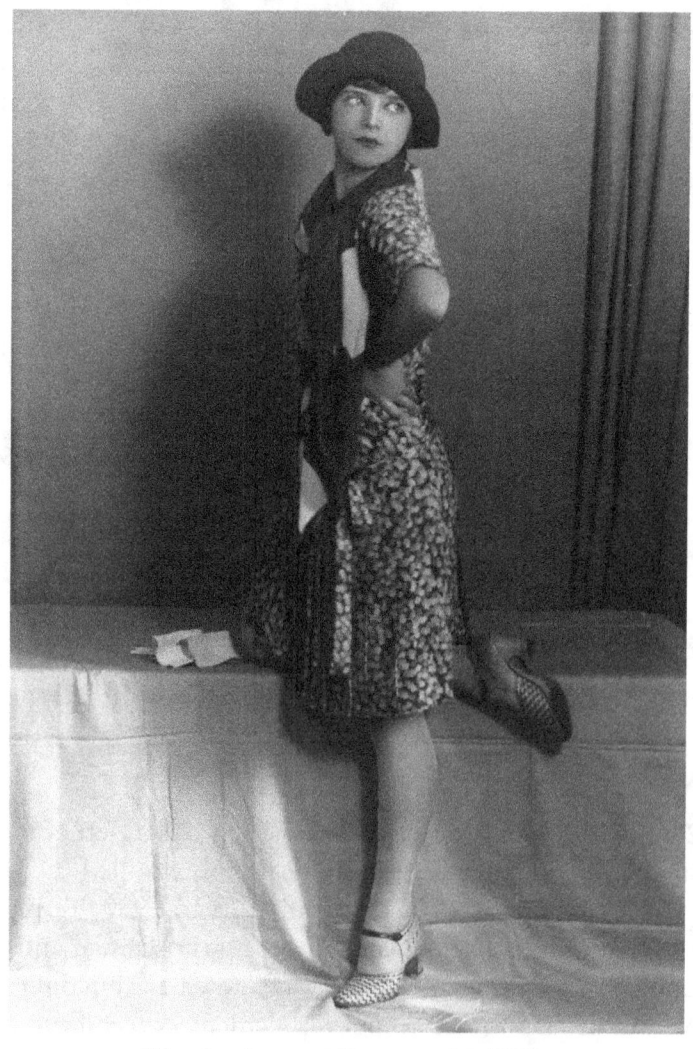

Magda, in a studio portrait, 1920's.

Dance as the Highest Calling

In 1927, Gertrud also spent time in Paris taking acrobatic theatre dance at The Folies Bergere School. The Folies Bergere was originally built as an opera house and opened on May 2, 1869. During the 1880s, a new form of entertainment was conceived by Edouard Marchand, which he called the music-hall revue. Beautiful women would be at the heart of Marchand's idea for the Folies. The American dancer Loie Fuller, who is famous for her innovation in theatrical lighting and her Serpentine Dance, starred at the Folies Bergere in the early 1890s.

In 1918, Paul Derval became the new artistic director and launched the careers of such notables as singer and actor Maurice Chevalier, singer Mistinguett, Fernadel, and the African-American expatriate singer, dancer, and entertainer, Josephine Baker.

Shows included trained dancers and acrobats. By the 1920s, the Folies Bergere had become a showcase for spectacular, cabaret performances and grand revues. Gertrud said that the performers wore elaborate costumes, which were very revealing and the shows often contained a great deal of nudity.

Folies Bergere School, 1927,
Gerti, centre left on the floor, with hands on her knees.

Gerti: Here I am at the Folies Bergere School. In Paris! How exciting! Ich liebe es or should I say J'aime ca! (I love it). My

French will have to improve now. My classes are acrobatic in nature and as such have the goal of improving the dance student's ability to perform theatrical movement for cabaret style shows. The practice studios we use are found upstairs after going through a warren of rooms near the top of the building. (You could easily get lost.)

Fortunately, I do well in the classes. I am extremely supple and flexible naturally. I have witnessed some girls trying to bend and stretch into positions with too much force which has led to injury. We do cartwheels, the splits, and paired flip overs to very lively music played by a pianist in the rehearsals. My ballet training is certainly a plus.

I am enjoying the camaraderie of the other students. I have made a good friend called Mimi. We are completely free to experiment with our own movement and dance together after the classes if the studio practice rooms are vacant. There is so much to learn from each other. Most girls have travelled around Europe and studied with other well-known schools and dancers. They inspire me to learn all I can while I am here in Paris.

I admire the professional dancers, who dance in the cabaret at night. I could be recruited after my apprenticeship. But I am not sure that this style of dance is what I am interested in pursuing. While the dancing is vivacious, the evoked sexuality and nudity is perhaps not for me. I need to rethink what exactly I am called to do and where. Mutti would have enjoyed the cabaret for its liberated spirit but perhaps not the way the girls are treated by the men.

Last night, students from the school were invited to an evening in the cabaret theatre to watch a show and it was fantastic. The performers wore the most risqué and suggestive costumes. One girl, who was very tall and slim, stood with a huge Russian wolfhound. She had on a long, white dress, which was completely open on the sides. You could see that she had nothing on underneath. People simply loved it. The audience was quite

Dance as the Highest Calling

unruly and at times shouted and cheered through the revue. The whole thing was thoroughly scandalous and to be greatly admired. Add the wonderful orchestra, the lights, the alcohol, and we girls had a marvellous evening.

A photograph of Gerti's fellow Folies Bergere School students, 1927.

Gerti (far right) Folies Bergere Dance School, 1927.

Our Love Affair with Dance

Folies Bergere Dance School, 1927, Gerti (far right).

Gerti (far right), Folies Bergere Dance School, 1927.

Dance as the Highest Calling

Folies Bergere Dance School, 1927, Gerti laughing, sitting centre on the floor, hands crossed over her legs.

Gerti (right front) with two unknown students, Folies Bergere School, 1927.

After studying in Paris at the Folies Bergere, Gertrud went to Dresden in 1928 to study modern dance with Mary Wigman. Mary Wigman (1886–1973) was a German dancer, choreographer, and dance instructor. A pioneer of expressionist modern dance, her work was hailed for bringing the deepest of existential experiences to the stage. She became one of the most iconic figures of Weimar German culture and is considered one of the most important figures in the history of European modern expressionist dance. According to dance historian Martin (1963), "Except for Isadora herself, no figure in the history of the modern dance occupies a higher position than Mary Wigman, in part, for her specific artistic creations, but mainly for her widening of the range of the art and the advancement of its underlying theory" (p. 144).

Gertrud in a studio photograph dated 1928.

Toepfer (1997) notes that Wigman was a prolific and successful performer. "During the 1920s… she produced nearly one hundred solo and group dances…" (p.108). Wigman was also a very successful teacher. "By

1927 she had 360 students enrolled at Dresden and more than 1200 enrolled at Wigman schools, operated by former students in Berlin, Frankfurt, Chemnitz, Riesa, Hamburg, Leipzig, Erfurt, Magdeburg, Munich, and Freiburg" (Toepfer, 1997, p. 108).

In recorded conversations from 1993, about Wigman's classes, Gertrud said, "The classes had about thirty students at a time and the warm up consisted of lots of bending, stretching, running, and leading with various body parts for at least half an hour before the main part of the class started." Gertrud also shared that, "The Wigman movement qualities or the foundations of Wigman's Ausdruckstanz were walking, gliding, falling or collapsing, various rhythms with the feet, jumping, skipping, turning or spinning, swinging, floating, and variations on the circle." She added that, "The Wigman movements were big sweeping gestures, masculine, and very strong and angular." Gertrud reminiscing remarked, "She liked Wigman's technique and style but it was too strong for her." She remembered that, "The students danced at least four to five hours a day and the Wigman classes always had structured improvisations."

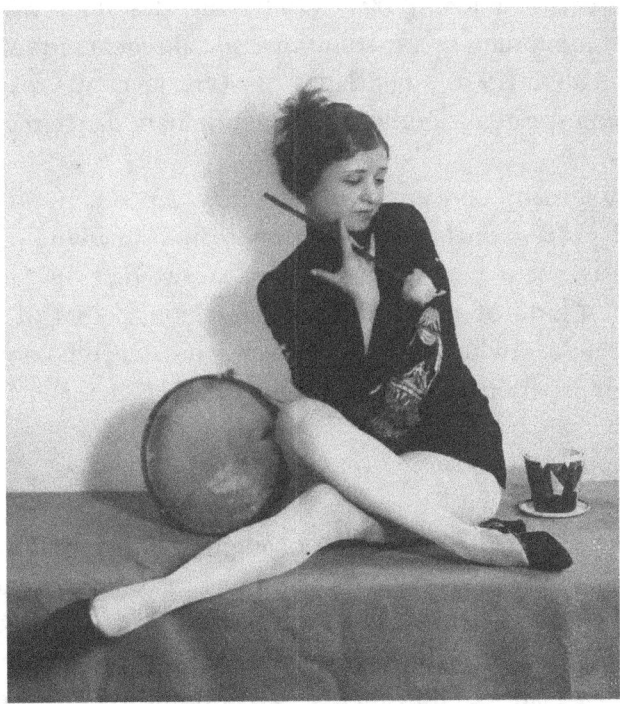

Gertrud poses with a Wigman inspired drum, 1928.

From the same taped conversations from 1993, Gertrud shared that, "Wigman wanted us to be individuals and her dance was different from other dance schools at the time, in that we danced barefoot and we were encouraged to make our dance our own." Gertrud related that, "Wigman liked to turn for half an hour every day as the Sufi dervishes and there was a performance every Sunday of student dances." She remarked with a wistful smile, "I would never miss this for anything and I loved the fact that Wigman students had the possibility to create and share their own dances with each other." Gertrud also mentioned that she liked Wigman's gong and drum accompaniment as, "Wigman didn't like music to dominate the movement."

Mary Wigman studied with Dalcroze and Rudolph Laban in her early years. "…she held on to Laban's use of improvisation and to his basic theory of the three elements—force, space and time—which became clearly recognizable components of her dance compositions and fundamental to her teaching. Wigman also adopted Laban's metaphysical idealism, using space as a metaphor for cosmic order" (Partsch-Bergsohn, 1994, p. 18).

Dance historian Randall (2005) additionally describes Wigman's vision for dance as functioning as a medium for social regeneration. Wigman believed, as did Laban (1976), that dance on some level was for every person and held a deep spiritual significance. For Wigman, dance represented life.

> Mary Wigman's conception of the new dance community included professional artists and interested amateurs. Specialist artists spent years pursuing the knowledge of "absolute dance," a kind of mystical knowledge akin to that of priests or priestesses who must be initiated into secret knowledge through experience. (Randall, 2005, p. 231)

Toepfer (1997) adds:

Wigman was great because she brought to dance an unprecedented magnitude of tragic feeling. For her, modern dance had to go well beyond the naive expressions of joy, innocence, and decorative idealism the public had come to expect since the heyday of Isadora Duncan: she tied conditions of ecstatic liberation to conditions of heroic sacrifice. (p. 110)

Dance as the Highest Calling

Gertrud concurred with Toepfer's assessment of Wigman in that she said, "At this period in my life, I felt the ballet was 'too sweet' and I felt the modern dance, especially with Wigman, provided far more room to be expressive and experiment with different types of movement." Wigman's influence on the Hahn sisters' dance philosophy and belief in dance as a liberating activity of emotion and expression stayed with them all of their lives.

Programme Card from A Fun Cabaret Evening, March 23, 1929, Karlsbad.

Translated this program reads 'Society Club Harmony' A Fun Cabaret Evening, Dancers Gerti and Magda Hahn, Artistic Director Karl Kohn, after the program, (Tanz fur Alle) Dance for All.

> **Gerti:** Magda and I have both returned to Karlsbad. Wigman's school was marvellous. The insights I gained just cannot be put into words but have been instilled into my body. It is as if the essence of what the dance really is was revealed to me.
>
> At the Wigman School, the dance classes served many functions. Some students sought out a cathartic experience, some to learn the new ways of the expressionist dance, others sought to find a connection to cosmic forces, but above all, everyone at the Wigman School was in search of truthful ex-

periences. Wigman focuses her dance on inner motivation and expression, not technique, which struck a deep chord for me. I have tried to convey all that I learned to Magda. She has happily embraced the Wigman philosophy as it advocates and affirms Dalcroze's ideals of the individuality of each person as a dancer.

I have once again been organizing the dance school and everyone has agreed to pull together to have another performance in March. I must say, it looks to be a very entertaining evening. I am enjoying visiting with my old friends and of course, seeing Papa, Magda, and my new beau, Yusuf.

PROGRAMM:

Der Direktor	Karl Kohn
Die Direktorin	Gerti Hahn
Die Musikanten	Fladerers 47 MS-Kapelle
Das Tanzgirl	Liesl Zentner
Karl Heinz Maria (des Direktors Sohn)	Franzl Lippert
Der Cowboy	Herta Zentner
Die neueste Film gedreht	Kurt Plowitz
musikal. begleitet	Kurt Maier
Der akrobatische Clown	Liesl Bernard
Der Schnellzeichner	Kurt Plowitz
Die Zigeunerin	Magda Hahn
Der Vortragskünstler	Kurt Maier
Die Primaballerina	Gerti Hahn
Der Zauberkünstler	Karl Kohn
(und „Sie")	Alice Kohn
Die Schlangenbänd'gerin	Trude Kohn
Die Musikclowns	Kohn—Maier
Die fünf Salto Mortalias	Gerti Hahn
	Magda Hahn
	Liesl Bernard
	Trude Kohn
	Liesl Zentner
Auszug der Komödianten	Die Truppe

Programme from A Fun Cabaret Evening, Karlsbad, March 23, 1929.

Translated from the programme, I note Gerti Hahn as one of the directors, Magda Hahn as The Gypsy, Gerti Hahn as The Prima Ballerina, and Gerti and Magda Hahn with three others as 'Die funf Salto Mortalias' roughly translated as (The Five Deadly Jumps or Somersaults) and as a finale the troupe in 'Auszug der Komodianten', (Abstract of the Comediennes).

**Gerti and two unknown performers, from
A Fun Cabaret Evening, Karlsbad, March 23, 1929.**

Gerti: This evening was truly a mixed cabaret. I first had the role of the female director, which was quite different from dancing as I had to spend time with the actors to rehearse lines. However, I felt up to the task and found the acting experience another feather in my cap. The production as a whole was maybe not entirely to my taste. But fun nonetheless. My good friend Liesl made the audience swoon as The Dance Girl and Magda was extra ordinary as The Gypsy. My Prima Ballerina was terribly clichéd with all the pirouettes and arabesques but I was told this is what the audience wants to see in a cabaret programme.

The costumes were indeed splendid and added to the theatricality and I must admit that the variety of the acts kept the audience amused and at times laughing out loud. The Cowboy was so tongue in cheek, bowed legs, a lasso and even rolling a cigarette. The Magician was actually much better than I expected and involved the audience which went over very well. I will have to thank Kurt and Karl for all their hard work on this production.

Despite everything going so wonderfully tonight, I had a funny, let down feeling when it was all over. The impermanency of the dance and everything in our lives struck me! Perhaps it is the fact that things will be changing soon. I have started to think more seriously about my future. What I mean is that Magda and I have decided to marry. Magda has agreed to marry her beau, Franz, and I have agreed to marry Yusuf. I do look forward to this but I must add that we are in no rush, our careers as dancers come first. And I know marrying could lead to separation from Papa and Magda, and who knows what I will do about the dance school. A shame really as it has been so successful. More troubling, lately Magda and I have had some disagreements which is so unusual for us...

I hope we are making the right decisions...

Meanwhile, I look with anticipation towards my summer plans. I must follow my Muse wherever she takes me!

Magda as The Gypsy in A Fun Cabaret Evening, March 23, 1929.

Magda as The Gypsy in A Fun Cabaret Evening with her fiancé Franz Weisskopf, March 23, 1929.

In the summer of 1929, Gertrud again left Karlsbad to travel and study dance and went to Hellerau-Laxenburg, a popular Dalcroze School, situated near Vienna. Toepfer (1997) notes, "In 1925 the Hellerau school accepted the invitation of the city of Vienna to relocate to Laxenburg Castle, which was its home until 1938, when the Nazis annexed Austria" (p. 120).

Gertrud related, "As I was there in the summer months, much of the school activities and classes were held outdoors. The school site was beautiful, like something out of a fairy tale. The school was in an old, stone castle surrounded by wonderfully kept lawns and a lake. We often danced and exercised outside on the grass and enjoyed the sun and fresh air."

She added, "Playing instruments and also developing one's rhythmic abilities while executing movement to music was stressed. The students, which were all women, were encouraged to swim and exercise outdoors as much as possible. Hellerau-Laxenburg was very much less regimented than my time at the Wigman School in that we had a lot more free time and could choose individual activities which appealed to us. I remember the school had wonderful teachers. These instructors gave me a fresh perspective on the Dalcroze exercises, lessons, and how to apply this to teaching dance and choreography."

Dance historian Toepfer (1997) also describes the Hellerau-Laxenburg School philosophy:

> Hellerau sought to free the female body without exhausting or depleting it. The school therefore condemned gymnastic acrobatics, dance virtuosity, and a focus on the perfection of movement: the female body possessed a different strength than did the male, and one measured it not by feats of acrobatic prowess but by an ability to move truthfully, confidently, and with adroit intelligence. (p. 119)

Noted by Toepfer (1997), and perhaps what attracted Gertrud to Hellerau-Laxenburg after dancing with Wigman, was that outstanding and well known Czech dancers and choreographers, such as Jarmilla Kroschlova, Valeria Kratina, and Rosalia Chladek, were instrumental in creating the curriculum taught at the school and there were often very successful performances at Hellerau-Laxenburg which attracted international interest. (pp. 120, 121)

Gerti at the Hellerau-Laxenburg School, 1929.

Gerti (far right with cigarette) at the Hellerau-Laxenburg School, 1929.

Dance as the Highest Calling

Hamming it up at Hellerau-Laxenburg (Gerti second from left), 1929.

Gerti at Hellerau-Laxenburg, 1929.

Gerti: Embracing the outdoors with recreation and dance activities these past months has been wonderful. Nature is a rejuvenating force. I needed to slow down after the Wigman School and gain some perspective as to what I want to do next.

I am being pressured, well not so much pressured, as requested by Magda and Papa to return to Karlsbad on a more permanent basis. They are right of course. We do miss each other and I should be attending more to my dance school.

Well, I know that all holidays must come to an end. Although, I view this experience at Hellerau-Laxenburg as much more than a holiday. My time here has reinforced all that I believe about Dalcroze's methods and system and has opened up my understanding of what Dalcroze hopes to achieve for humanity with movement and exercise. Movement should be a liberating experience for everyone!

I must also return to Karlsbad to spend some time with my fiancée Yusuf. He has said he understands that I must travel to study and learn all that is new and innovative in the dance world. He unfortunately added that he hopes my travelling will get all of this business out of my system before we settle down together and are married. Hmm, I don't think he knows me as well as he thinks he does. I will never get studying dance and performing 'out of my system'. The dance is an integral part of who I am. There will always be much that is new to learn.

As Ida Herion, my heroine in the dance, so aptly states:

In dance, man (sic) deeply penetrates into the centre of his very own nature. Harmoniously connected to the light forces that flood the universe, experience itself pervades in the Dance as a dance, the vibrating body-soul becomes a vibrating world circuit. As artists like Diefenbach and Fidus, pioneering in lines and through profoundly beautiful shapes, that now blossom into time. (Translated from German, from Getanzte

Dance as the Highest Calling

Harmonien' (Danced Harmonics) Dance photographs by Paul Jsenfels, of the Tanzschule (Dance School) of Ida Herion, published in Stuttgart in 1927, p. 3.)

Hellerau-Laxenburg School students. (Gerti, center back, standing beside a woman wearing a black exercise suit), 1929.

The above quote from Getanzte Harmonien illustrates the type of dance literature that permeated German speaking artistic circles of the 1920s and strongly influenced Magda and Gertrud's ideas and philosophy about dance. It is interesting to note the mention of Karl Wilhelm Diefenbach (1851–1913) and Fidus (1868–1948) the pseudonym of Hugo Reinhold Karl Johann Hoppener. Both of these artists were German symbolists and art nouveau painters, as well as radical socialist reformers of the Weimar period. Diefenbach and Fidus' paintings and illustrations are stunning examples of the reciprocal influence that dance and visual art had on one another in this era. The work of Diefenbach and Fidus illustrate many striking images of the body and dance.

The Hahn sisters thoroughly embraced the artistic life, now more openly available to women in the 1920s, and said that they treasured their memories of travel and the diverse dance schools they had attended. In our numerous conversations in the early 1990s, I observed that Gertrud and Magda retained a passion for the avant-garde. They were always interested in exploring many subjects, which included dance, music, art, literature, and film. In Vancouver, during the 1960s and 1970s, Magda worked as a censor for foreign films in German and French. The sisters were also very open and accepting about sexuality and nudity. They had embraced the freer lifestyle of the 'golden twenties', as it was called in Germany, and had been immersed in the culture of artists, which included meeting and working with all sorts of flamboyant and creative people from all walks of life. Nothing seemed to shock or surprise them about the so called 'modern' times of the swinging sixties and onward for they had seen it all before.

The Hahn sisters, throughout the 1920s, as many dancers did at the time, had many studio photographs taken. I appreciate the few semi-nude photographs I was given of them, with permission to share them publicly, as evidence of their openness to nudity. In Germany, nudism is known as Freikoerperkultur, or Free Body Culture. "Germany's passion for clotheslessness finds its origins in late-19th-century health drives when stripping off was seen as part of a route to fitness and sunbathing a possible cure for TB and rheumatism." (Krueger, 2018, p. 1) However, in the Nazi era, laws were passed to limit nudism as nudism was seen as part of the immorality of the Weimar state.

Toepfer (1997) extensively discusses Nacktkultur (Naked Culture) in relation to dance in the Weimar period in Germany between 1910 and 1935 and states that, "The uniquely Germanic construction of the modern body involved two large categories of performance: nudity and physical movement, particularly ideas about movement introduced by the most turbulent dance culture in history. The Germans powerfully emphasized nudity and movement as the decisive elements bestowing modernity upon the body." (p. 7). Toepfer (1997) adds, "A major sector of Nacktkultur regarded nudism as an aspect of feminism and as a force promoting a new, modern identity for women" (p. 39). The Hahn sisters were undoubtedly influenced by the progressive views regarding nudism in the 1920s and seem to have embraced this widely flourishing modern attitude of showing the naked body as vital and beautiful in photographs and performances to enhance the body's artistic merits. The sisters said they did not dance nude but were unashamed and happy to show their 'nudes' as Gertrud called the photographs they had kept from their youth.

Dance as the Highest Calling

Gertrud posing for a semi-nude dance photograph, 1920s.

Gerti: The nudes we have taken were all in fun and to explore the beauty of the body. Magda and I have been the photographer for each other, most of the time. But really, baring one's soul is much harder than baring one's body, especially when dancing. Most people have been to a cabaret show and seen nude dancing, which has its popularity. These shows are perhaps titillating to some, but one gets tired of it quickly unless the performers are talented dancers or singers and exude a stage presence and personality that is exemplary. To successfully share yourself with an audience is not as simple as removing one's clothing. An open and unguarded offering of one's authentic self to an audience, these are the moments where one may feel more vulnerable and exposed. True art comes from the inside.

Magda in an artistic semi-nude photograph, late 1920s.

Magda: To be truly free in the dance one must embrace one's whole body and soul completely. There is a special feeling when one accepts one's body unashamedly. The times have changed for women. We are freer to do what we wish, to dance naked if that is what one wants. But I still feel there should be an underlying awareness that the body is a dancer's own, to be upheld as a means of sharing the dancer's art. This body only belongs to the audience for brief moments. The dancer is not for the audience to ogle or think sexual thoughts about, while he or she is 'baring' or revealing his or her soul and perhaps uncovering his or her skin in expressing an inner vision or interpreting a choreography. (Except at the Folies Bergere, Gerti!) I am teasing her. I will be serious again.

The dance is an artistic expression with the body, clothed or unclothed but always to be venerated. My Mutti's words echo in my mind. "Love yourself whole heartedly, and other's will love you too." "Stand up for your beliefs and defend your art, for in our art one finds the true meaning of life." Oh, I wish Mutti was here to hug.

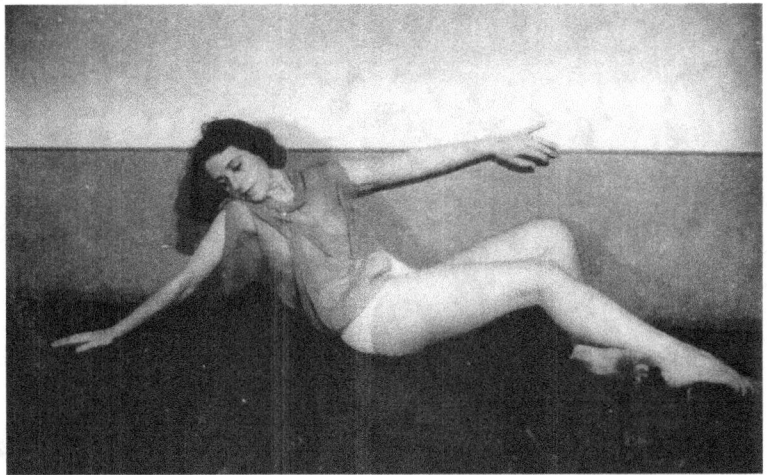

Magda in an artistic semi-nude photograph, late 1920s.

Magda: And speaking of nakedness and dance, here I must make mention of the inspiring work of Ida Herion, whom I greatly admire. In conjunction with photographer Paul Jsenfels, Jsenfels and Herion have recently published a book of uplifting, nude dance photographs. This wonderful publication features an artistic vision of the youthful, unclothed, dancing body in all its sublime and resplendent glory. Herion states, "A sacred joy in the body whose source is deep in the soul. Now the days are coming up, where dance permeates our lives again as a joyous art. The climax of the erotic joy of movement and the sustained wave of connectedness to new, noble festive forms."... "Dance is a reconciling bond between physical and spiritual culture." (Jsenfels, Herion, 1927, p. 3). Translated from German from 'Getanzte Harmonien' (Danced Harmonics) dance photographs by Paul Jsenfels, of the Tanzschule (Dance School) of Ida Herion, published in Stuttgart in 1927.

The Hahn Dance School in Karlsbad continued to flourish in the late 1920s and early 1930s. The sisters took many artistic photographs of their pupils during this period to illustrate exercises and movement ideas.

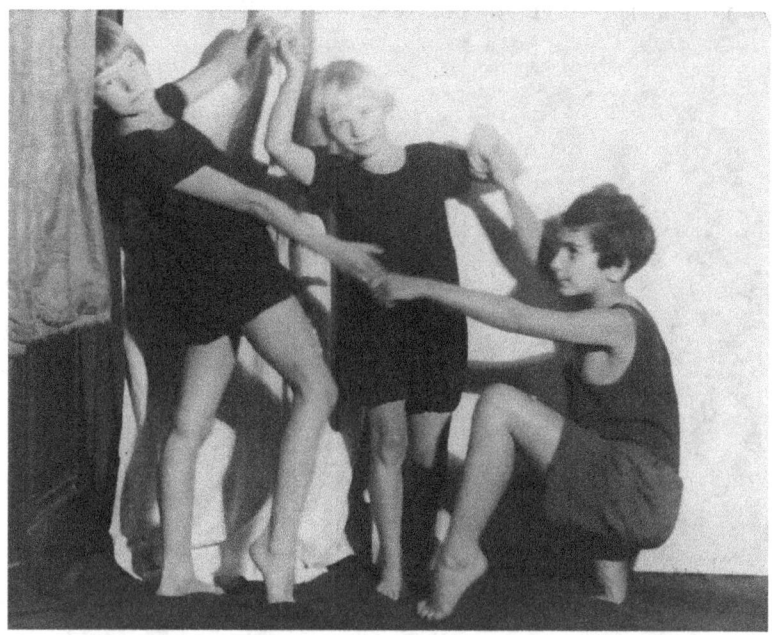

Young dance students at the Hahn Dance School, 1920s, Karlsbad.

...the educator should endeavour to develop the temperament and character of his pupils as they are revealed in the four periods of childhood and adolescence, to restore wholly to the body the primitive rhythms of the personality, to combat all resistances, intellectual and physical, to correct their faults or turn them into good qualities. (Jacques-Dalcroze, 1930, p. 83)

Dance as the Highest Calling

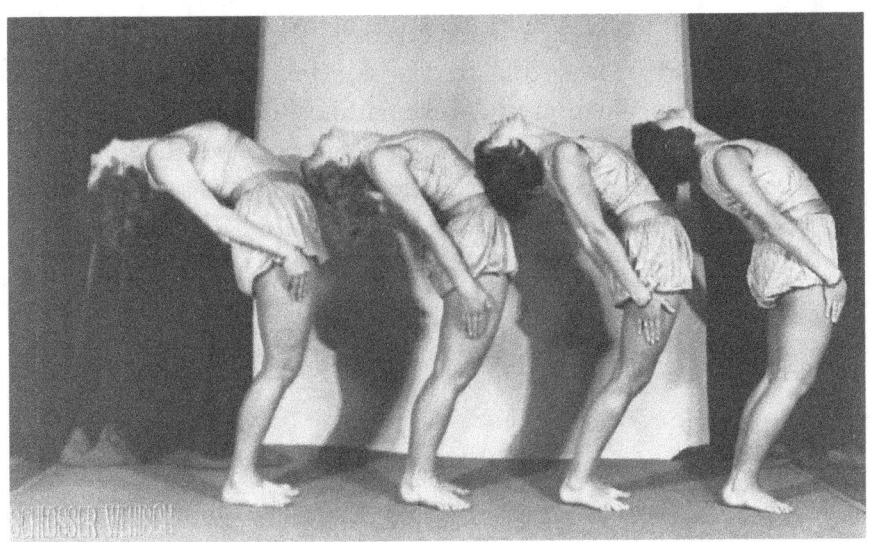

Magda (second from right) at the
Hahn Dance School, Karlsbad, around 1930.

Magda (far right kneeling on the floor) with students at the
Karlsbad Hahn Dance School, around 1930.

This general harmony of our cerebral, physical, and spiritual forces assures for us the free possession of ourselves, develops our imagination, and quite naturally transports our sensations and feelings, conceptions and actions, into the domain of art. Art is an intimate correlation with life: it is the outward projection of love and the knowledge of beauty and truth. (Jacques-Dalcroze, 1930, p.93)

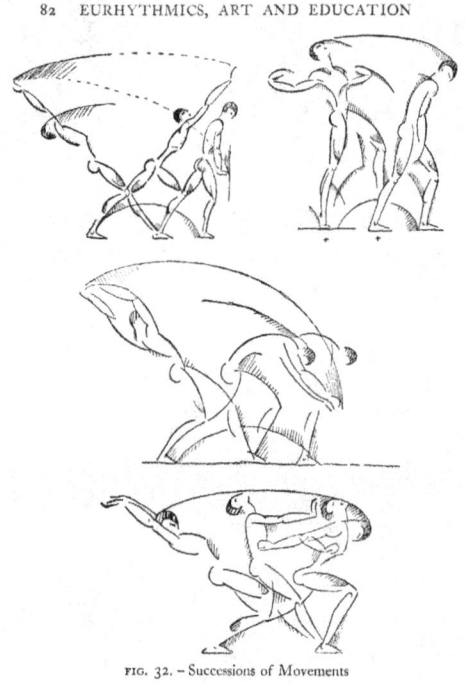

FIG. 32. – Successions of Movements

(Jacques-Dalcroze, 1930, p.82)

The Greeks attached great importance to rhythmic movements: they recognized the beneficent influence of a rhythmic education of both body and mind, and they also knew that this rhythmic education was capable of influencing the inner life of man. Plato says: "Rhythm, ie. The expression of order and symmetry, penetrates the way of the body into the soul and into the entire man, revealing to him the harmony of his whole personality. (Jacques-Dalcroze, 1930, p.102)

Dance as the Highest Calling

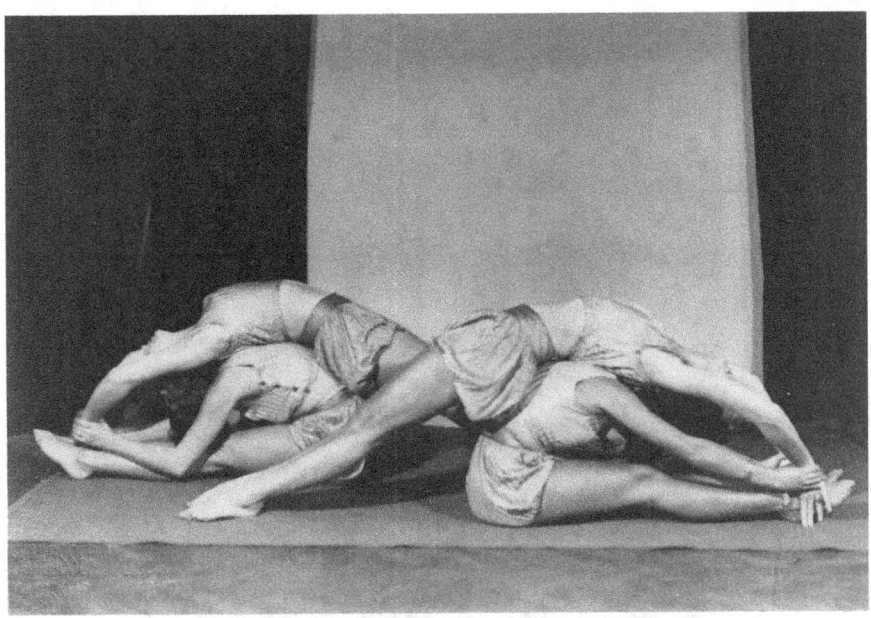

Magda and students demonstrating exercises at the Hahn Dance School, Karlsbad, around 1930.

Gerti, second from the right. Magda wearing a white top far left, with unknown students, at the Hahn Karlsbad Dance School, around 1930.

Our Love Affair with Dance

Magda posing outdoors. Written on the back in German, translated as: "The woman from the south sea island looks into the far away distance. She hopes to see her darling loved one soon." June 29, 1930.

"Dance in God's free nature. There everything is completely different then inside, the human becomes simpler, the spatial far. A string is struck, which sounds like surrender." Translated from German from (Jsenfels, Herion, 1927, p. 2).

Magda: I embrace the sun, the fresh air, and all of nature. I love to move and dance outside as much as possible. This unification of the moving body and the natural world is to experience life as a part of the universal cycle of existence, constantly transforming and in motion. I am a sun worshipper. I say this with no apology. I am told I will be as wrinkled as a prune when I am old. But if this is the price to pay, I will gladly pay it. To stay out of the sun, that is like telling a fish not to swim in water. I can't! And while I worship the heat, the light, and the life giving qualities of all of nature, more than this, I am thankful and have grace in my heart for my art and ability as a dancer which enables me to taste the best of being alive.

Magda posing outdoors. Karlsbad, June 29, 1930.

That's what it is all about: the pure language of animated lines, and at the right moment retaining the feeling of springtime. Natural grace, budding development, young, strong humanity, ignited by culture to art. (Translated from German from (Jsenfels, Herion, 1927, p. 2)

Magda, exercising outdoors, early 1930s.

Magda, outdoors, with unknown Hahn Dance School students, early 1930s.

Dance as the Highest Calling

Magda, second from the left, with unknown students, early 1930s.

Research into the development and the spread of Wilhelmine and Weimar body culture ideals reveals that the formation and belief in body culture at this time was not created or limited to just a few innovative and well known dancers or movement philosophers' contributions but rather to a whole array of unique participants and believers, most of whom have been unfortunately consigned to oblivion.

Toepfer (1997) states, "Much of the powerful Weimar dance culture has been undeservedly forgotten because scholars cannot compile thick dossiers on many personalities and therefore cannot confine their perceptions of dance to those manifestations (or documentations) of it that produce a life story about which one can write at length". Further, "...the vast majority of these have left so little trace that no one can reconstruct them" (pp. 2–3).

Toepfer (1997) additionally explains how the body culture in Germany and Austria in the Weimar period had a vast diversity of teaching styles and philosophies. "The tendency to reduce the Weimar dance culture to the activities of a few major figures—for example, Mary Wigman, Kurt Jooss, and Rudolph Laban—gives a very incomplete view of how dance and attitudes toward the body produced a modern culture within a particular

European social context" (Toepfer, 1997, p. 2).

Toepfer (1997) mentions that there were hundreds of dance schools and solo and group performing artists in the time between 1910 to 1935 and documentation is very limited because of the ephemeral nature of the dance. For most dancers of this period, their dance only existed for brief moments on a stage. Toepfer (1997) relates that dancers did not want to film their work in the fear that someone would copy them. Photographs and a very limited number of films are all that is left to mark the passage and contributions of the many significant Weimar culture dance artists.

The Hahn sisters managed to study with many of the most famous dance schools of the Weimar era, both in ballet and modern dance. It is gratifying to have so many photographs and reminiscences of their lives so as to have been able to piece together a chronological and coherent record of events, which illuminate their personal dance history in this fascinating time.

The Hahn sisters were two of the many thousands of young women searching for inspiration and self-realization through the dance in the 1920s and early 1930s in Europe. The notion of rhythmic gymnastics and dance as transformational, a link to the inner spirit, and a means of affirming the body and one's life force seems to have been a universal philosophy in many of the dance schools of this era. Toepfer (1997) aptly describes Germanic body culture as, "A mystical belief in the body as a salvational force" (p. 383). In my estimation, the Hahn sisters believed this to be true and this philosophy or belief was to become an integral part of their teaching. 'The dance' was always spoken of with great reverence.

The dance philosophies of the Weimar body culture were spread mainly through a profusion of published writings and photographs. Photographs and postcards of dancers were popular and an excellent way to advertise a dancer's work as not everyone was able to view the live performances.

Toepfer (1997) shares:

Modern dance culture emphatically preferred photography as the medium for transmitting the new image of dance. The emancipatory authority of modern dance achieved its most convincing representation when aligned with the expanding expressive capacity of photographic technology, which also had a stake in modernism insofar as its own ambition to attain the status of art was concerned. (p. 374)

Dance as the Highest Calling

As well as retaining historic photographs of the Hahn sisters from their time in Europe, I am grateful to have been given two publications the Hahn sisters kept from the Weimar era, which illustrate some of the material that propagated different dance and movement philosophies during this time. The first is Ausdrucksgymnastik (Expressive Gymnastics) by Rudolf Bode, published in 1922 in Munich. This publication is in German and has fifty-five pages of text and sixteen pages of accompanying photographs of men and women in gymnastic poses to illustrate the types of exercises Bode believed would benefit the body. Bode (1881–1970), according to Toepfer (1997), "was a student of Dalcroze at Hellerau in 1911–1912. By 1913, when he established his own school in Munich, Bode opposed the methods of his teacher and embarked on a pedagogy that developed bodily rhythms independently of music" (p. 127).

The second publication, which I have already quoted from, is Getanzte Harmonien (Danced Harmonics), a series of dance photographs by Paul Jsenfels, featuring the dancers of Ida Herion's Tanzschule (Dance School), published in Stuttgart in 1927. This publication of photographs is a treasure trove of outstanding dance photographs of the period, which represented and modeled for the Hahn sisters a reverence for the body as an instrument to express art. The photographs show youthful male and female dancers, singularly and in groups, clothed and unclothed, artfully posed in nature and against the backdrop of a beautiful country villa. The images illustrate the beauty of the naked body and dance movements. There is only a brief three page introduction in German included at the beginning of the book, which in detail describes the splendour and fairy tale quality of a villa in the mountains as an ideal indoor and outdoor setting for the photographs. The author draws a connection between the harmony of nature and the harmony and appropriateness of dancing naked in a natural setting. The last few lines of the text read (in a rough translation):

> Dance is a cheering embrace of this all too fast fleeing, luminous life—yes, yes, to the glory of the young-flaming arc between body and spirit. Dance is the quiet, priestly walk to the holy self—to solitude and clarity. Where dance flows from the inner experience, a wave glides silently into the current of the stream of creation (eternity). (Jsenfels, Herion, 1927, p. 3)

This is a fitting and poetic description of the dance photographs contained in this book and echoes the passion the Hahn sisters reflected as participants in the dance culture of this time and throughout the rest of their lives.

My understanding of why the Hahn sisters in their late teens and twenties attended so many diverse schools of movement was somewhat clarified by Toepfer (1997) as he states, "In the early 1920s, many people realized that competing theories of bodily movement were equally persuasive, even if they contradicted each other. Some students went from Hellerau to Laban or from Mensendieck to Hellerau or from a Wigman school to a Laban school" (p. 129).

During the latter half of the 1920s, the sisters related that in between studying at the various dance schools they attended around Europe, they would return to Karlsbad to teach at their school. They incorporated much of the dance technique and philosophies they learned in their travels as dance students into a Hahn methodology, which became a blend of Dalcroze exercises, ballet technique, and modern dance. During the late 1920s and early 1930s, the sisters said that they continued to have many successful performances in Karlsbad.

Magda demonstrating exercises at
the Hahn Karlsbad Dance School, early 1930s.

Magda demonstrating exercises at
the Hahn Karlsbad Dance School, early 1930s.

Magda: The Dalcroze method of rhythmic gymnastics is an aesthetic blend of dance movements and gymnastics. Rhythmic gymnastics has proven to be a beneficial method for dance and music students alike, utilizing our natural instincts for rhythm in the acquisition of an intimate knowledge of musical construction. For the dancer, the sequences lead the student to a heightening of body awareness and an association of rhythm with the complete physical body. Very importantly, the exercises reinforce kinaesthetic feeling. Rhythm or a body connection to the music is emphasized so that music is felt from the top of the head, down to the feet and toes. A deeper understanding of the relationship between dance and music will then resonate inside the body and for the dancer enable a deeper expression of the music.

The goals of the rhythmic curriculum will not only teach the dancer to feel the nuances of music but develop musculature and gross motor skills. The possibilities are attuned to the individual desires of the student.

In the Dalcroze system, each different kind of note in a musical composition, for example, a quarter, half, or whole note, can be expressed by certain motions of the arms; such as three four time with the right arm, and four-four time with the left arm. Additionally, each measure can be translated into steps or a series of steps, swinging up onto the toes and down to the heels. These exercises will bring out the hidden, inner sense of rhythm. The music and bodily expression may be then so closely related that together they may form a whole.

The scope of the method when applied to children is remarkable. Improved co-ordination, phrasing, and the ability to shade the dance with feeling. Dalcroze Eurhythmics never becomes an automatic group of exercises because the series of movements are only the means to expressing music and dance ideas, which are infinite.

FIG. 9. – Different Ways of Skipping

(Jacques-Dalcroze, 1930, p. 24)

Gertrud: As Dalcroze states so beautifully:

Those who, by a special form of education, wish to help their fellow-beings to rehabilitate the cult of moving beauty, ought to take more care not to deprive aesthetic emotion of hereditary instinctive elements... To create a work of art we need a superior intellect. This intellect is the product of the equilibrium and the harmony we should try to introduce into our movements and therefore into our minds. The way to attain this end is to study the laws of rhythm, which include the laws of art, and which, once we have mastered them, will be the means of embellishing and ennobling our everyday life. (Jacques-Dalcroze, 1930, p. 191)

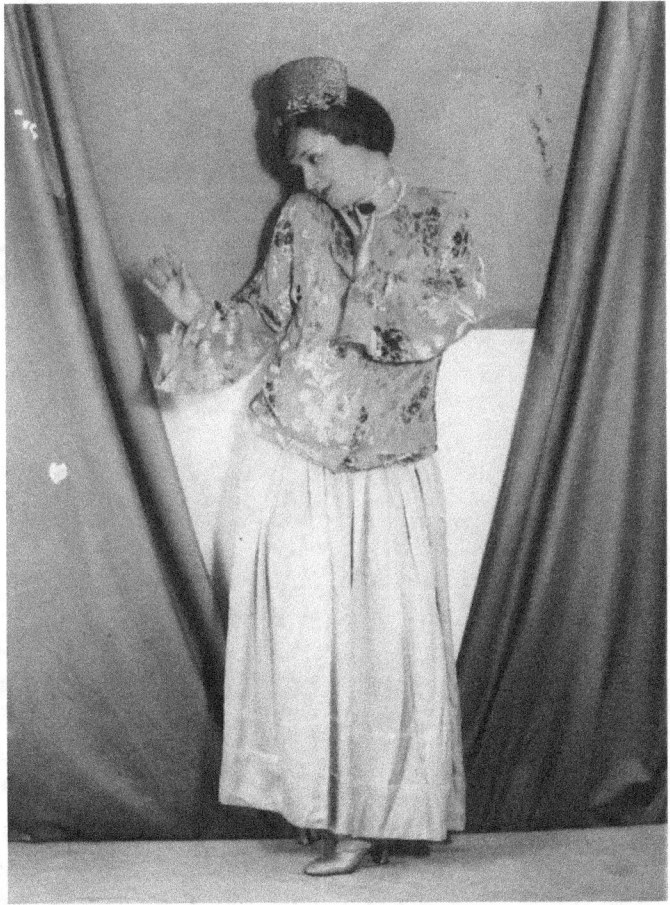

Gertrud in an unknown character dance, Karlsbad 1931.

The dance is a living language... an artistic message soaring above the ground of reality in order to speak, on a higher level, in images and allegories of man's innermost emotions and need for communication. Above all, the dance asks for direct communication without any detours. Because its bearer and intermediary is man himself, and because his instrument of expression is the human body. Whose natural movement forms the material for the dance, the only material which is his own and his own to use. (Wigman, 1966, p. 10)

Magda in a photograph from an unknown study, Karlsbad 1931.

Dance as the Highest Calling

Magda in a photograph from an unknown study, Karlsbad 1931.

Magda in a photograph from an unknown study, Karlsbad 1931.

Magda: I am here, in these present moments with the dance. I am also embracing change. The doors to transition have swung open and Gerti and I cannot stay in our liminal spaces any longer. We must go through. This is not always the happiest time for everyone. There will be separations. But positively, I look back and see we have had wonderful experiences dancing as single women and now we embrace our future as dancing wives.

I reflect on the dance and particularly the ballet, as it is my first love. The ballet, in its present form, has really survived many changes, has lasted longer than most dance styles and will probably continue for a long time to come. The structure of ballet is so well designed, thought out, and laid down, that it not only helps the individual teacher to teach along the identical lines of any other teacher of ballet, but it makes it easier for the student to study. Because of the definite rules that ballet must follow, it also simplifies the task of the examiner and brings greater comprehension to the onlooker. This is the great advantage ballet has over modern creative dance. Or should I say, this is the great disadvantage of modern creative dance that at present it seems to have no hard and fast rules. This dance is wild and free and still in its formation, only dependent on the choreographer's imagination.

And ballet, perhaps for the very reason of extreme perfection, high standard, and great popularity, will in its strictly classical form, be more and more challenged by many new and different styles and forms. We have seen this happen in every field of art: painting, sculpture, writing, architecture, and music.

So I too, as the ballet, will be open to change and survive. As the ballet, I will retain my structure and beliefs, retain my high standards but also accept new challenges in form and perfection. And as the modern dance, which is still seeking its own identity, I will also seek a new identity and embrace change and create my own new rules. I will create a new life. Above all, I will always stay enveloped in the dance.

Dance as the Highest Calling

Gerti on stage in an unknown work, Karlsbad 1931.

Gerti: Life brings changes and people must adjust and adapt. This it seems is inevitable. But the Muse of the dance calling me will never change. What is to come after I marry, I do not know. But whatever changes occur, I will retain my integrity in what I believe, which is that art is the greatest calling in life. Now in this new epoch of the dance, changes in its presentation have been drastic. Every dance has become the property of the dancer, and every dancer has worked to make his or her particular style the accepted style or the new trend. So far, this ambition has not been fully realized and their genuine efforts to establish the modern dance have not yet been rewarded. As a result, the modern dance is a mixture of different styles. It has not yet got a rigid thesis of movement, presentation, or technique. This is only in the making, although it is slowly gaining ground and Terpsichore's temple will again have new bricks built upon her ancient ones. But this time the bricks will be brought from Siva's temple, (oh yes, especially as I am to reside in India with Yusuf after we marry) and the Muses of all the creative arts will join hands because the new conception of the dance is no longer just a fairy tale but a creation taken from life as we live it today. And that is really a very natural outcome, when you think of it, for all styles change with the times. It is nothing extraordinary that this should also happen with the dance or with our lives.

PART 3

6

THE PROTECTIVE SHIELD OF TERPSICHORE
WHEREIN TERPSICHORE MEETS SIVA

Magda, Gertrud, and Yusuf Mitha, Karlsbad 1932.

In my continued conversations with the Hanova sisters, I learned that in 1932 the sisters both finally married. Magda wed Franz Weisskopf, a fellow Czech, and Gertrud married Yusuf Mitha, an Indian lawyer from Bombay, who was a graduate of Cambridge University in England. Gertrud said that Yusuf's father was also a doctor, educated in England, and was a close friend of the Hahn sisters' father. In a taped interview from 1993, and the reader must remember that Gertrud was born in 1903, so she was ninety years old at this time, Gertrud said wistfully, "Magda and I did almost everything together, but for some reason, we both were unable to attend each other's weddings." I did not ask for more details about this as I sensed this was a very private memory. But Gertrud did mention that after her marriage in 1932, she sold the Hahn Dance School in Karlsbad in preparation for her moving to India with her husband Yusuf.

Shortly after being married, Magda and her husband Franz moved to Teplitz, Czechoslovakia. Teplitz, also a spa town, is located in the North Bohemia region, near the border with the German state of Saxony.

Undoubtedly by 1932, Gertrud and Magda had heard about the unsettling political situation in Germany with the rise of the Nazi Party. But the rapid approach and severity of what was to come to Bohemia and Czechoslovakia could not have been imagined by anyone. The Hahn family's Jewish heritage was not something they hid or were ashamed of. Being Jewish was just one aspect of their background. At this time, the sisters identified themselves primarily as modern women, artists, and foremost dancers. In the early 1930s, Jewish people in Europe could never have conceived of how having a Jewish heritage was going to affect their future lives so drastically.

Gerti with her husband Yusuf Mitha, 1932.

Gerti: I love my husband dearly and know a wife is expected to follow her spouse to his homeland but I cannot yet imagine what living in India will be like for me. Yusuf has not been home for many years and he seems so English really. Not at all what I think of as an Indian person. He speaks English very well and prefers English food, clothes, and literature above all others. He is helping me to learn to speak this language, which he said I must be able to do in India if I want to do anything of significance. What that will be, who can say? I have packed everything I own of value which includes my mementos, photographs, sheet music, and costumes, all in huge compartmentalized trunks. I will be prepared and ready to perform and perhaps teach when I arrive in Bombay.

I miss Magda terribly. What will I do without her? It is as if part of me is missing. But she is now married to Franz and has started her own new life in Teplitz. She seems happy from her letters, but I worry. Europe seems so different now. There is so much disturbance and political manoeuvring. I feel there is an underlying and invisible layer of fear spreading out from Germany. The papers report terrible things and Karlsbad seems no longer the safe haven I grew up in. There are now nasty men. They shout nasty slogans and are saying ugly things about Jews. I am glad I am leaving Europe right now and will be able to get away from all this craziness. I will start a new life with my husband and escape all this mayhem. Even though I am going into the unknown, I am not afraid, rather I see this as a fresh adventure. I leave behind many wonderful memories of my former life and say adieu and auf weidersehen to my dancing days in Europe. But I implore the powers that be to look after Papa, Magda, and Franz.

Although the Hahn sisters often said they were not at all political or religious, they must have been aware of the changing political situations and events that were taking place in Europe after WWI. As they travelled in Czechoslovakia, Germany, Austria, and France to study dance in the 1920s, they inevitably were faced with disturbing news concerning the rise of the Nazi party in Germany and its anti-semitic doctrine.

To briefly clarify the chain of events that took place and led up to WWII, and which ultimately led the Hahn family to flee Europe, in 1918 the First World War ended and Kaiser Wilhelm abdicated. Germany and the allied powers signed the Treaty of Versailles. Germany was ordered to pay large reparations for war damages.

> German propaganda had not prepared the nation for defeat, resulting in a sense of injured German national pride. Those military and political leaders who were responsible claimed that Germany had been "stabbed in the back" by its left wing politicians, Communists, and Jews. When a new government, The Weimar Republic, tried to establish a democratic course, extreme political parties from both the right and left struggled violently for control. The new regime could neither handle the depressed economy nor the rampant lawlessness and disorder. (Florida Center for Instructional Technology, 2019, p. 1)

In 1920, Adolph Hitler joined the National Socialist German Worker's Party (NSDAP), called the Nazi Party for short. In 1921, he became the leader of the NSDAP and took the title of Fuhrer. Hitler and the NSDAP attempted to overthrow the Bavarian government in 1923. Hitler was jailed for 9 months and started to write Mein Kampf (My Struggle). His book details his radical ideas of German nationalism, antisemitism, and anti-bolshevism.

From 1929–1930, the world experienced the start of the Great Depression and nearly four million Germans faced unemployment. In 1930, with promises of a restored economy, the Nazi party gained 18.3% of the vote in the Reichstag and in 1932 was elected as the largest party. Adolph Hitler was appointed Chancellor of Germany on January 30, 1933. On March 20, 1933, Dachau, Germany's first concentration camp was completed. On April 1, 1933, Germans were told to boycott Jewish shops and businesses. By November 24, 1933, the homeless and the unemployed in Germany were being sent to concentration camps. On August 2, 1934, Hitler made himself Fuhrer of Germany.

In late 1932, Gertrud and her husband Yusuf, left Europe for Bombay, India, the home of Yusuf's family. Almost a year later in 1933, Gertrud and Magda's father, Gustav Hahn, fled Karlsbad to London and requested funds from Gertrud to join her and her new relatives in India. Early in 1934, Magda and her husband, Franz, fled Teplitz and followed Gertrud

The Protective Shield of Terpsichore, Wherein Terpsichore Meets Siva

and Gustav Hahn to India.

Fortunately for them, the Hahn family paid heed to the alarming warning signs of Jewish persecution and had the means to escape Europe. Others were not so fortunate. In the Sudeten area of Czechoslovakia, by 1933, the rising antisemitism and rapidly changing political situation had become intolerable and dangerous for those of Jewish heritage.

The Sudetenland, the area inhabited by Bohemian Germans, which included Karlsbad and Teplitz, saw the rise of right-wing political groups like the German National Socialist Worker's Party in the early 1930s. This area began to urge for a unification with Germany. And the Sudeten area was annexed by Nazi Germany in 1938 and at the same time the victimization and expulsion of the Jewish population began with the demolition of the Teplitz synagogue, the largest synagogue in Bohemia. In 1939, as war was declared, the remaining Jews were deported to Theresienstad concentration camp in German-occupied Czechoslovakia and later sent to and exterminated at Auschwitz in German-occupied Poland. After the war in 1945, the ethnic Germans in the area lost everything and were forced to move out of Czechoslovakia. The Hahn sisters were reluctant to talk about these terrible times, but they did say they never returned to Karlsbad or Teplitz.

Gertrud with two unknown friends, on the ship to Bombay, 1932.

Gertrud, on the ship to Bombay, 1932.

Gerti: "I welcome the mysteries of the East into my being." (I think if I say this enough times it will be true.) I do look forward to my new life in India. Yusuf says there are many kinds of dancing to experience and I will enjoy the society. But what of Europe? Is it to be wiped from my memory? It is truly horrifying what I hear is happening. All the people I know, how are they holding up under such slander? Will there be war, again?

I must be positive although it is my nature to look at things pessimistically. Magda has always been the optimist. We seemed to balance each other out. Now we are not together I feel strange. It is as if part of me is missing. Even when we were in different parts of Europe dancing, I felt her near me in spirit. I do know how to keep up appearances, but my darker nature is appearing on this voyage. I try to stay out on deck in the fresh air all that I can. The warm breezes and sunshine give me the feeling of hope, that all will be well. All I can do is try to envision a bright future, for all of us, and throw off these negative sensibilities. But I confess there seems to be too much evil in the world right now.

Gertrud was welcomed to India with many garlands, 1932.

Gerti: Well, we have arrived! The heat and humidity is much greater than I could have ever imagined. It seems European and Indian people do their business in Bombay very early in the morning and then just lounge around or rest all afternoon indoors. In the early evening, the cooler temperatures of the night arrive and activity picks up again. Most evenings, so far, there has been a formal dinner at the Mitha home with many relatives or friends in attendance, who want to meet me and visit with Yusuf. We wear proper dinner clothes and drink cocktails. And the Indian food is marvellous! Gott sei Dank! (Thank God!) The curries, the sauces, the breads, and rice dishes very much suit my palate. The ship board food was so bland and boring, turnips, boiled potatoes, and chipped beef for dinners, very English from Yusuf's description.

I am inundated with cards for social calls. It seems everyone wants me to come for tea so they can meet the girl Yusuf married from Czechoslovakia. I have already ventured out to some theatre and European dance performances. But what I really want to see is Indian dance. Yusuf said he is arranging tickets for us to see a famous Indian dancer called Menaka, which will be very soon. But I am growing impatient to meet anyone who has the least interest in dancing. I am also quite anxious to find a studio space. I intend to open a Hahn Dance School as soon as possible.

Yusuf's family is very formal. When I meet with anyone, they first bow their head with palms together and say "Namaste". Conversations are a bit stilted and limited by my English being a language I am not entirely comfortable with yet. When we arrived, Yusuf's parents were extremely welcoming and gracious to me. Of course, I knew Mr. Mitha already. And, as is the custom here, there are numerous aunties, uncles, cousins, and what have you, all living in one Mitha family house. We have our own rooms in one wing. There are so many servants. I cannot remember all of their names. It seems one cannot go to the facilities without someone watching your every move. Ha! Ha!

The Protective Shield of Terpsichore, Wherein Terpsichore Meets Siva

Gustav Hahn aboard ship in transit to Bombay, India 1933.

Gertrud: When we received the telegram from Papa, I was furious. How dare those people we have known all of our lives, and that Papa has helped in their direst moments, act so callously. We have immediately wired him a ticket and money for travel. He said his bank accounts were frozen because he was a Jew. What is going on in Europe has shaken me to my core. I cannot imagine this Europe. The chaos and disorder, the lawlessness, and the boldness of these men to harass and harm good people so openly. And it seems that no one is stopping them. Papa has now left London and is on his way to Bombay. I must persuade Magda to leave also. It takes so long to get or receive a letter these days, so I have sent a telegram and implored her to come to India! To leave as quickly as possible! She must convince Franz!

Magda and her husband Franz Weisskopf. Written on the back of the photograph, Weihnachten 1933 (Christmas 1933).

Magda: I have married Franz. Only Papa and Franz's family were in attendance in a small ceremony. Despite our family now being separated, I feel I made the right choice. We have moved to Teplitz for Franz's work and Gerti and Yusuf have married and moved to India. I worry about Gerti on the long journey to India but Papa also. He is now living alone in Karlsbad.

Yusuf is a wonderful man from a good family but India is so far away. I know Yusuf will look after Gerti but I miss her and Papa so much. Will she be free to dance now that she is married? Will I? Our husbands both assure us we are free to do as we wish. But I feel a constraint, maybe all in my own mind, to act as if I am a happy wife. The expectations and duties of being married seem suddenly overwhelming. My dreams of dancing and teaching seem to be falling away. The world seems to be on a crazy path. So much seems uncertain. I must keep to what I love to do. For the time being, my goal will be to find a dance school to teach at here in Teplitz.

And now, I am trembling in horror! I have just read in a desperate telegram from Papa, that he was stranded in London, almost penniless, and that he has with the Mitha family's help, embarked for India to join Gerti and Yusuf. He said, "I have escaped. My life was no longer safe in Karlsbad. You must join us soon! Do not delay!" I am deeply shaken by this news…

Events seem to be moving so quickly. Our lives have changed so much. And Mein Gott, the things happening in Europe seem unbelievable. So far we have been trying to ignore all the unpleasantness. It seems ludicrous that we would move to India. But our safe and happy lives seem suddenly unsafe and perhaps we should consider a trip, just until all this political posturing blows over. Seeing Gerti and Papa will be marvellous. The philosophy of Dalcroze will continue to sustain me.

To live life fully both mind and body must be free. Physical and intellectual liberty are not exclusively evidenced in expansive fashion by primitive impulses; the steady pursuit of an idea, as also the slow, elastic and measured development of a movement, give evidence of the free possession of a clairvoyant, prevoyant mind, which knows how to skirt obstacles and choose out new paths, always with a clear perception of the goal to be reached. (Jacques-Dalcroze, 1930, p. 81)

Magda and her husband Franz Weisskopf, in a playful moment. Teplitz, Czechoslovakia 1933.

Bombay, now known as Mumbai, as the name was changed in 1995 to throw off the unwanted legacy of British colonial rule, is a port city situated on the west coast of India and the capital of the Indian state of Maharashtra. It is presently India's most populated city and the heart of the Bollywood film industry.

Bombay has a long history of occupation, which includes being under Muslim rule until approximately 1534, Portuguese and Spanish occupation until approximately 1661, and the long held possession of Britain until August 15, 1947, when India was partitioned and declared independent. The British Empire acquired Bombay from King John IV of Portugal in 1661 when the marriage treaty of Charles II of England and Catherine of Portugal placed Bombay in British possession as a part of Catherine's dowry.

From what the Hanova sisters told me, the Bombay of 1932, for Europeans, was an extremely privileged existence. The sisters, now married and connected to a respectable and professional family, were readily accepted into Bombay society. They enjoyed a special status as Czechoslovakian patriots, refugees, and dance artists.

In 1932, India was, and is perhaps still, a country of extremely strict and enforced caste and social barriers. While Europe and Britain have their own rigid class systems in place, India's appear to be far more unforgiving. The sisters grew up with wealth and middle class values, were multilingual, and had an interest in many artistic pursuits, and so from what they said fit easily into the Indian, British, and European societies in Bombay.

It is of interest to note that Gertrud was married to an Indian Muslim, who had been educated in Britain, as had his father. It was unusual at this time for a white women to marry an Indian man. Gertrud said the Mitha family was accepting of her but she never mentioned if she was shown any prejudice for her marriage by anyone while in India. From what I know of the Hahn sisters, they would have probably not cared what other people thought of them in a general sense. They were very self-contained and the opinion of each other was what seemed to really matter to them. Of course, this self-containment did not extend to any reviews of their dance presentations. They cared very much how they were perceived as dance artists and kept all newspaper reviews of their performances.

Shortly after arriving in Bombay, Gertrud set up a dance studio teaching a Modern Central European Style and also taught Eurythmics at the Fellowship School. Without pause, she continued her life of teaching and performing dance in Bombay. After Magda arrived in 1934, the sisters were once again united to pursue their dance goals together. Gertrud said that she took Magda to the Indian dance studio of Thakure Naba Kumar Sinha, a teacher of Manipuri dance, the very next day after Magda arrived from Europe. In the spirit of always wanting to learn new forms of movement and dance, both sisters embraced the study of yoga and instruction in the many diverse Indian dance styles.

In India there are four major schools of dance technique, Bharata Natyam, Kathakali, Manipuri, and Kathak, each having its own particular dance characteristics, special rhythms, and musical accompaniment. To become proficient in any one school requires a minimum of dedicated study for seven years. Indian dance differs from European dance forms in that Indian dance has a religious origin and is permeated with Hindu thought, stories, and philosophy.

Bharata Natyam, from Tail Nadu, the most academic form, has strictly stylized and forceful movements and emphatic, elaborate hand gestures. This style also has rechakas, or sliding neck movements, and a constantly fluctuating tempi of foot beats, which are accentuated by ankle bells. Kathakali, from Kerala, evolved from early temple forms in the 17th century and is based on Hindu sacred stories that combine devotion, drama, dance, music, costumes, and makeup. Manipuri, known as the most graceful style, follows the path of eight and the foot movements generate a light touch on the ground. Kathak, from northern and western India, from Sanskrit means 'teller of stories'. This style emphasizes rhythmic foot movements. The ankles are also adorned with small bells, and the stories are told through a developed vocabulary based on the gestures of arms, upper body movements, facial expressions, and bends and turns.

Through the sisters' avid pursuit of mastering Indian dance during the 1930s and 1940s, they became friends of classical revivalist Indian dance performers such as Ram Gopal, Menaka, Uday Shankar, and K.K. Shetty. An excerpt from a programme from Menaka's Indian Ballet in 1941 aptly describes Indian dance.

> There is nothing woolly or pretty pretty about Indian dancing. It is, in fact, a vigorous dance of great exactitude both as regards its pattern and timing. The beautiful gestures produced by the hands, arms, eyes, and eyebrows, moved in the strict intricate timing of classical Indian music, give it a distinction all its own.

A brochure cover for the Manipuri dance school Gertrud first attended in 1932 in Bombay. Gertrud's teacher was Thakure Naba Kumar Sinha who was Madame Menaka's ballet master. "Manipuri Dance—a sacred dance of devotion to harmonize with the dignity of every respectable society."

Gerti: I have started to take Indian dance classes with a Mr. Thakure Naba Kumar Sinha, who is a very talented dance artist. He does not speak any of the languages I speak well, except one, the language of the dance. So I go to his studio with my servant early in the morning, when it is still not too hot for vigorous actions and I copy his movements. He has a small orchestra of three, which play us the rhythms he requests. I repeat after him what he says of the rhythms in his language and follow his steps and arm movements with my own. The Indian dance is so unlike European movement. It has a flow and cadence all its own. I feel as if I have entered into a special and do I dare use the word 'sacred' or sanctified place when we begin my lesson. As I finish and leave the class, as is the custom to thank him, I bow with my hands together in front of my chest as if in prayer, and say "Namaste". I have learned this represents the belief that there is a divine spark within each of us located in the heart and saying "Namaste" acknowledges the soul in one by the soul in another. How apt and respectfully poetic. After my saying my "Namaste", the spell in the studio is broken and I return to the heat, noise, and odours of the real world outside, until we meet again.

A poster for A Unique Programme of Choice Indian and European Dances, by Enakshi Ram Rao and Gertie Hahnova, one of Gertrud's first public performances on April 5th, 1933 in Bombay.

Billing details: A Dance Recital In Aid of Charity at the Sir Cowasji Jehangir Hall Tuesday, the 5th April 1933. Seats at Rs. (Rupees) 5, 3, 2, 1.

Inside the programme amongst other celebrated artist names:
Peasant Dance Miss Gertie Hahnova
Eurhythmic Class Demonstration by the Fellowship School Children trained by Miss Gertie Hahnova.

Gertrud in Bohemian dance costume, Bombay 1933.

In 1933, Gerti Hahn now starts to bill herself as Gertie Hahnova. As mentioned, in Czech and other Slavic languages, the suffix 'ova' is traditionally added to the last names of all females. It is an ending which is present to this day and literally means 'belonging to' the male, be it husband or father. But it seems that the name change was Gertrud's way of making it clear that her nationality was Czechoslovakian and the name 'Hanova' in various spellings was used from 1933 onward by both Gertrud and Magda for the stage.

Gertrud in Slavic Peasant Costume, 1933.

Gerti: My first major performance in Bombay was for a Dance Recital In Aid of Charity at the Sir Cowasji Jehangir Hall. The audience of dance enthusiasts was a mixture of European and Indian people, many whom I graciously met at the reception following the event. My students from the Fellowship School did an exceptional job demonstrating Dalcroze Eurhythmics. The success of this performance has reinforced my resolve and belief that the dance will always be my calling. Wherever I might find myself, I will keep performing, teaching, and taking dance classes. I know this to be my destiny, which I will not let anything interrupt or deter. I see possibilities here in Bombay. But one must get into the right set and know how to publicize oneself. I will start with what I know, the ballet, modern dance, and of course Dalcroze rhythmic gymnastics. I'm sure people here will welcome and appreciate a new dance artist joining their circle.

Gerti: Yusuf is wonderful and gives me everything I could wish for. In our home, there are many servants, always under foot. Each servant has a specific job and will not do anything else but that job. Now I live in India, I have come to realize that it will take some time to fully understand the ways of this very different country and culture.

In the Indian dance classes, I am learning the stories of the Hindu Gods and this leads to an explanation of the movements and expressions. I observe closely and try to duplicate what I see. But more importantly, I feel these new movements deep within. I have come to understand that in Siva and Terpsichore we worship the same Muse.

Gertrud in traditional Indian sari, mid 1930's.

The Protective Shield of Terpsichore, Wherein Terpsichore Meets Siva

Gerti 1934: I am overjoyed! Magda and Franz have finally arrived in Bombay and I am feeling much better as to their safety. The very next day after she disembarked from the steamer, I took Magda to Thakure Naba Kumar Sinha's dance studio for a lesson. We attended, as is my usual practice, very early in the morning to avoid the heat. The class began with floor exercises and to my horror a scorpion scuttled right up to where I was sitting. I jumped up and ran over to the bar covered windows, (the bars are to keep out tigers) and another dancer pulled off her chuppal (her sandal) and with no effort or fuss killed the scorpion dead. Well, what was I to do? I calmly pretended all was in order and went back to my place and continued to practice the floor exercises. Magda had her mouth hanging open at first but took my lead and without blinking an eye, my sister is very pragmatic, continued practising the new movements.

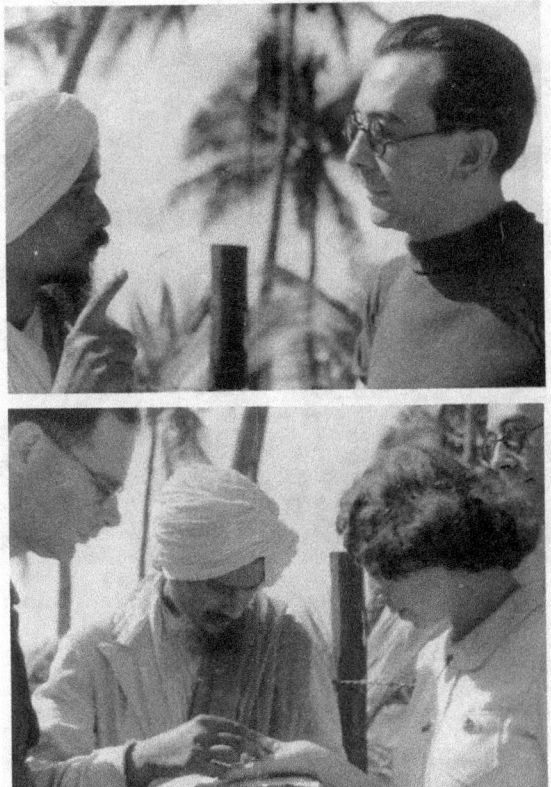

Franz and Magda having their fortunes told, 1934.

Magda: We are here in Bombay, at last! It was so wonderful to be reunited with Gerti and Papa. Just to sit in their presence and feel safe and unworried about anything was such a joyous feeling. And I simply love the sun and the heat in this climate. Bombay is so intriguing, so unlike Europe. I am fascinated with the people and customs. I cannot resist going out every day to find some new and exotic market or shop to poke around in. Gerti says we should stay inside and rest during the hottest part of the day, but I cannot. There is so much to see and do that I feel compelled to go exploring. Gerti has already taken me to an Indian dance class and I was captivated. The music and movement were so unfamiliar from what I know, but still there was something I recognized. I felt a resonance, which delighted me. My first class was like a new door opening, beckoning me to try something refreshingly different in my experiences of the Terpsichorean Arts.

Magda's husband Franz Weisskopf with Indian transportation. Mid 1930s, Bombay.

To give some background to Indian classical dance, at the turn of the twentieth century, Indian classical dance had all but disappeared or been dismissed by the public, as the dancers were considered to be no more than temple prostitutes. In the 1920s and 1930s, a revival took place inspired by famed poet and performer Rabindranath Tagore in Bengal, Valathol Narayan Memon in Kerala, and Sadhona Bose established the Kathak School of Dance in Maharashatra, where Bombay (Mumbai) is located. Indian classical dance now started to become more respectable and middle-class, educated women ventured to study this ancient art form.

The revered Indian poet Rabindranath Tagore, an unknown woman (centre), and famed classical Indian dancer Menaka (far right). Photograph from the Hanova collection.

> Dance My Heart!
> Dance, my heart, dance today with joy!
> The streams of love fill the days and nights with music,
> And the world is listening to its melodies.
> Mad with joy, life and death dance to the rhythm of this music.
> The hills and the sea and the earth dance.
> The world of man dances in laughter and tears.
> Why put on the robe of the monk, and live aloof from the world in lonely pride?
> Behold! My heart dances in the delight of a hundred arts; and the Creator is well pleased.
>
> (Tagore, 2019, p. 1)

Interestingly, the united efforts of foreigners were also involved in the revival of Indian classical dance. The famous Russian ballerina, Anna Pavlova, and American dancer La Meri were both instrumental in encouraging and supporting Indian dance artists.

La Meri (1899–1988) discovered and supported classical Indian dancer Ram Gopal. La Meri was known as the 'queen' of ethnic dance and traveled extensively all over the world learning dances from many cultures. She earned a reputation as one of the foremost experts in the ethnic-dance field.

Ram Gopal (1912–2003) was born in Bangalore in the South of India. He was the son of a Rajput lawyer father and a Burmese mother. He performed mostly as a soloist and was one of the first Indian dancers to tour extensively in Europe and America in the 1930s. He will be remembered as a major figure in the revival and restoration of Indian dance. Ram Gopal studied Bharata Natyam, Kathakali, Kathak, and Manipuri dance techniques and blended these classical Indian styles with balletic choreography. As a choreographer, he is known best for his productions, Legend of the Taj Mahal, Dance of the Setting Sun, and Dances of India. During WWII, Ram Gopal returned to India and for seven years annually toured India striving to revive interest in Indian dance. He returned to Europe after the war and settled in the UK where he continued to perform and create a positive atmosphere for the appreciation of the Indian dance arts. Ram Gopal will be remembered for his dedication and tireless work in rejuvenating the dance of India.

Ram Gopal, from a programme in the Hahn sisters' collection, London 1956.

Gertrud related an engaging story about meeting Ram Gopal. She said he was visiting Bombay, she didn't mention which year this was, and the sisters invited him to their dance studio. Gertrud said they got on very well and showed each other their dance styles and talked for quite some time. After a few hours, Ram Gopal's secretary hurried in to tell him he must leave to attend a meeting with the Maja Raja. Gertrud laughed as she

217

related that Ram Gopal said to his secretary, "The Maja Raja can wait. The Hahn sisters are much more interesting to talk to."

As mentioned Anna Pavlova, the famed Russian ballerina, also supported the revival of Indian dance. She toured the world extensively in the 1920s and 1930s. In the early 1920s, while performing in India, she looked for authentic classical Indian dance but was told it was all but dead. Some years later, while in London, Pavlova met a young Indian set designer called Uday Shankar (1900–1977), the brother of famous sitar player Ravi, and encouraged him to develop his interest and abilities in the Indian dance arts. "Working with Pavlova shaped Uday into a disciplined artist and familiarized him with the essential elements in successful stagecraft" (Joshi, 2012, p. 3). Shankar became one of the most famous touring Indian dance artists of this period and is called the Father of neo-classical or contemporary dance in India.

Programme of Uday Shankar's 'All India Tour' 1939 from the Hanova collection.

Dance has occupied in India from time immemorial a most important place in the cultural achievements of her people. Having a background of cosmic symbology and drawing inspiration from the whole of nature, it has been a constant source of inspiration to great sculpture and painting in the past. In the rhythmic evolution of the universe India sees eternal dance—the dance of Siva, Lord of dancers, who dances in the heart of the world, releasing those who love him from earthly bondage and bestowing on them eternal bliss. (Uday Shankar, programme notes, 1939).

In 1927, Pavlova also met Leila Sokhey, an Anglo-Indian woman, who later became famous as Madame Menaka. With Pavlova's friendship and backing Menaka also became a world famous dancer, touring with Pavlova and reviving the classical dances of Kathakali, Manipuri, and Bharata Natyam. Menaka was honoured with the first prize for her dance production at the Berlin Dance Olympiad in 1936 and is remembered for creating a renaissance in the Indian dance arts.

Pavlova also supported Rukmini Devi in touring the world with Bharata Natyam. Historian Joshi (2012) comments that, "With boundless creativity and a wealth of traditional resources, these three artists (Shankar, Menaka, and Devi) elegantly demonstrated to the world the timeless élan of India's art and culture, helping to dispel the notion of India as a primitive and inferior country suitable for foreign colonial rule" (p. 5).

Menaka was a particularly close friend of the Hanova sisters in Bombay and greatly inspired the sisters to pursue studying Indian dance forms. The sisters were introduced to Menaka by Thakore Navkumar Singha, Gertrud's first teacher of Indian dance, who was Menaka's ballet master. Magda and Gertrud kept an album devoted to Menaka memorabilia, programmes, personal photographs, and correspondence, which reveal that they shared one another's dance studio spaces and worked together on dance presentations. Gertrud in her memories of Menaka said, "Menaka's innovation was to bring Indian dance to a wider audience, to give it a new respectability, and to make Indian dance come alive once more. In 1934, she toured the whole of India and the Far East and again took her Ballet to Europe in 1936. She traversed the continent and gave over 750 performances in two years. Menaka devoted her life to restore the dance of her country to its former prominence."

Menaka with Nilkanta. Photograph from the Hanova Menaka memorabilia.

The Protective Shield of Terpsichore, Wherein Terpsichore Meets Siva

From the Hanova memorabilia, a poster advertising a Menaka performance at the Royal Opera House, April 3, 1933, Bombay. Perhaps the first performance in which Gertrud saw Menaka perform.

A photograph from the Hanova sisters Menaka album inscribed: "Magda, with love from Menaka".

Magda: When I first met Leila Sokey, better known as Madame Menaka, I was immediately struck by her composure and calm manner. She had a serene presence. She was and is a quiet and thoughtful woman. But it was when I first saw her dance that I realized 'this' was her true way of communicating. As I observed her detailed and intricate movements, rhythms, and expressions, I could see the noble eons of India's glorious past unfold before me. I stand in awe of this venerable form of dance. This art of India can be strong and fierce, beautiful and tender, with flow and pause, and then relentless in its rhythmic passion. In this movement, I behold an ancient symbolic language connected to the sacred and an expression of the deep spiritually of the Indian people. The motions are magnificent and so unlike European dance, in that the eyes, neck, hands, and torso all play such significant roles in adding to the story being told.

Menaka in a photograph from the Hanova collection.

Our Love Affair with Dance

The Hanova sisters said they mixed freely in Bombay society with people and artists of all kinds, who were European or Indian. The sisters enjoyed an active social life. They mentioned they were invited to many functions, such as garden parties, teas, and dance performances which included meeting the Raja Narsinggirji.

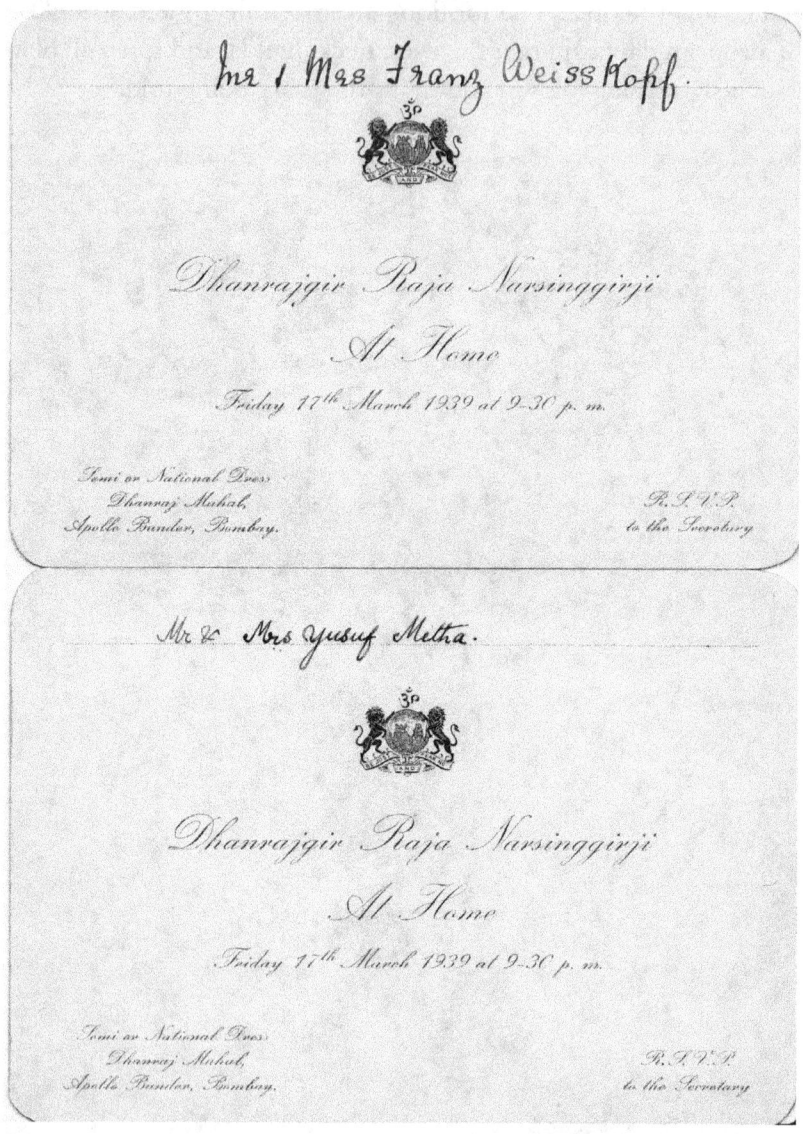

Formal invitations to Dhanrajgir Raja Narsinggirji At Home for Friday 17th March 1939, for Mr. & Mrs. Franz Weisskopf and Mr. & Mrs. Yusuf Mitha.

The Protective Shield of Terpsichore, Wherein Terpsichore Meets Siva

Gerti: It was wonderful to meet His Highness, The Raja Narsinggirji. He is also considered to be the King of Hyderabad in Telangana, the state bordering Maharashtra. We were so honoured to tour his new art deco styled Dhanraj Mahal which was only recently built. It is said to be one of the largest and costliest buildings ever constructed in Bombay. Raja Narsingh is a philanthropist and very charming. We were glad to be invited to this gathering. However, I was not pleased that the Raja was more interested in discussing the Nazi takeover of our country and politics in Europe than about discussing our dancing here in India. I certainly did not need to be reminded of what has happened in Czechoslovakia only days ago. Germany has invaded our homeland much to our abhorrence.

Gertrud gathering supplies for an excursion, Bombay 1930s.

225

Gerti: As I walk through the early morning market and assemble supplies for our trip to the hill station, the air is already shimmering with heat. The light is bright and intense. As always, the streets are a swirl of colour and sound. The chatter of Marathi, Gujarati, Hindi, and occasionally English, sound in my ears. The spicy aroma of food frying in oil permeates the air. Yusuf insists I do not eat anything from a stall. He says they are unsanitary. But the food smells so good. Beautiful fabrics hang everywhere in small tailor shops with hand turned sewing machines at the ready. The crowds of people coming and going jostle each other. Hands are thrust out with cries of "Baksheesh, Memsahib!" Bleak faces peer up at me, but I have been living in India for some time now and with sadness turn away. My servant scolds the beggars to leave me alone and hands them small coins. The rich and the poor are completely separated here and live worlds apart.

My world is one of plenty. Only the other day, Yusuf brought me a beautiful, tiger skin rug for a present. I, to my chagrin, haughtily told him to take it away as I didn't like it. What possessed me to be so rude to him? Yusuf is always polite and gracious to me. I must seem so ungrateful, but lately I am driven by black moods and seem to take offense at the slightest small thing. I imagine I am unhappy with my life. Something is missing. What that is, I cannot say. I feel the walls closing in on me some days. Yusuf loves me and wants children, but for me that is out of the question. The terrible events in Europe are far away but on my mind nonetheless.

My thoughts turn to those we knew in the dance world in Europe and I also often wonder about our students, friends, and neighbours in Karlsbad. Do they miss us? Do they wonder what became of us? I have received very few letters lately but the ones that have gotten through make me shudder at the descriptions of the way the Jewish people have been treated by the German invasion. These are people just like me. It is incredible that the beauty and love for the arts that we shared with so many has turned to hate and denigration.

The Protective Shield of Terpsichore, Wherein Terpsichore Meets Siva

March 26, 1939.

Manipur School Of Dancing

RECITAL IN BOMBAY

Lovers of Indian dancing in Bombay will be pleased to learn that a recital, arranged by Pandit Navakumar Singh the Manipur Dance teacher, is to be given in Bombay about the third week of April in some local cinema.

Pandit Navakumar himself is taking part, with his son, Narendra Kumar, now in the Menaka Ballet, and a number of his pupils. They include Leela Row, who gave a number of recitals in Europe, Ramila Shroff, well known in Bombay, Vimala, Malati, Damayanti and Benita, Usha and Lata Munshi, and a few European ladies who have been taking regular lessons from the dance master. They are Esther Wolse, Doris Walter Jepson, Gertrude Hahnova and Magda Hahnova.

The programme, comprising various types of dancing of the Manipur School—which has won great appreciation from audiences in Bombay—will provide an opportunity of seeing the Manipur School of Dancing in all its different styles, thus providing an interesting comparative study with the other existing schools of dancing in India.

The Manipur School of Dancing advertises an upcoming recital on March 26, 1939. Gertrude Hahnova and Magda Hahnova are mentioned as two of the European ladies who have been taking regular classes and will be performing.

Gertrud and Magda pose in Indian dance costume, 1930s.

Besides studying Indian dance and teaching European styles of dance in Bombay at their own dance school and at private schools, Magda and Gertrud broadcast an exercise and body sculpture program called Keep Fit from 1936 until late 1940. Magda played the piano while Gertrud instructed listeners as to how they could and should become physically fit.

The Protective Shield of Terpsichore, Wherein Terpsichore Meets Siva

Magda and Gertrud broadcasting at the Bombay radio station studio. The sisters Keep Fit program aired from 1936 to late 1940.

An excerpt from the Hanova sisters radio show, Keep Fit, informs us:

> In the Hanova System, one starts with exercises. One strives for the highest achievement in the physical sense, whether it be for developing, correcting, or maintaining the physical co-ordination of the body. These are designed for children or adults of both sexes, to enable them to get the maximum effect with the minimum of effort, and to keep muscles and ligaments in a healthy state, and to prevent aging. To do exercises is a "Must"

for everybody, from the growing child, to the dancers, for the sports-minded, and last, but not least, for the tired, hard-working man or woman. Exercises are a "Must", but—and this is most important—they should be enjoyed and executed correctly with a proper knowledge of each and every single effect and purpose. Only then can they make one elated and happy and there is truth in the saying: "In a healthy body lives a healthy mind." But the Hanovas say, vice versa, "Train your mind and you can train your body for even greater happiness."

Magda and Gertrud at the Bombay radio station studio, with a fellow employee, some time between 1936 and late 1940.

The Protective Shield of Terpsichore, Wherein Terpsichore Meets Siva

In another insightful excerpt from the Hanova sisters' radio program, Gertrud shares more of the Hanova philosophy of body sculpture:

> Let us start with Body Sculpture. For this, forming and moulding, stretching, bending, loosening, and swinging are literally, 'sculpting' the body. Movements form the link between Body Sculpture and The Dance. They improve poise and confidence and are of great value to anyone in the theatre on or off stage, on the sport's field, or in ordinary private life. They are technically controlled and are themselves a form in their own right. The dance arts in every epoch choose their own pattern and adjust themselves to the modern world. Art must ever express itself over again in a modern style.

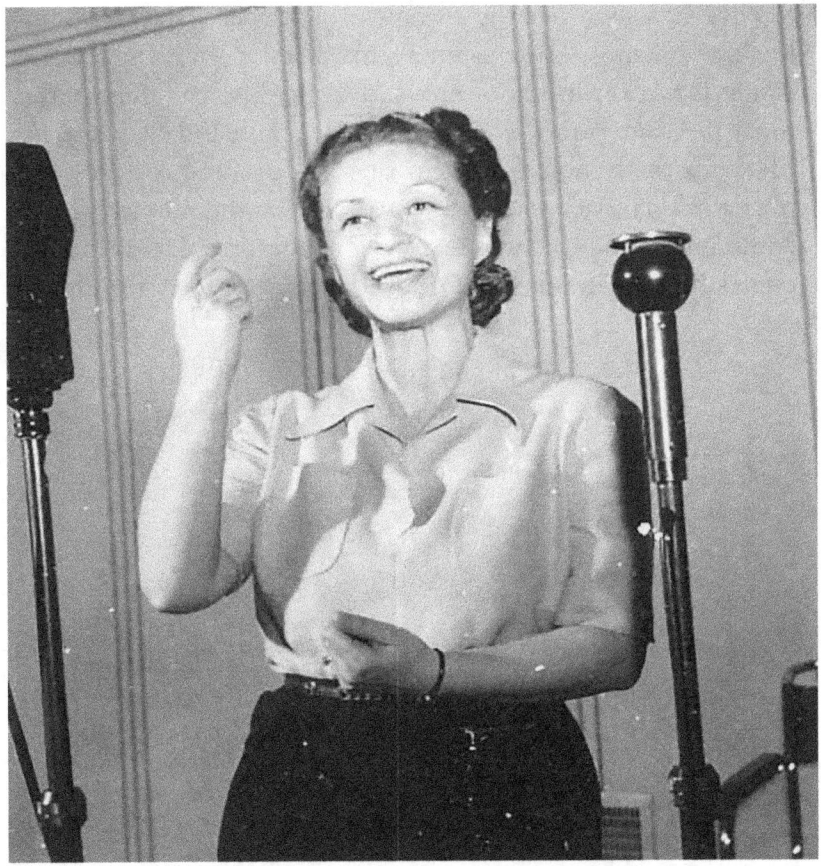

Gertrud broadcasting the Hanova radio program, Keep Fit.

Magda and Gertrud's radio program came to an end in late 1940, due Gertrud related to the war effort needing the air ways. The following quotes are from The Times of India, the first is praising the sisters' program, the second is lamenting the end of their popular show.

> Thursday: waking with rosy-fingered dawn for the "Keep Fit", course, Miss Gertrude Hanovah's exotic accent, and intimate mike manner. Almost thou persuades me to try "touching the floor with my head": but consideration like an angel came, and I just enjoyed the piano (gymnopedies). A great course this, you should try it, sometime." (The Times of India, May 28, 1940.)

> Miss Gertrude Hanovah's early morning physical jerks have come to an end. They made one of the longest and most attractive series put over by a single broadcaster. I shall miss the luxury of lying in bed listening to Miss Hanovah telling me to get down on the floor and Go To It. She has one of the most pleasant voices on AIR and the command of a variety of sympathetic noises to help one through the tortures she prescribes. Her scripts and the way she fits them to music are admirable. I hope it will not be long before Miss Hanovah comes back. (The Times of India, December 10, 1940)

Magda and Gertrud pose with a 'handi', an Indian cooking pot, 1939.

The Protective Shield of Terpsichore, Wherein Terpsichore Meets Siva

**Gertrud and Magda pose on the Mitha balcony, 1939.
The costumes pictured in these photographs were designed by the sisters.
The skirts were made of many panels of fabric and when the sisters
turned, the skirts expanded out in an exquisite, full circle of material.
They said they loved to create their own ensembles for the stage.**

To understand the circumstances which precipitated the start of WWII, I outline the following events. On March 2, 1938, German troops annexed Austria for the Third Reich. Hitler said his mandate was to unite all German speaking countries in Europe, even though under the terms of the Treaty of Versailles, Germany and Austria were forbidden to be unified. Next, Hitler invaded Czechoslovakia on March 15, 1939 and took over Bohemia, another German speaking area, and established a protectorate over Slovakia. When the German army invaded Poland on September 1, 1939, Britain and France declared war on Germany, as they realized Hitler had been lying about his intentions to only seek unification with German speaking countries. As India was a colony of Britain, Indian regiments served as part of the allied forces. As war broke out, the Hanova sisters now donated all of their dance performance receipts to the European and Czechoslovakian war effort as did many other artists in Bombay.

Magda poses in costume from an unknown work, Bombay 1939.

Magda: Despite that the world is in turmoil, Gerti and I stay resolute in our dedication to the dance. Without art, humanity has no meaningful future. We will continue to dance our way to inner and outer peace and tranquillity.

The Protective Shield of Terpsichore, Wherein Terpsichore Meets Siva

Magda and her husband Franz Weisskopf in Bombay during WW II.

Magda: Since the declaration of war in September, I have been volunteering for the Red Cross and Franz has joined up with the British forces. Gerti, Papa, and I may be out of the way of any real danger, but I feel I must do something to support the war effort. I shiver in horror as we read about what is happening in Europe. Gerti and I unquestionably will be giving all of our box office receipts to support worthy war causes. It cannot be stressed enough how much we are grateful to be here in India, but we sadly miss our homeland and our carefree dancing days in Europe.

One can only wonder in sorrow at the chaos and the deliberate and unprovoked attacks on the Jewish people in Europe. Our family is Jewish as part of our heritage. But as modern women, we have chosen not to observe any religious practices. Being Jewish has just been one aspect of our cultural background, which we have never felt the need to hide or proclaim. Gerti and I have focused on being dance artists. It is certainly hard to believe a whole group of people, just like us, have been targeted because of their family lineage. We have heard in the news that not just Jews but homosexuals, artists, gypsies, and free thinkers of all kinds have also been attacked and imprisoned by the Nazi regime. I cannot comprehend this madness. My heart bleeds for everyone.

During the Second World War, India was controlled by the United Kingdom, which sent over two and a half million Indian soldiers to fight under British command against Axis powers. Indians fought with distinction in Europe, North Africa, and in the South Asian region defending India against Japan. Over 87, 000 Indian soldiers died in World War II.

Of interest, The Indian National Congress led by Mohanda Karamchand Gandhi, denounced Nazi Germany but also British Imperialism and said they would not support or fight with Britain until India was made independent. The Congress refused to cooperate in any way with the war effort and so the government arrested over 60,000 national and local Congress leaders, who were jailed until June 1945. Gandhi was allowed to leave prison in May 1944 because of his poor health. However, The Muslim League, which supported the advocacy for a separate Muslim nation, worked closely with the British authorities.

The Protective Shield of Terpsichore, Wherein Terpsichore Meets Siva

Franz Weisskopf in uniform. On the back of the photograph, Franz humorously wrote, "An "aristocratic" look" for my "royal" sis-in-law! Franz".

Mohandas Gandhi and unknown companions walking along the Bombay beach in front of the Mitha beach house. Gertrud said Gandhi was their beach house neighbour. Photo by Gertrud Hanova, 1939.

Our Love Affair with Dance

Gandhi was the pre eminent political and ideological leader of India during the Indian independence movement, which finally led to India breaking away from British rule and becoming a united and independent nation in 1947. He is famous for employing non-violent civil disobedience and inspiring civil rights and freedom around the world. Gertrud said she snapped these pictures of him walking by their Bombay beach house in the early morning. Gandhi was tragically assassinated in 1948.

A photograph of Gandhi and an unknown companion walking on the Bombay beach. Photo by Gertrud Hanova, 1939.

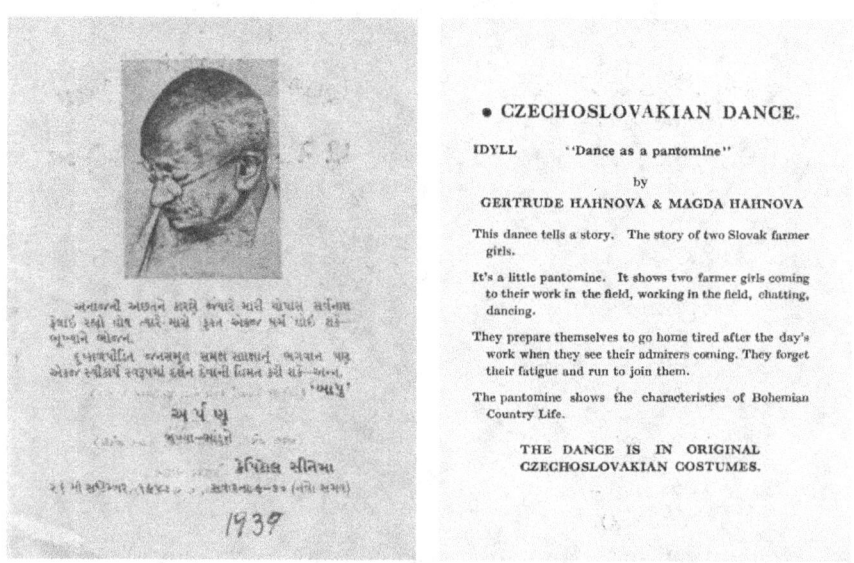

A programme cover and inner page from a Hanova performance in 1939 in Bombay. The cover picture is of Mahatma Mohandas Karamchand Gandhi.

Gerti: Once again we will perform our dance, Idyll, on a bill with many other acts for the war effort. Although I cannot say that anything appears to be 'idyllic'. We are actually shattered beyond belief by news that has filtered in to us from letters from friends in Europe. Our beloved homeland has been polluted and desecrated by men who wish to be powerful and are merciless. Lies are told and believed by many. Neighbours are no longer friends but enemies. I have faith that all those I loved have fled to safety. And what of art or a reverence for the beauty of movement. These things do not appear to have any bearing on anything or to be in anyone's mind anymore. We must uphold the ideals that there are still things in this world that are worthy of artistic merit and that have important meaning and go far beyond bloodshed and senseless violence. I will keep performing to show the public how to keep faith with our troops and those who fight against tyranny.

Magda and Gertrud consistently performed for Bombay audiences throughout their sixteen years of residence in India. During the war years, box office receipts from their performances were donated to the war effort. The sisters were also often invited to be part of concerts showcasing a variety of dance artists, during and after the war, in which the monies raised were inevitably given to charitable causes.

From a programme dated January 24, 1940, I discovered that the sisters performed with The Pupils of Navkumar Singha's Manipuri Dancing Class at the Capitol Theatre. This concert was called 'A Programme for Vraj-Vihar'. Programme notes list Gertrude Hahnova and Magda Hahnova in Puja Nritya. This piece is described as 'Two pujarinis worship God and put flowers and saphron at his feet'.

I reflect that in 1940, the sisters had now been studying Indian dance for several years and had advanced in their skill and mastery. Nevertheless, it was undoubtedly still an honour to be included in these public performances with Indian dancers.

In my Indian dance lessons with the Hanova sisters, I remember Gertrud showing me how to bend back and stretch my fingers to warm up the hands to gain the correct flexibility and style for the mudras or Indian hand gestures. She said she thought the European could learn Indian dance but would never be able to execute the movements as well as an Indian dancer.

> **THE TIMES OF INDIA**
> **JANUARY 25, 1940.**
>
> ### MANIPURI DANCES AT "CAPITOL"
> #### Interesting Recital
>
> The stylised technique of the Manipuri dance, rendered mainly to the accompaniment of the *mridang*, has a fascination all its own—with its graceful swings and curves and the fluid expression of the body.
>
> As a form of folk-dancing, with a limited range, it would hardly be extensive enough to cover a complete recital, but the ingenious master, Thakur Navkumar, has succeeded in weaving a full and interesting programme out of it—and amidst his pupils many a budding and graceful dancer can be detected. Gertrude Hanova and Magda Hanova, well-known dancers, have adapted themselves to the Indian technique in a truly admirable manner, and their movements in the Puja Dance were sinuous and expressive. Medha Yodh dances with a sweeping grace which reveals her great talent. Leela Rao, the tennis "star" proves her versatility by adding dancing to her many accomplishments.
>
> The two group dances and the Manipuri *garba*, with the glittering costumes and fine movements, were very picturesque ensemble numbers. Thakore Navkumar is to be congratulated on his efforts in popularising the Manipuri dance.

January 25th, 1940, a review of a Hanova performance captioned Manipuri Dances at "Capitol" Interesting Recital.

The stylized technique of the Manipuri dance, rendered mainly to the accompaniment of the *mridang*, has a fascination all its own—with its graceful swings and curves and the fluid expression of the body... Gertrude Hanova and Magda Hanova, well-known dancers, have adapted themselves to the Indian technique in a truly admirable manner, and their movements in the Puja Dance were sinuous and expressive.

Gertrud and Magda perform Puja Nritya, January 24, 1940.

Despite a full schedule of teaching and performing with their own dance school, Magda and Gertrud also found time to instruct physical fitness, rhythmic gymnastics, and dance at private schools in Bombay for most of the 1930s and 1940s.

Magda far left, standing on the top row with students from The Modern Preparatory School, 1940.

Magda taught at The Modern Preparatory School and at The Alexandra Girls' English Institution as Mrs. Weisskopf. Her credentials were listed as 'Schools of Physical Culture training and the Continents'. (Alexandra School Annual report from 1942–43) Gertrud taught at the Fellowship School and at the Cathedral and John Connon Girls' School. There is evidence from the many private school lecture demonstration programmes the sisters kept that Magda and Gertrud arranged numerous performances for the public to showcase their teaching of dance and eurhythmics.

Magda: The children at the private schools where I teach, absolutely love to exercise and dance. They tell me mine is their favourite class. I know this to be true because students crave to move their bodies and have a need to be freed from sitting with pen and ink in hand all day.

With the music of a pianist to accompany us, I have introduced many European composers to the students. The scores I have selected, mostly marches and waltzes, have the swinging rhythms and ideal beats to practice Dalcroze Eurhythmics. The students are very supple and responsive. I demonstrate and they immediately are able to follow. The younger students especially seem to grasp the essence of what I am intending, which is an inner enjoyment of the movement and music in combination to further expand the soul and spirit. The students are easily swept up with feeling as we unite in creating a fantastic movement choir.

Recently, I organized a lecture demonstration showcasing the older students from The Alexandra Girls' English Institution. This, as always, is an excellent way to educate the parents and the other teachers on staff. The girls admirably showed that dance is to free the soul and to express oneself unreservedly. The students had a natural grace and flow with all of their movements. They beautifully performed the dances we worked on with much exuberance. Their vitality and liveliness were commendable. The girls seemed to carry the spirit of Isadora herself!

Isadora has sadly now passed on with many other notable dancers. But her authentic philosophy promoting the freeing nature of the dance will ever prevail. Isadora's adopted daughter, Irma, has quite recently published some of Isadora's words for posterity.

Photograph from The Alexandra Girls' English Institution pamphlet, 1940. "Choreography by Magda Hanova."

Irma Duncan states most eloquently:

Isadora did for movement in relation to the dance, what Chaucer did for the English language. They both achieved a purifying and releasing process, rendering more articulate a vehicle which had previously been bound up and limited...

This great artist developed two things: First her principle of movement, by using motions familiar to all races, such as walking, running, skipping, jumping, kneeling, reclining and rising. Second, she used this theory as a means to a new expression in the dance art. These ideas had far reaching educational results. They demonstrated the ennobling effect of natural movement on physical development, and achieved amazing results in the field of the physical and spiritual education of children. Her ideas in this particular scope have been confused with her ideas on the art of dancing. To move is one thing, to dance is another. (Irma Duncan, 1937, p. x)

Magda, demonstrating jumps for students at
The Modern Preparatory School, Bombay, 1940s.

The Protective Shield of Terpsichore, Wherein Terpsichore Meets Siva

Magda demonstrating jumps at The Modern Preparatory School, 1940s.

Magda: We are outdoors for many classes, moving in the gloriously fresh, early morning spaces, freeing ourselves of stationary learning to explore lessons in dynamics and motion.

Magda: As Gerti and I progress in our study of Indian dance, we have also been acquiring an understanding of yoga. I have been told that following this path is a process to transformation, self-mastery, and self-realization. These attributes may all lead one on a spiritual journey. Our guru (teacher) has explained with great patience that channels are cleared within the self through the exercises and meditation to illuminate the divine. I cannot help compare this method to the practices of dancing.

Perhaps I do not fully understand what an Indian mystic or guru may be trying to explain concerning reaching a spiritual goal of transcendence. But I do understand the benefits of the postures (asanas), the breathing, and cleansing oneself of bad feelings through this meditation to facilitate relaxation and peace. It is much like the philosophy of Dalcroze. One is trying to find a balance inside so one may live life fully on the outside.

And although the war continues to rage on in Europe, I am coping by applying this meditation to clear and cleanse my mind and body. Much like what Isadora Duncan revealed, that the dancer after a stilling and searching of the inner body may discover a power, or subtle inner force, stemming from the center, which when tapped into may lead to greater artistic expression and vibrancy. So similarly the teachings of yoga, speak of prana, life's vital energy, which may be expanded through yoga exercises and meditation, leading to feelings of increased vigor and tranquillity.

My comparison of Eastern and European movement and exercise methodologies are revealing universal philosophies, which have similar goals, although Indian practices are far older. Nonetheless, I feel extremely privileged to have learned what we have of Indian movement, music, and mysticism and to conversely share what we know of European dance and exercise methods. The dance and movement in its many forms will continue to intrigue me and lead to my serenity and a dynamic animation wherever I abide.

The Protective Shield of Terpsichore, Wherein Terpsichore Meets Siva

An article, from February 28, 1941, in The Sporting Times, advertising the next upcoming performance by the Misses Gertrude and Magda Hanova. 'Physical Culture Display by Czech Artistes at Excelsior Cinema."

Bombay is to have a unique type of entertainment at the Excelsior Theatre on March 13, 1941. It has been arranged by two well-known Czech lady physical culturists—the Misses Gertrude and Magda Hanova. These artistes, who have frequently broadcast on the All India Radio, have been trained under the best masters in Europe. They have arranged their programme to show the relation of physical exercises to classical dancing. It has been planned as follows: Physical exercises on rhythmical movements and classical dances… The scenery and costumes are both novel and exquisite and have been designed by the artistes themselves. All those interested in physical culture and dancing should make it a point to see this show which promises to have strong continental flavour.

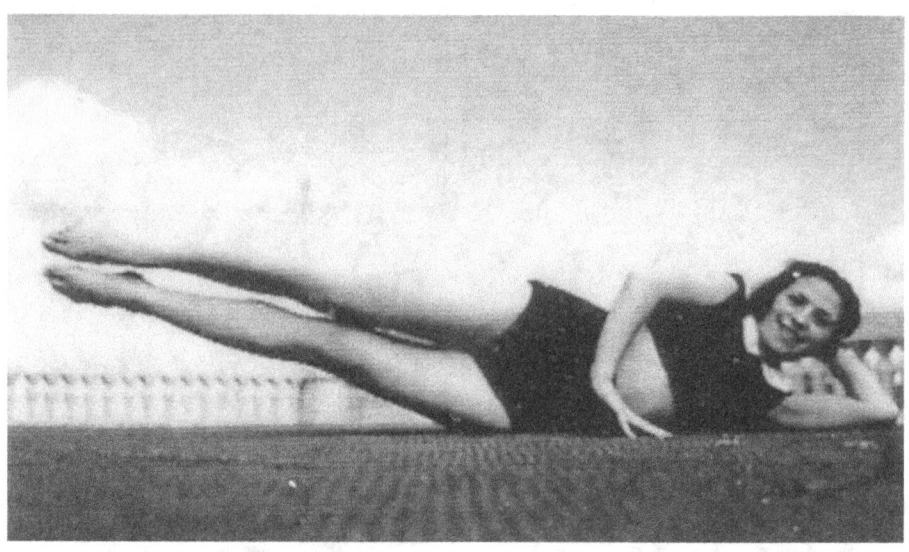
Magda demonstrating exercises on the Mitha balcony, 1941.

Magda, in a promotional photograph demonstrating a yoga pose for the sisters' next performance at the Excelsior Theatre, March 1941.

The Protective Shield of Terpsichore, Wherein Terpsichore Meets Siva

As most artists of the day, the Hanova sisters advertised in all the local papers before a performance. The Bombay Chronicle, February 28, 1941 reported, "How physical culture can be made as enjoyable as sport by being adapted to rhythm and music, will be demonstrated by Miss Gertrude Hahnova and her sister Magda Hahnova, at a show given by them at the Excelsior at 6:30 p.m. next Thursday, March 13. Nearly half the programme consists of a variety of classical dances with an Indian dance in Manipuri style."

Also in The Times of India, March 8, 1941, the sisters advertised a "Recital of Classical Dances and Rhythmical Movements by Gertrude Hahnova and Magda Hahnova (well known for the "Keep Fit" on the All India Radio)".

Gerti: I contemplate that in performing for the public, our presentations have become more than showing the benefits of exercise or the beauty of movement. Our concerts have become, as the Indian dancer professes, a sacred offering. I reflect that Hindu mystical values have slowly seeped into my being without my seeming to have noticed.

The Hindu believes that the soul reincarnates, evolving through many births, until all karmas have been resolved, and the soul finally transcends to a higher place. And the Hindu's belief that the universe undergoes endless cycles of creation, preservation, and destruction seem very real as I hear news of the war and the deaths of many soldiers and innocent civilians all over the world. As Indian dance is based on the epic tales and mythology of the Hindu scriptures, the Indian dance is consequently a form of worship for the Indian dancer and seen as a revered and genuine path to their salvation. As the Indian dance artist says so beautifully, "Dance is one facet of God's light to follow".

This pearl of wisdom deeply resonates with me although I retain no affiliation with any traditional religion. But while dancing in the Indian style, I gain a soul understanding of the mysteries of Hinduism. I feel a deep reverence for the Indian dance that is not unlike the awe I have felt in times past while dancing outdoors in the splendour of nature. The Earth and its wonders are accordingly my temple and dancing on its surface has always been my true act of devotion and worship.

My husband Yusuf is a Muslim. This did not seem to matter too much when we were in Europe. And I have tried to understand the ways of his religion, which differ greatly from the Hindu. His beliefs interestingly stem from those of the Jews and Christians. All three religions are considered to be people of the 'book'. The Muslim interestingly believes Abraham and Jesus to be prophets and that Mohammed, 'Peace Be Upon Him' as Yusuf would say now he is back in India, is the last prophet sent by God. As in the Jewish and Christian faiths there are many rules to follow. In all three faiths, women inevitably take a back seat to men. Needless to say, I don't fit into the traditions of being a proper Muslim wife. Yusuf said he doesn't care, but the longer we are in his country, the more I see his European mannerisms being shed. He craves a family and cannot understand my singular devotion to the dance. He is still wonderful to me but we are maybe not as close. Perhaps marriage goes this way?

Anyway, what interests me the most about the Muslim faith is the mystical branch called the Sufi and the Sufi spinning. I remember seeing Mary Wigman practice these dervish turns. At the time, I thought Wigman eccentric in her movement but loved her bold and brilliant dances and the liberation of spirit she seemed to exude. I did not understand or correlate her ritual of spiralling, to her finding a deeper inspiration for her work. I did not realize this was her offering.

Now I am taking a closer look and see the turning in a new light. Through the dance, the Sufi Dervishes of the Mevlevi order are performing a physical meditation, an act of worship. They seek to achieve the wisdom and love of God. I see now that in our own way, Magda and I have always felt the dance to be a link to a spiritual harmony, which I do not see as connected to any one religion.

This link, forged through the dance, connects us to a greater cosmic force, a cosmic force which may have many names. I reflect on the Hindu belief that there is but one true god, the supreme spirit, called Brahman. But that there are multiple paths to reaching this god. I had an epiphany that worship is also deeply personal and may be enacted through many forms. The dance is our way of honouring and venerating this life we have been given. I am at peace with everyone believing what they may. We must all celebrate our lives in any way we can.

I have heard it said that the true dancer of Manipuri has reached a stage where the earthly audience has ceased to matter and the dancer is only conscious of the deity of the temple. As a European dancer, I have also gone beyond the applause and audience appreciation to experience this knowing, this inner hallowed feeling while dancing. But I must admit that to evoke a response from my audience, to move them in some way will always retain some importance for me. Perhaps I hope to transfer this glorious feeling achieved through the dance to the onlooker.

Programme for a Recital of Classical Dances and Rhythmical Movements March 13, 1941. The photograph is from the Hanova sisters dance 'Idyll'.

This dance tells a story of two Slovak farm girls. It shows the girls working in the field, chatting and dancing. Tired after the day's work, they prepare to go home when they see their admirers coming. They forget their fatigue and run to join them.

The Protective Shield of Terpsichore, Wherein Terpsichore Meets Siva

The pantomime shows the characteristics of Bohemian Country Life. (Programme notes describing Idyll, March 13, 1941)

I note that the term 'dance idyll' was a concept originating with Magda's former dance teacher, Ellen Tels. According to Toepfer (1997), "Tels "dance idylls" attracted audiences in Germany, Austria, and even England between 1911 and 1914, partly because she aligned pantomimic movement with literary scenarios" (p. 179).

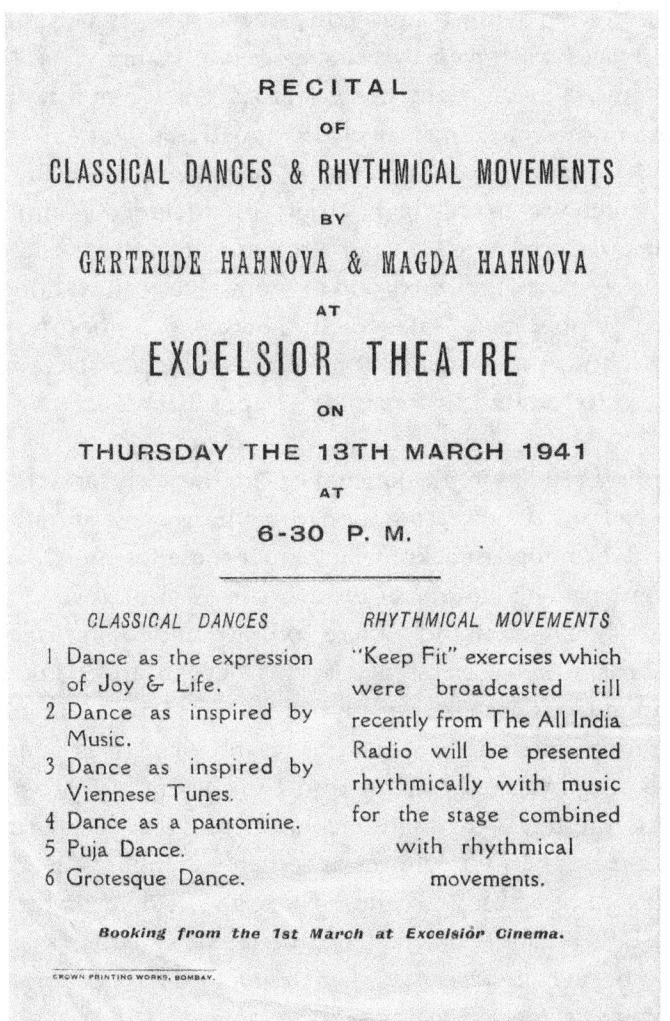

The bill listing the dances for a Hahnova Recital of Classical Dances and Rhythmical Movements, March 13th, 1941.

Magda and Gertrud's dance programmes in India invariably consisted of first showing exercises of what they called the Central European style, then rhythmical movements which were based on Dalcroze Eurhythmics, and then Classical Dances. In this program they danced Slavonic Dances with music by Dvorak, the Viennese Waltz with music by Strauss, two Classical Indian Dances, and A Dance of Fun with their students.

A review in the Bombay Sentinel, dated Friday, March 14, 1941, states:

> An interesting demonstration of "Keep Fit" exercises and classical dances was given by Miss Gertrude Hahnova and Magda Hahnova at the Excelsior yesterday. Exercises for all parts of the body were impressively demonstrated by the sisters to the accompaniment of music. A large section of the audience which was mainly high society and included a number of young girls, applauded the performance. It must be stated that these exercises which are good in themselves can be done only by the "Upper class" of society. There was a good response to the show and it was announced that the profits would be donated to the Red Cross and the Leper Home.

Magda: I reflect on the concept of 'high society' and the term 'upper class', which is mentioned in the review of our latest presentation. I must acknowledge that these terms are a reality in Bombay. The European residents live within a strict structure of behaviours and adhere to quite unbending rules and standards, which are assigned by their level in this community. Indian citizens are also severely divided, maybe more so than the Europeans, into a system of castes or classes which are solidly immovable. Coming from Europe and the artist's life, part of me tends to stand back and view this compartmentalization by the two cultures and their inhabitants, as equally unfair and disturbing. By these rules, an accident of birth has one's fate firmly decided. I don't believe in either system. I feel, especially as a woman, that we need to have the power to define ourselves and make our own destiny.

Part of our calling as dancers and dance teachers is to educate everyone, not just a select few who claim superiority through wealth or class. Perhaps people who consider themselves 'high society' do have more knowledge concerning the arts, but anyone can develop an appreciation. And anyone may become enlightened to the merits of attending performances. Here I must not leave out that additionally anyone may enjoy dance classes to attain good physical and mental health. A fully functioning body and mind are only achieved through activity, movement, and exercise.

In another positive review of the March 13th performance, The Bombay Chronicle, from March 15, 1941 reported, "A lively programme of physical exercises, rhythmical movements, and dances. The Hanova sisters executed the various items with facile movement and remarkable ease."

And the Sunday Standard, March 16, 1941 stated:

> The programme for the evening was judiciously divided into three groups consisting of bodily exercises, rhythmical movements, and classical dances—European as well as Indian. The exercises were broadcast until recently from the All-India Radio in their "Keep Fit" series. The exercises, though based on such famous schools as Dalcroze, Wigman, Duncan, Ellen Tels, etc., are essentially their own. That the Hahnova sisters' possess a rare combination of technique and art was evidenced by their presentation of classical stage dances. These dances comprised the Dance as the Expression of Joy and Life, Dance inspired by Viennese tunes, Dance as a Pantomime, and an Indian Manipuri number entitled Pujarin which was especially composed by Thakur Navkumar Singh and Narendra Kumar Singh.

Gertrud: Reviews! What is the public to think of what the reviewer has printed, really? Unless one was in attendance, the terms 'facile' or 'remarkable ease' cannot adequately describe what was experienced by the audience in the theatre. It is my opinion that the audience or reviewer using words, cannot completely or accurately tell of their experience because witnessing an artistic work is first visceral and not immediately deliberated or thought about. What I mean is that a dance is experienced in the moment. Moments which hopefully uplift or move an audience and then this audience leaves the theatre with memories and emotions of their experience, which are impossible to completely share with others who were not in attendance. A reviewer is required to use language to interpret and share their experience. Saying a dance performance was 'lovely', 'graceful', or 'interesting' does not really tell the reader anything concrete. I hunger for someone of education in the dance to really explain to the public what they saw, experienced, or found to have merit, or on the other hand, was unworthy of viewing. We read only platitudes and vague descriptions which only give an unclear thumbs up or down.

I must remember not to share these thoughts with anyone except Magda, as the papers are actually all sympathetic to our cause and highly positive considering that most don't really seem to understand what we are doing or why. I have asked Magda if she thinks we are making a difference. Of course she says, "Yes". And then she reminds me of our Mutti, who was so cheerful and encouraging. Our dear mother, who always told us to follow our hearts and to fulfill our destiny. Magda seems so accepting of our life here in India. I do try to be at peace with our place in this world despite the war, hatred of our kind, and men who want to rule unmercifully over others.

I feel the choreography we are creating now is actually quite marvellous and perhaps because of the war our new pieces have been inspired by our homeland, European composers, and all that we learned dancing in Europe. We will never forget our beginnings. But the extra ordinary thing about our life in India is that we have been exposed to so many wonderful new ideas concerning the dance that we might never have heard of in Europe. Here, we have been able to expand, stretch, and heighten our abilities to achieve something I feel quite surpasses the remarkable. Reviews do not seem that important when I think on these things.

The Protective Shield of Terpsichore, Wherein Terpsichore Meets Siva

Gertrud and Magda in a pose from Viennese Waltz, 1941.

Gertrud and Magda in a pose from Viennese Waltz, 1941.

**Dancing on the balcony of the Mitha house.
From the Viennese Waltz, 1941.**

Magda: We are so fortunate to continue our work here in India, which is a celebration of all that is the dance. I try not to think about Europe. After all, we have been in India almost seven years now. But thoughts of all we knew, who we knew, what was, and what has become of it all, cannot be helped. I have to believe that the war will be over soon and we will be able to travel again and enjoy freedom in the world.

It is in the waltz that freedom can be achieved in movement. The flow of the turns and rotations, reminding one of the Sufi, bring on a languorous meditation. The one, two, three of the change steps, beat time with their concentration on the rhythms inherent in the music to create a liberation of the limbs. Our Viennese Waltz has a plastic choreography and is a true tribute to Terpsichore as one gets swept up in the music's surge, swirl, and swell. And each time we perform this dance, the performance is slightly different. Not different in time, rhythm, or essence but a subtlety of interpretation. How can this be? The Muse is alive and channels her response and inspiration. Gerti and I are so aware of each other while dancing this piece that we could have our eyes closed and still intuit

The Protective Shield of Terpsichore, Wherein Terpsichore Meets Siva

exactly when we will meet and part, join and separate, or dance side by side. I read in a magazine that in Europe they say the ballroom version of the Viennese Waltz is outdated, but I saw a return of the waltz's popularity before we left. However, the Hanova style of dance welcomes all beauty of movement and so the waltz and Herr Strauss will never seem old but be enfolded in our arms with love, forever.

Magda and Gertrud pose for The Illustrated Weekly of India, August 1941.

The caption reads: "This striking dance pose photograph is by Mr. Habib Ibrihim Rahimtoola, F.R.P.S, of Bombay, a very successful exhibitor in photographic exhibitions overseas."

Gertrud: We were so pleased to have our photograph published in The Illustrated Weekly of India. The publicity has been excellent for our school and reputation. But what I really enjoyed the most was seeing the dance portrayed so prominently and joyously, so people will say, "Dancing appears to be something marvellous!" "Perhaps we should try it."

Magda at a Bombay Society Tea, October 28, 1941.

Magda: I am still actively soliciting funds for the war effort. Going to teas and benefits are all part of being seen and recognized and then being able to issue invitations to our performances. We also try to support other worthy causes which fund those impoverished and made homeless by the war. Bombay has now become the residence of many Europeans driven to escape the unwarranted hate and unworthy persecution by men with insane political ambitions. Gerti and I try not to dwell too much on our homeland and what has become of our friends and fellow artists. But word filters in and what we have heard sinks my heart. So much of beauty, free thinking, and noble art has been lost. The people of our land have been turned away from truth and decency by lies and false promises, which profess that their lives will be better without certain so called 'tainted' peoples living amongst them. We are Jews by heritage, never denying this or ashamed of our forefathers and mothers. Choosing to follow the Muse as our spiritual inspiration is not a conflict. As modern women we have this choice. Targeting any people is scapegoating for purely political aims. I reflect on my identity. I am with no apology a Jew by heritage, but above all I am a dance artist. No one should have to hide or deny who they are in this life.

UNITED NATIONS FETE IN BOMBAY December 5, 1942.

Pictures from The Evening News of India. The caption states: Lady Lumley opened the United Nations Fete organized by the Ladies Committee of the Bombay War Gifts Fund at the P.V. M. Gymkhana and the Cooperage yesterday. The picture on the left shows His Excellency the Governor with Lady Lumley and Lady Blackwell at the march past of representatives of the United Nations at which His Excellency took the salute. Centre: A dance by the Czechs. (Featuring Franz Weisskopf, Magda and Gertrude Hahnova). Right: Sir Homi Mehta trying his luck at the Hoop-la stall.

Czech dancers, Franz Weisskopf, Magda, and Gertrud, center right with unknown fellow Czech participants, December 5, 1942.

From the Czechoslovakian Information Service Paper (Bombay, January 1, 1943. Vol. 5):

We the children of Czechoslovakia confidently awaiting our liberation send greetings to all friends of our country with trustingly expectant wishes from afar for a bright and victorious New Year.

Nazi Vandalism in Prague. All memorial medals and tablets of historical significance in Prague have been confiscated by the Nazis and smelted. Bilck's monument of Moses, Dvorak's Semik, and Maratka's monument of Legionnaires met with the same fate.

United Nations Fete in Bombay. The pre-Christmas activities in Bombay reached their climax in the United Nations Fete which took place in the Princess Victoria Mary Gymkhana from 4th to 6th December. It was a veritable world's fair on a small scale, attractive, ingenious, imbued with the spirit of co-operation. The fete was sponsored by the Ladies' Committee of the War Gifts Fund under the chairmanship of Lady Blackwell, and consisted of stalls with a decorative scheme, each stall representing one of the Allied Nations. Czechoslovakia was represented by a typical village market place, surrounded by country buildings with gables and arcades giving ideal shelter and picturesque frame to various stalls and shops. In the centre of the market there was a dance floor on which, several times each day, the popular Czech folk dance called "Beseda" was performed by the ladies of the Czechoslovakian Society of Bombay, dressed in gorgeous national costumes. This was a particularly attractive number on the programme and always had a big crowd come to the Czechoslovak section when the "Beseda" was danced. The music was furnished by a village band from Batanagar.

Magda, Franz Weisskopf, an unknown Czech dancer, and Gertrud perform at the United Nations Fete, Bombay, December 5, 1942.

Amongst the other attractions in the Czechoslovak section were the shooting gallery with Hitler, Goering, and Goebbels as targets, a stall serving tasty sausages made according to well-known Czech recipes, a beer house, a shop selling most delicious pastry, cakes, and a stall with embroideries, toys, ornaments, and fineries. From the Czechoslovakian Information Service Paper, (January 1, 1943. Vol. 5).

Gertrud: I feel guilt but also relief because we are so far away from all the horror of the war. What we have heard has happened in Bohemia seems impossible. So many have died or disappeared. And the community of believers, those who held art to be the highest source of humanities worthwhile presence, seem to have passed into oblivion. I am receiving no letters back from so many friends. The dancers, musicians, artists, composers, and writers we remember and always will remember, what has happened to them? How can all of their precious work be wiped away so quickly? I lament as I look back and realize the golden age of my youth has passed with all else in Europe. I have just had my fortieth birthday. But I don't feel old yet! For there is still so much to create, to dance, and explore. I yearn for and remember those days in which I was so young and naive, not fully appreciating the beauty of peace and the freedom to pursue artistic goals. I could not have ever foreseen or conceived of what has happened in the world today. But as we put our energies into holding the torch of artistic accomplishment aloft, the torch of creativity and virtuosity, and the torch of freedom to be ourselves with no shame, I thank our Muse that we are here in India and not being ground into dust as others we have known.

Magda: Of late, Gerti and I are frequently asked to organize and perform at events in support of the war effort. We often present our favourites, which are dance works that have been in our repertoire for many years. You would think we might grow tired of performing these pieces? Or the public would grow tired of seeing them? But to the contrary, we are told the public loves to see Idyll or the Viennese Waltz again and again. Perhaps because these two dances, in particular, represent happier times and echo a Europe that might be gone forever.

The Protective Shield of Terpsichore, Wherein Terpsichore Meets Siva

**Gertrud (standing far left) with the staff of
the Cathedral and John Connon Girls' High School, 1943.**

In a programme for the Cathedral and John Connon Girls' High School Concert, on the 25th and 26th of March 1943, I note on the bill, Miss Gertrude and Miss Magda Hahnova in their Dance 'Idyll'. Gertrud was employed at this school for many years while in India.

> **Gertrud:** Here I am with the rest of the staff. This photograph was for the yearbook. I enjoy teaching the older girls. We are creating much of substance together. This job is keeping me busy and focused on something other than myself. The war drags on…
>
> And though I may get down hearted, in the midst of it all, I do truly appreciate the brilliance of youth in the girls I am teaching. They are still sweet and untouched by the ugliness of the world. They revel in the music, exercises, and dancing, enjoying all I have to show them, begging for just one more

minute or hour of creating together. Was I like this? Yes, although it seems I only see those days 'through a glass darkly.' Ha, I must be feeling really low to be quoting the Bible. So, I remind myself that we had such a happy home, happy parents, and so much pleasure in our youthful dancing. This war must end eventually...

THE VICTORIA MEMORIAL
SCHOOL FOR THE BLIND

AN
ENTERTAINMENT
WILL BE HELD AT
THE ST. XAVIER'S HALL
ON
MONDAY 6th MARCH 1944 AT 6-30 P. M.

The Programme will consist of
PART I.

1 (a) "Coppelia"
   (b) "Sylphides"   .... Ballet Dances
   IRIS WINDHAM
   (English Ballet Dancer and holder of the Advanced Certificate of the Royal Academy of Dancing.)

2 Songs - Selected
   HENRY BARNES

3 (a) Viennese Valse
   (b) Czechoslovakian Dance
   MAGDA & GERTRUDE HANOVA
   (Well-known for their modern classical style of dancing.)

4 (a) Sinfonia .... Bach
   (b) Gavotte .... Rameau   .... Oboe
   HENRY POWIS

PART II.

TABLEAUX of OMAR KHYYAM
(Repeated by special request)

Admission : **Rs. 10, 7, 5, 3** (Reserved)
           Rs. 2 (Unreserved)
PLAN AT MESSRS. S. ROSE & CO. LTD., RAMPART ROW—TEL. 20395.

This bill from the Hanova memorabilia is evidence of the sisters continued and busy performing life. This was an Entertainment held at The St. Xavier's Hall, March 6th, 1944 in aid of a School for the Blind. On the bill No. 3. (a) Viennese Valse (b) Czechoslovakian Dance Magda & Gertrude Hanova.

Gertrud: I feel I have embraced much that is India, but I often still feel that I am looking on from the outside. The Indian person has such a stoic quality. They seem to accept life as it comes. I cannot, although I try. On our recent, very long rail journey to Allahabad to perform with Menaka, I learned so much from her of tolerance. She focused solely on the positive, as did Magda. I long to share in their attitude of acceptance. Unfortunately, I found faced with the crushing heat and the soot and dirt flying into my face and hair on the train, I could not help but wish for cool and rainy climes. A bright outlook was definitely out of my reach.

But it was an honour to perform with Menaka and see more of the country. We danced at a music festival to raise monies for the Red Cross. My personal reason for going was to get away from everything for a brief respite. I find waiting for the war to end to be nerve-racking. I so much want everyone's life to return to normal. Although our 'normal' may never arrive. I fear that the homeland we knew is lost forever.

Magda: It was an lengthy journey travelling by train, first north and then to the west, before we finally arrived in Allahabad to perform for a Red Cross charity event. Menaka and Ram Narayan shared their exceptional talent and stood out above the other performers. They garnered much admiration and applause. I continue to deeply respect Menaka for her strength and determination in all that she undertakes. It is to her credit that Gerti and I have come so far in our abilities to dance in the Indian styles. We have come to love the mysticism, the stories, and intricacies of the Indian dance and enjoy the renewed appreciation and deserved reverence by the public in which Indian dance is now being held. Menaka has promoted Indian dance to the exclusion of her health and wealth. Other dancers are now arising on the scene to claim credit for this revival, but we know Menaka deserves the most praise as she has been a tireless and long term advocate for the Indian dance arts, travelling the whole world to proclaim its merits.

Menaka, in a promotional photograph, for the Allahabad Benefit, April 1944.

The Protective Shield of Terpsichore, Wherein Terpsichore Meets Siva

"In a promotional photograph for the Allahabad Red Cross Benefit, Gertrud Hahnova and Magda Hahnova pose in their Viennese Valse costumes. On the programme for the Allahabad Benefit, The Nrityalayam Menaka Indian Dance Center will present Menaka and Ram Narayan, first prize winners of International Dance Olympiad, 1936, and Shervanti, accompanied by Kamal, Gangull and Vishnu Shiroka. And danced by the Hanova sisters, the Viennese Waltz."
The Leader Newspaper, April 1944.

GALA WEEK

IN AID OF

RED CROSS FUND AND POLICE CHARITIES
MUSICAL DANCE FESTIVAL

ON

April 6th, 7th & 8th at 9 p.m.

UNDER THE PRESIDENTSHIP OF

D. R. BHATTACHARYA, PH.D., D.Sc., F.N.A., F.Z., S.F.N.I., F.I.A.,
PROFESSOR OF ZOOLOGY, ALLAHABAD UNIVERSITY

Programme for April 6th, 1944—

1. SHAHNAI—Professor NAND LAL and Party of Benares—30 minutes
2. NRITYALAYAM MENAKA DANCE CENTRE, BOMBAY, will present—
   (a) Jhaptal—Miss Shevanti
   (b) Parbat Vdharan—Ram Narain
   (c) Virah Milap—Miss Shevanti, Menaka and Ram Narain
3. VIENNESE WALTZ & CZECHOSLOVAKIAN DANCE—Hanova Sisters
4. DANCE—Miss Jayakar of Lahore
5. VOCAL SONG—Kumar Gandharva of Bombay
6. LIGHT POPULAR MUSIC—Kumar Sachin Dev Burman of Calcutta
7. MUSIC—Umar Khan of Lucknow
8. DANCE—S. R Mawalankar Sisters of Allahabad

ORGANIZERS—

S. K. ANAND, Esq.,
M.Sc., LL.B.,
Dy. Supdt. of Police, C. I. D.,
U. P., Allahabad.

K. S. ABDUL RASHID KHAN,
City Dy. Supdt. of Police, Allahabad.

The programme for a Musical Dance Festival in which Menaka and the Hanova sisters performed in Allahabad, April 6, 1944.

The Protective Shield of Terpsichore, Wherein Terpsichore Meets Siva

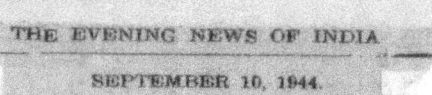

Good press from The Evening News of India advertising the Hanova sisters next upcoming show on September 10, 1944.

"Festival Dance"—a modern plastic ballet—one of the many colourful items in the recital of modern gymnastics, rhythmical movements, and classical dance to take place at 10:15 this morning at the Excelsior Theatre. Gertrud Hanova and Magda Hanova will have a leading part, and the show is in aid of the Czechoslovakian Relief Fund and the Bhumijan Seva Mandal.

The Sunday Standard, September 10, 1944, in support of the upcoming show also reported, "Both the gymnastics and rhythmical movements are designed to develop "the body beautiful", and a supple lissome grace."

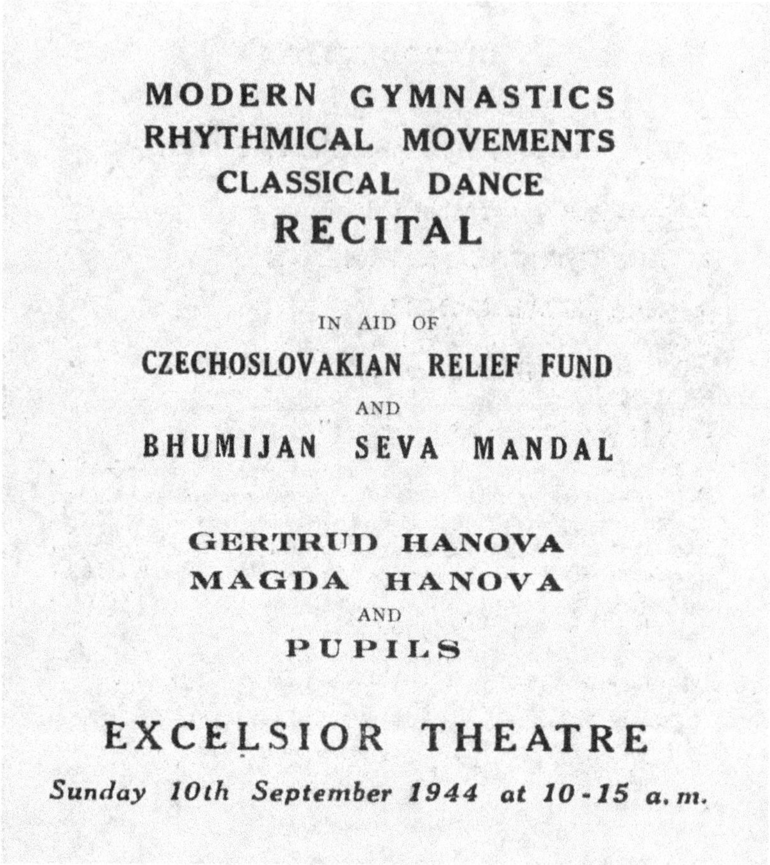

> **MODERN GYMNASTICS**
> **RHYTHMICAL MOVEMENTS**
> **CLASSICAL DANCE**
> # RECITAL
>
> IN AID OF
> **CZECHOSLOVAKIAN RELIEF FUND**
> AND
> **BHUMIJAN SEVA MANDAL**
>
> GERTRUD HANOVA
> MAGDA HANOVA
> AND
> PUPILS
>
> **EXCELSIOR THEATRE**
> *Sunday 10th September 1944 at 10-15 a.m.*

Programme cover for a Recital in aid of Czechoslovakian Relief Fund and Bhumijan Seva Mandal, featuring Gertrud and Magda Hanova and pupils demonstrating Modern Gymnastics, Rhythmical Movements, and Classical Dance, Bombay, September 10th, 1944.

On the bill, Part I Modern Gymnastics, Part II Rhythmical Movements, which had three presentations: Arm Movements, Three Groups in Triple Time, and Studie. Part III Classical Dance, which consisted of five dances: Viennese Waltz, Idyll, Festival in modern plastic ballet, Akayli muth yaio Radha Yamuna Ki Tir in Kathak North Indian Classical Technique, and Dance of Fun.

An excerpt from the programme notes reads: "Modern Gymnastics". "Exercises for everyone—they are essential for building up the body and for health, beauty and happiness. Many different systems of Physical Culture exist. We have formed our own system, which has been built up by us through intensive studies in various schools in Europe. Physical Exercises give the body poise, charm, grace, and personality. They are also used for sports, art, education, and medical purposes. Physical Exercises carried out in the correct way will bring all the muscles, tendons, ligaments, and the components of the body into work and will therefore automatically reduce fat as well as develop neglected parts. They help to assume control over the entire body."

Gertrude Hahnova

Magda Hahnova

A publicity photo for the Hanova sisters' Recital on September 10, 1944. This pose is from Dance of Fun, one of the Classical Dances on the programme.

Our Love Affair with Dance

Photographs from Studie, Music by Handel's Largo.
"Simple, graceful, harmonic movements inspired through music, laid out in a choreographical way." (Programme notes describing Studie.)

Gertrud and Magda in a pose from Studie, September 1944.

Gertrud in a pose from Studie, September 1944.

Magda in a pose from Studie, September 1944.

Magda: As Studie begins, I listen to the slow, steady tempo of Handel's Largo and hear the words 'Ombra mai fu'. This aria is from Handel's opera Xerxes and the main character is admiring the shade of a plane tree. Gerti and I joke that the word Ombra is so slowly drawn out that it reminds us of Om which is the holy or sacred mantra of Hindu meditation. This is ironically beautiful because Handel's Largo does feel sacred. Indeed, this music leads the dancer on a pilgrimage of faith. A contemplation of all that is solemn and heartfelt.

As this dance unfolds, Gerti and I retain an invisible connection as we traverse the stage together. Our movements complement each other and we have an acute awareness of time, which is sustained and measured, as our graceful movements gradually extend and unfold on the stage. In the dance space, we use all levels, creating momentary tableaux of harmony and opposition. Our dynamics are deliberately soft and then strong, which unites the piece to a crescendo that is not sweet but blessed. Dare I say, the mysticism of our Hebrew ancestors flows through us in this dance and we unite with the audience as the choreography spills slowly forth with ceremony, creating a venerated, raised consciousness. We are symbolically back in the garden.

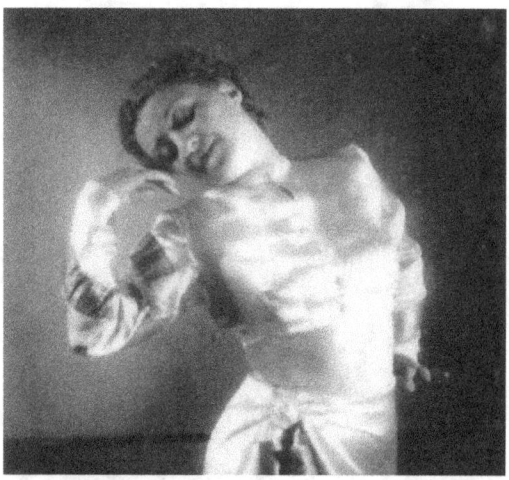

Gertrud posing from Studie, 1944.

The Protective Shield of Terpsichore, Wherein Terpsichore Meets Siva

Magda posing from Studie, September 1944.

Gertrud and Magda in a photograph from a performance of Studie, 1944.

Gertrud: We continue to create and perform new choreography and I marvel at how one of our latest works, Studie, has come about. Magda and I, of course, have been shaken in these perilous times by the news in the papers, letters from abroad, and stories we hear of a crumbling Europe, flattened by the Nazi war machine. This is all very frightening. It is in my nature to succumb to despair and worry. Magda, to the contrary, while affected and saddened to hear of the many countries fallen to Hitler's evil, has rallied her spirit. She has emphatically said she is determined to control and shape our future by creating dances that are inspirational and that promote a peaceful existence for all humanity. In Magda's reading about the Indian people's desire to free themselves of British rule she came across this striking quote by the leader of the Indian Independence Movement, Mohandas Gandhi.

"We but mirror the world. All the tendencies present in the outer world are to be found in the world of our body. If we could change ourselves, the tendencies in the world would also change. As a man changes his nature, so does the attitude of the world change towards him. This is the divine mystery supreme. A wonderful thing it is and the source of our happiness. We need not wait to see what others do." (Gandhi, 1913, 1964, p.158)

Consequently, my sister has convinced me, we must reflect tranquillity, not fear from the world. Our new work is therefore a dance that represents a metaphorical, spiritual path of unity which for us is not based on any formal religious teaching. The dance composition, Studie, is indeed a study and a holy expedition in contemplation, harmony, and balance.

We are often asked about our religious beliefs in India, where everyone is something, and I must say that people are thus pigeonholed by others when they reveal their creed. Magda and I staunchly refuse to profess faith in anything but our Muse. As Gandhi, with the world of our bodies, we strive to change the world through reflecting beauty and peace with dance.

Dance And Gymnastics

Reprinted from the Kaiser-I-Hind of 17th September 1944.

The dance recital of the sisters, Gertrude and Magda Hanova and their pupils on Sunday last at the Excelsior theatre was quite a remarkable performance very much appreciated by the public of Bombay. It was a beautiful demonstration of modern gymnastics and rhythmic movement for the building up of a healthy and harmonious body, which is important not only to the future dancer but to everyone who wants to develop an all-round personality.

A development of the sense of rhythm and of an understanding of the beauty of movement is important to everyone who wants to enjoy art which in all its variety of aspects is essentially built upon rhythm and beauty of movement in time and space.

The youthful pupils of the Dance Academy of G. and M. Hanova, showed a very high standard of achievement. Everything was good but the most impressive items of the programme were the "Three groups in triple time" and the amusing "Dance of fun."

The sisters are not only first class teachers but also charming and graceful dancers, as they demonstrated in their lovely and ethereal "Viennese Waltz" and the lively little pantomime to Dvorak's music.

A rare achievement for European dancers and a graceful tribute to their country of adoption, India, was the Indian dance in Kathak technique performed by the Hanova Sisters with skill and understanding. The costumes designed by the sisters were beautiful.

A review of the September 10, 1944 Hanova performance at the Excelsior Theater in the Kaiser-I-Hind, September 1944.

Our Love Affair with Dance

A review in The Evening News of India, September 11, 1944 of the Hanova Dance School Recital on September 10, 1944.

For sheer beauty of rhythm, music, and colour, the recital by the Hanova Sisters and their pupils at the Excelsior yesterday morning was one of the finest shows Bombay has seen in quite a long time. The Slavonic dance, Viennese Waltz, the Festival Dance, a combination dance by three groups of pupils, and the Indian dance by the Hanova Sisters were some of the highlights of an exceedingly entertaining programme.

In an additional review by The Bombay Man's Diary, in The Evening News Of India, Saturday, September 16, 1944 it was reported:

> Undoubtedly the Hanova Sisters have the art and a real flair for presenting it with the zest and grace and je ne sais quoi, which dancing demands but seldom receives from so many of its votaries one sees hereabouts... It was clear at first sight that their's is no display of unbridled exuberance but an art developed with years of disciplined training of body, limb, and muscle inspired by minds filled with need for artistic expression.
>
> Their pupils showed ample evidence of the right method—and the result was a display of dancing that was really exhilarating. I was glad to learn this morning from Dr. Urban, Consul for Czechoslovakia, that the recital was as successful financially as it was artistically.

The Sunday Standard, September 10, 1944, stated in their review:

> A most pleasing feature of the programme is the elimination of monotony from routine exercises by doing them all to gay, jazzy tunes-mostly modern song hits. Exercises and dance technique was striking ... for the spirit of "joie de vivre" about them... The classical dances are mainly Slavonic, interspersed with a beautiful Indian number, and a delightfully grotesque Dance of Fun. The Slavonic dances, with their characteristic Czech musical idioms, are interpreted with fire and abandon, and joyous verve.
>
> Ramnarayan of Menaka's Troupe is responsible for the arrangement and choreography of the Indian dance: The Hanova sisters excel themselves in this, catching the difficult Ajantaesque poses with polished and practised ease.

Our Love Affair with Dance

A press clipping in the Blitz newspaper, Bombay, January 20, 1945, to advertise an upcoming Cultural Exhibition. "The Hanova Sisters will take a major part on the European Dance side of the Exhibition."

The Hanova sisters participated in an International Cultural Exhibition from January 19th through to February 2, 1945. The Illustrated Weekly of India, January 14, 1945, reported: "A unique exhibition portraying the cultural progress and heritage of no fewer than 17 countries from the four continents will be held in Bombay organized by the Goodwill Committee of the Rotary Club... The exhibition will display the varied accomplishments of each of the participating nations in the cultural field... and as a final treat at the Excelsior Theatre with the presentation of "The Golden Gate" by Gertrude and Magda Hanova for the European ballet and Menaka and Ramnarayan for Indian dance. This show combines the two classical styles in a single ballet, and will be in the nature of hymn to Art."

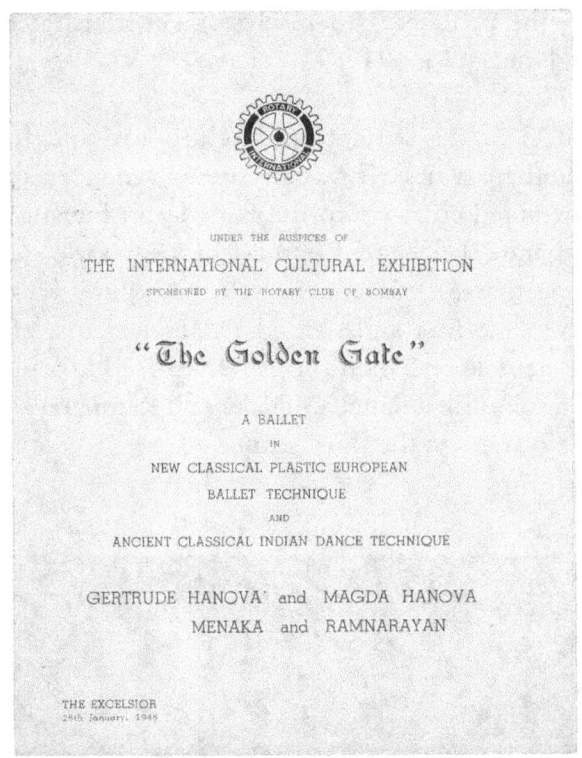

The programme cover for "The Golden Gate" A Ballet in New Classical Plastic European Technique and Ancient Classical Indian Dance Technique. January 25, 1945 at The Excelsior Theatre.

This novel ballet called "The Golden Gate", will feature both European and Indian classical techniques, an experiment which should be of great interest and which should prove that the arts of even such distinct civilizations, may be successfully combined.

Menaka and Ramnarayan, the well-known dancers, will take part in the Indian section of the ballet and the European section will be taken care of by those talented dancers, Gertrude and Magda Hanova. The whole show is planned on a fantasy depicting the importance of the art of the dance as the basis of human culture. The four principals between them were responsible for the choreography, music, and decor, all of which is original. The cast consists of no fewer than 70 performers, including the producers themselves. (The Illustrated Weekly of India, January 14, 1945)

The Golden Gate was a mixture of European and Indian dance on one program, perhaps a first. It was an interwoven story about The Golden Gate, the imagined entrance to the Kingdom of Dance. The program consisted of separate dances of Central European style and Indian dance. Gertrud told me that Magda and herself, plus pupils from the Hanova School, danced in the first and second scenes which were danced in the Central European style and then the sisters danced in a piece in the third scene, which was all Indian dance. Menaka and Ramnarayan were the Indian principal performers in the third scene.

Gertrud and Magda in The Golden Gate Ballet, January 25th, 1945.

Gertrud: Our dream of uniting Indian Classical Dance and European Dance on one stage has finally manifested. Without Menaka this would not have been possible. She was our catalyst. Our shared vision in this experiment has been successful. Our hope, to show the harmony and accord between eastern and western dance has been realized. For Magda and I, this performance has been particularly meaningful because it ascertains our conviction in the universality of the dance, as dance is present in every human culture. This deeper and underlying message will perhaps go over the heads of some of the audience, but for many they will gain a confirmation of the place the dance arts should hold for all people in life. There is a great necessity for us to continue to share these ideals in education and for society in general.

A review of The Golden Gate Ballet Experiment in Companionate Dance Technique:

> "The Golden Gate" which was presented at the Excelsior Theatre on Thursday, under the auspices of the International Cultural Exhibition sponsored by the Rotary Club of Bombay was the first attempt of its kind to produce a ballet in the European and Indian classical dance technique. It placed the dance technique of Europe and India in proper perspective, and provided a fine opportunity to the audience to appreciate the merits of both. (The Bombay Chronicle. January 31, 1945)

Ramnarayan and Menaka in promotional photos for The Golden Gate Ballet.

Inside the programme for The Bombay Homoeopathic Association Silver Jubilee Celebrations Variety Entertainment, which featured the Hanova Dance School, March 17, 1945.

The Hanova Dance School performed twice in March of 1945. First, at the Excelsior Theater on March 9th and then on March 17th for the Bombay Homoeopathic Association Silver Jubilee which featured the Hanova sisters' pupils as well as other dance academies. A review of the March 9th performance from The Bombay Man's Diary reported:

> **Eurhythmics** There was a highly appreciative attendance at the Excelsior Theatre yesterday morning for the display of gymnastics, eurhythmics, and dancing by the well-known Hanova Sisters and their pupils who ranged from tiny tots to teen-agers. For grown-ups obsessed by that middle-aged dread (and spread!) the Hanova Sisters and the older pupils showed, with plastic grace, how both can be tackled without tiring or tedious effort, and with much delight. The cool unhurried ease of the performers, who went through a varied assortment of evolutions which it would be a libel to label "jerks", to music chosen

from the Great Masters, was a feast for eye, ear, and soul.

The programme was planned to display the educational effect of this kind of training upon young persons, caught really tender—from the first "exercises", and essays in expression and group dancing, to the final finished ballet—all excellent and well polished in a degree that invited comparison with some of the heavy-footed gambolling to which we are treated, not infrequently, under the guise of ballet and classical dancing. Outstanding was an Indian dance by the Sisters, who went through its intricate patterns with creditable grace and kinetic fidelity. (The Times of India, March 10, 1945)

Gertrud and Magda: Finally the war has ended!!! September 2, 1945 will be remembered by all here in exile with relief and hope as we pray that the world will return to some semblance of what it was before the horrors, terrible persecutions, and tyranny began. War has brought many changes for everyone. There was a life before the war, a life during the war, and now we speculate as to what life will be like for us after the war?

Gertrud and Magda (center) with two unknown dance students from the Hanova Dance School, Bombay 1945.

Gertrud: In India, as all over the world, changes have occurred because of the war, but it seems that here in India, there are now many more changes to come. The call for the withdrawal of colonial rule is being loudly demanded by the Indian people of all castes and stations in life, fuelled by the demands of politicians and bolstered by charismatic leaders of all religions. Voices are raised, the papers are full of protests and demands, and the people are extremely agitated. The Indian citizen clearly wants the end of British rule and to regain control over their own country and destiny. "The Raj is to leave!", they shout. It seems that we escaped the direct impact of the war in Europe, but now we must face another kind of war, an internal war. The Indian National Congress was crushed by the government in 1942, but now it is regaining its voice as Gandhi is out of prison and very active once again. The 'quit' India campaign is renewing its strength. Our position here suddenly does not seem so solid. Yusuf says, "Inshallah, if God wills. Do not worry, everything in life has uncertainty…" I wait pessimistically as is my nature, to see what will happen next.

A portrait of Magda, Bombay 1945.

Magda: I of course rejoice with everyone that the war has ended, but I cannot keep from wondering how all the damage and loss will be restored. While we continue to dance the waltz and revel in the beauty of movement, I think of those who will never waltz again. It seems it was our fate to escape Europe and come to India. We barely eluded the terror and violence. We have been privileged to enjoy our freedom in India, while others lost their lives. In truth, it is a miracle that Franz and I left Teplitz when we did. I pause to wonder at the ways of fate. Ah so, enough of doom and gloom, I look to the future and not the past. We have several performances coming up to round out the year. We are on the programme for the Bombay YWCA for their Garden Fete Entertainment on November 3rd, to dance our 'Idyll', and at the Taj Mahal Hotel on December 3rd to perform our 'Waltzes' for the International Social Club.

After the war ended, the Hanova sisters continued to teach dance and perform with their pupils in Bombay and enjoyed many social engagements. Gertrud said she was honoured to meet Her Highness The Begum Aga Khan at a garden party on December 5th, 1945.

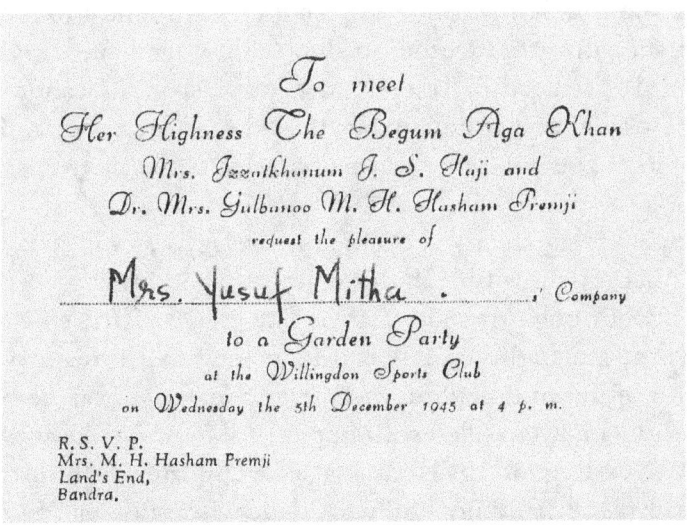

Invitation to meet Her Highness The Begum Aga Khan for Mrs. Yusuf Mitha to a Garden Party on December 5th, 1945 at 4 p.m.

Gertrud: I have been invited to meet Her Highness The Begum Aga Khan (the wife of the Aga Khan) at a garden party. This is a great honour for me. The Aga Khan is the royal title of the spiritual leader of the Shia Ismailia, a sect of the Muslim faith, which Yusuf and his family belong to. In addition, the Aga Khan is a very important diplomat and the president of the All-India Muslim League.

The Begum Aga Khan is the fourth wife of the Sultan Muhammad Shah, the Aga Khan. In the Muslim faith, divorce is permitted when both parties agree and the Aga Khan and his third wife were divorced by mutual consent. The Begum Aga Khan and the Sultan have only been married since 1944. She is said to be very tall and beautiful and remarkably is from Sete, France. Her maiden name was Yvette Blanche Labrousse.

Of course, the papers are full of her story. At the age of twenty-four she became Miss Lyon and one year later Miss France. She travelled the world as a beauty queen and loved Egypt the most, where she decided to live in the late 1930s.

The Begum Om Habibeh Aga Khan is very much younger than the Aga Khan. But I believe love has found love. I read that she converted to the Muslim faith while living in Cairo, and this occurred before she met her husband. I cannot imagine doing this, although Yusuf said that since we are both people of the book my conversion was not necessary.

The papers say the royal couple met in Egypt. I will always remember my short time in this country, when I was on my way to India through the Suez Canal. The image of the expansive and beautiful harbour of Port Said will stay in my memory forever. On that momentous voyage, my marriage was new and my thoughts were filled with hope for the future. Ah well... I heard The Begum Aga Khan is also a supporter of the arts, especially music, and hopefully the dance. I cannot wait to meet her. I will have to practice my French with Magda.

The Protective Shield of Terpsichore, Wherein Terpsichore Meets Siva

Two ads announcing upcoming Hanova performances on February 24th and March 3, 1946, in the The Bombay Chronicle, February 23, 1946.

The caption from the photograph states, "One of the items in the Dance Recital of classical dances and rhythmical movements which the Hanova Sisters will give at the Excelsior Theatre on Sunday (Feb. 24) morning in aid of the Dadar School for the Blind and Czechoslovakian Children's Funds".

The newspaper photograph is of a scene from the Dance Pantomime: Once Upon A Time, "Set in a market place, a disguised princess with her maidens enjoys the freedom of being incognito until her father, the Caliph enters and she dances with abandon and is discovered." (From the Hanova dance recital programme notes, March 3, 1946)

Our Love Affair with Dance

Three press clippings about the Hanova recitals in aid of Czechoslovakian Children and the Dadar School for the Blind, February 24th and March 3, 1946.

"The famous Hanova Sisters, Gertrud and Magda, snapped during one of their brilliant acts. They will perform at the Excelsior theatre tomorrow at 10:15 a.m." (March 2, 1946, The Morning Standard)

"The Hanova Sisters in a graceful pose from one of their many items in the programme which they presented with their pupils at the Excelsior Theatre on Sunday morning. The proceeds are devoted to the Czechoslovak Children's fund and the Victoria Memorial School for the Blind." (The Bombay Chronicle, March 2, 1946)

"Magda Hanova, of the famous Hanova sisters, who assisted by their pupils, will give a dance recital to-day at the Excelsior at 10-15 a.m. The proceeds will be divided between the Dadar School of Blind and Czech refugee children." (The Sunday Standard, February 24, 1946)

The Protective Shield of Terpsichore, Wherein Terpsichore Meets Siva

Programme for Modern Gymnastics, Rhythmical Movements, Classical Dances Recital in Aid of Czechoslovakian Children and Dadar School for the Blind, February 24th and March 3, 1946.

Part 1: Modern Gymnastics: 1. March to Health and Beauty 2. Children's Gymnastic 3. Keep Fit Exercises 4. Combined Exercises

Part II: Dance Technique: 1. Basics of the Classical Dance 2. Relationship of Two Classical Styles—The ancient Indian (Manipuri) and the modern European (Gertrud Hanova Magda Hanova)

Part III. 1. Chorus of Movements (accompanied by Percussion Rhythmic) 2. Children's Study with Percussion and Music (Dvorak) 3. Study with Drum, Cymbals, and Gong (Magda and Gertrud Hanova and pupils) 4. Three Sketches (Chopin) 5. Musical Interlude 6. Theme and Variations (Handel arranged by Brahms)

Part IV. Classical Dances: 1. Viennese Waltz (Gertrud and Magda Hanova) 2. Happy Birthday (Gertrud and Magda Hanova)

Our Love Affair with Dance

Part V: Dance Pantomime: Once Upon A Time. Danced by the full cast of pupils with Magda as a gypsy and Gertrud as a dancer. (From this description, it seems the sisters revived their roles from their Karlsbad production in 1925.)

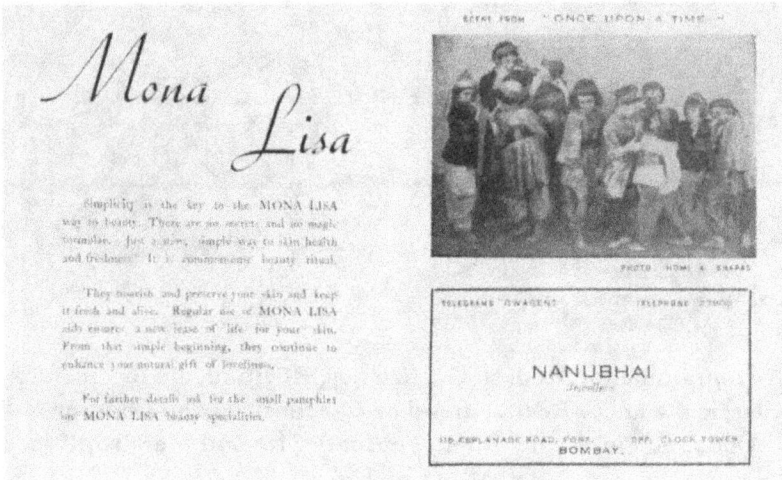

Inside the programme showing a photograph of the Hanova students in Once Upon A Time.

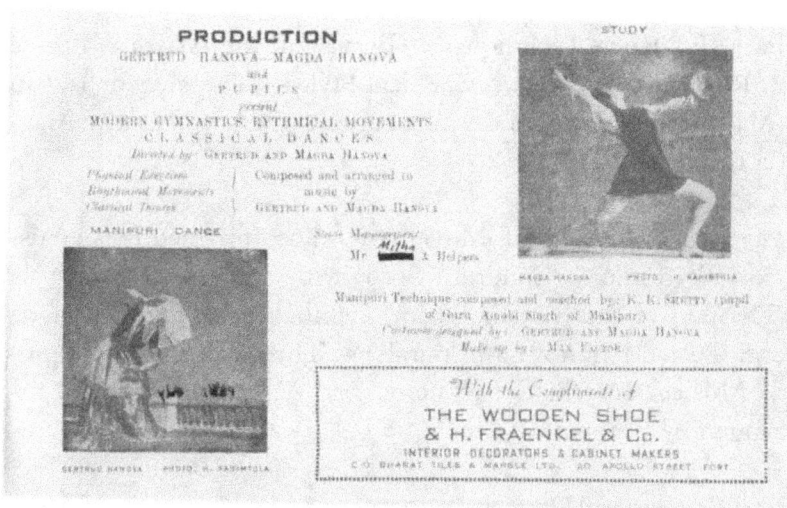

The back page of the programme showing Magda with cymbals and Gertrud in Manipuri costume.

In this extensive Hanova Dance School recital on February 24th and March 3rd, 1946, the Hanova sisters continued with the set programme they had developed over their many years of performing, by first showing examples of modern gymnastics, dance technique, and rhythmical movements. Then the sisters performed dances which had become standards on their programmes, such as the Viennese Waltz, and introduced new works, in this case, Study with Drum, Cymbals, and Gong, Happy Birthday, and the full cast performing a dance drama, Once Upon A Time. The sisters' mandate was always to educate the public about the benefits and methods of movement before showing any set choreography.

Magda and Gertrud, in a pose from Study with Drum, Cymbals, and Gong, March 1946.

Magda: Study with Drum, Cymbals, and Gong has stirred something deep within me. This new choreography again celebrates the reverential qualities of life. Our inclusion of the drum and cymbals in this dance evokes memories of a time long past. However, Gerti and I have co-created something, which has a fresh feeling and spans the old to the new. Our past impressions of life have become rejuvenated expressions of our existence with the dawning of a new world era of peace. We have turned our natural rhythms, our experiences, and the stimulation of all our senses into an aesthetic rendition of our present. This present is hopeful and calls to our audience as collaborators to join us in viewing these brief moments of performance as an engagement, a promise that we will be conjoined in our sharing of this art. The performers and audience are thus united as cohabitators in the work.

Magda and Gertrud, in a pose from Study with Drum, Cymbals, and Gong, March 1946.

The Protective Shield of Terpsichore, Wherein Terpsichore Meets Siva

The Kaiser-i-Hind English Section
March 24, 1946.

One Of the Hanova Sisters

★

Gymnastical Movements In Dancing

Recently, the public of Bombay had a rare occasion to see a dance performance of very high standard by the Sisters Hanova and their pupils. As last year, the programme was very varied and contained many new attractive items. Very interesting was the demonstration of gymnastical movements useful for everybody who cares for her health and fitness. The second part of the programme — rhythmical movements—had the beauty of music made visible, a flowing and lovely design.

The gaiety and nostalgic beauty of the Viennese Waltz performed by the Sisters Hanova was like a dream of Gay Vienna lost now forever in the mists of the past, Czech dance in colourful costumes performed also by the sisters was a joy to the eyes. They also danced a Manipuri dance which was very much applauded.

A picture out of 1001 Nights was the dance drama—a day in the market of Harun-al-Rashid's Baghdad or Basara with gypsy dance, Khalif and little thieves and even a modern tourist! It was full of dramatic movement and lovely design.

A review from 'The Kaiser-i-Hind English Section' March 24, 1946 of the March 3, 1946 Hanova School performance.

The article reads: "Recently the public of Bombay had a rare occasion to see the dance performance of very high standard by the Sisters Hanova and their pupils. As last year, the programme was very varied and contained many new attractive items... A picture out of 1001 Nights was the dance drama—a day in the market of Harun-al-Rashid's Baghdad or Basara with gypsy dance, Khalif, and little thieves, and even a modern tourist! It was full of dramatic movement and lovely design." (The Kaiser-i-Hind English Section, March 24, 1946)

Gertrud in a publicity photo for 'BUDDHA-JIVAN' "Renunciation of Buddha", a Dance Drama to be held at the Princess Theatre on April 30, 1946 at 10:00 am, presented by the pupils of Guru Navakumar Singha and his Sons Narendra Kumar and Khagendra Kumar. On the bill: Sj: Narendra Kumar Singha, Mrs. Gertrude Hanova, and Mrs. Magda Hanova.

Magda: It is a privilege to be included once more in a performance by our first mentor of Indian dance, Mr. Singha. I look back on my arrival in India many years ago. As I landed in this far away country I was unsure in what direction the dance would lead me. Thankfully, my concerns were immediately put to rest. I remember the very next day after my arrival, Gerti took me to my first Indian dance class at Mr. Singha's dance school. That morning in Mr. Singha's studio, I was filled with elation. From this initial experience, I knew right away, I had a future with this new and exotic Muse.

Gertrud: Again, with great appreciation, we were asked to join Guru Navakumar Singha and his school to perform. We have come far in learning the Indian Dance, that is, for Europeans. I feel sometimes that we have barely touched the surface as the Indian dance is such a multi layered endeavour. But despite our inadequacies, the spiritual essence in this dance overshadows any feelings of deficiency. I say this from a non-religious place, as I am not a Hindu or Muslim but a Jew, who worships the dance arts. Indian dance, undoubtedly, has an underlying aura of sanctity and worship. For that is what this dance started as and will continue to be. The observer does not have to be religious in nature to see its value. On the contrary, this dance will bring the observer to believe in something greater than themselves, which all art is capable of doing.

Unexpectedly, the Hanova sisters' good friend, Menaka, died suddenly on May 30, 1947, at the age of 48. The Bombay Chronicle Weekly paper, dated June 15, 1947, poignantly reported her passing with a multi-paged tribute honouring her work. With reverence the paper announced, "With the breath of her enthusiasm Menaka fanned to flames the dying art of Indian dance till its rosy glow suffused the entire world" (p. 15).

On the front page of the paper, there is a photograph of Menaka with her fellow touring partner, the famous Russian ballerina, Anna Pavlova. Inside the paper, a headline reads, 'The Passing of an Apsara.' An Apsara is a celestial dancer which inhabits the heavens in Hindu mythology. The Hahn sisters said they felt her loss immensely as Menaka had been their close friend and mentor throughout their time in India.

Our Love Affair with Dance

The front page of the Bombay Chronicle, June 15, 1947, showing Menaka and Pavlova together. From the Hahn sister's Menaka memorabilia.

The Bombay Chronicle. "In the death of Madame Menaka (Lady Leila Sokhey) the world loses one of its top-most ballerinas, and India a classic dance exponent. She represented the glory of dance that is Kathak."

The Protective Shield of Terpsichore, Wherein Terpsichore Meets Siva

A photograph of **Menaka** from the **Hahn** sister's memorabilia.

From The Bombay Chronicle Weekly June 15, 1947:

A good friend of Pavlova and having first-hand knowledge of the creation of her ballets, Menaka saw vast possibilities in the Indian classic technique for the creation of Indian ballets. "Krishna Leela," and "Kaliya Damanam," the fight between Krishana and Kaliya, the serpent, were the first ballets which blazed the trail in the dance horizon. In 1932, Menaka first visited the Continent and gave performances in European capitals. In London she gave a recital to the Indian delegates of the Round table Conference and opened the eyes of her countrymen to her valuable cultural mission in Europe.

Magda: We have lost our dear friend Menaka and words cannot convey the depth of our sorrow. She was so much to India. So much to Gerti and I. She was more than a dancer. She was a woman, who had the living goddess of the dance reside inside her. Her legacy will be felt for generations as the dance in India has come alive again because of her dedication and far reaching vision. Menaka, our Leila Sokhey, in reviving the Indian dance, has revived the Indian people and brought to their remembrance their spiritual connection between the living body and the spirit.

A photograph of Menaka from the Hanova private collection.

Gertrud: A light has gone out with Menaka's passing. Something has faltered in me. My spirit has been dampened down. I no longer seem to have the same feeling for India now Menaka has gone. Am I being too melodramatic in thinking these thoughts? I seek some solace. I want to be surrounded by the comforts of home. But where is home now exactly? I have heard that the Europe I knew is gone forever. But still I yearn for my old continental life. I want to go to a bakery to buy

The Protective Shield of Terpsichore, Wherein Terpsichore Meets Siva

kolache or a fasnacht, a dairy to buy milk, a butcher shop to buy schnitzel, or to see a performance at a Berlin theatre. I yearn to say to someone in German, "Wie geht es ihnen heute?"(How are you today?) "Schones Wetter haben wir." (Nice weather we are having.) I wish to experience real winter again and see snow and ice and wear a heavy, wool coat and scarf. The loss of Menaka is somehow tied up with the loss of my young self. Her death has tipped me over some invisible edge. Her passing is like a sharp, hard stone in my belly and my hope is that this feeling will dull someday to just a long, awful ache. Ah so, I must show a strong, stoic face to the world. It is not my habit to reveal my feelings. But inside I cry.

A photograph of the Menaka Ballett from the Hanova collection.

Throughout their sixteen year residence in Bombay, the Hahn sisters' dance careers flourished with their live radio program from 1936 until 1940, their consistent study and performance of Indian dance, and their teaching of European Dance and Eurhythmics at private schools. The sisters also prioritized teaching students at their Hanova Dance School and creating new choreography for themselves and their students, which was shown at many public performances. The following photographs are from unknown works taken in the 1940s at the Hanova Dance School in Bombay. Gertrud and Magda were often the photographers. These pictures illustrate the sisters' consistent productivity and artistry in this period of their lives in India.

Magda, Hanova Bombay Dance School, 1946.

**Magda, right, and an unknown student.
Hanova Bombay Dance School, 1946.**

The Protective Shield of Terpsichore, Wherein Terpsichore Meets Siva

Magda with an unknown Hanova dancer.
Hanova Bombay Dance School, 1946.

Magda, standing, with an unknown Hanova dancer.
Hanova Bombay Dance School, 1946.

Magda center, Hanova Bombay Dance School, late 1940s.

Gertrud, Hanova Bombay Dance School, late 1940s.

Gertrud, Hanova Bombay Dance School, late 1940s.

Magda, Hanova Bombay Dance School, late 1940s.

Magda: The depth of this work is visceral. This dance has mysteriously appeared, as a rejuvenation, a renewed discovery of myself through this art making. To label it as a spiritual experience is too simple. I come away feeling almost redeemed...

Gertrud, Hanova Bombay Dance School, late 1940s.

Gertrud: I am exploring myself through my art. In communion with my inward feelings rather than my intellect. I mine all that I know to allow the core of what I need to communicate to emerge. In this creation, I have manifested in the physical my ideas and emotions to share my story. This story is known by all humanity already, but in the recognition of the plot and outcome the viewer rediscovers themselves somehow. There is a deep satisfaction, a need that is met by embracing this storied art. "Every utterance and every gesture that each one of us makes is a work of art." (Collingwood, p. 285, 1938)

Our Love Affair with Dance

Magda and Gertrud, in an unknown work, late 1940s.

Gertrud (far right) with two unknown Hanova students, 1948.

The Protective Shield of Terpsichore, Wherein Terpsichore Meets Siva

Gertrud, far right, with two unknown Hanova dancers.
Hanova Bombay Dance School, 1948.

Magda and Gertrud (center) in an unknown dance work.
Hanova Bombay Dance School, 1948.

Magda: We have created so many beautiful dance works in Bombay. They reflect our constant relationship with the Muse and our understanding that life is made meaningful through art making. We are living our art every day and its formation is our joy and fulfillment. To know the dance, one must be continuously in motion, discovering and rediscovering the sensations of the body. This stimulus is essential to awaken perceptions and so allow one's creativity to emerge and flow.

Magda, on the left, with an unknown Hanova dancer.
Hanova Bombay Dance School, 1948.

Gertrud: It has been truly marvellous to lead the life we have lived here in India. We have produced so much significant choreography for ourselves and our pupils and continue to have many performances. Our school has maintained a strong philosophy of movement and stresses health and body sculpture through modern physical exercises, modern rhythmical movement, and Central European dance. Life is good. But...? I must confess I feel uneasy and brood over the future of my life, on what seems lately, this far away continent.

Partition has come to India. The newspapers tell many horror stories of neighbour killing neighbour. Of mothers and daughters dying at the hands of their own family so that they would not fall into the hands of the 'other' religion. The Hindu and the Muslim have been forced to separate. I wonder who is behind this crazy idea. The India I have known did not seem to be unhappy with the arrangement as it was. People seemed to have respect for each other and their differences.

We have so far remained out of the melee. Yusuf and his family are firmly established in Bombay which is thankfully far from the new boundaries. We have been told we are not in any danger. I try not to complain or speak of my fear. But I am apprehensive as it seems that another dark cloud is gathering over my head as it did when we lost Menaka.

Magda is my salvation. She is always sunny and positive and tells me in English, "To look on the bright side". If only it was that easy. People are indeed complex and self-analysis seems pointless. I feel unhappy. There it is. Plain and simple. Why? I don't know. Of course, the situation in the country is appalling! But I must say, it seems I have a sense of disquiet and anxiety that stems from something else. To pull up the rug and look underneath is just not to my taste. So again I turn to my Muse, in an endeavour to dance away my negativity. The world is chaotic right now, perhaps I am reflecting this chaos in my feelings of restlessness and agitation?

Our Love Affair with Dance

Magda at the Hanova Dance studio in Bombay, 1948.

Gertrud at the Hanova Dance studio in Bombay, 1948.

Gertrud: I feel compelled to further record my thoughts in regards to India and partition. This has been a momentous event in the history of the Indian subcontinent. It seems to have been driven by the elite in British government, Indian politicians, and agitators, who created in the people's minds a wish for something unnecessary. People should be careful what they wish for. Promises of prosperity, freedom, and the absence of religious conflict are not always easy to attain. I do understand why the Indian would desire the British to leave them to their own governance, after all who wants to be a second class person in their own country. But now if one can believe the papers, the partition has descended into chaos. On June 3, 1947, the Viceroy Lord Mountbatten announced partition of India into two countries, an Islamic Pakistan and a Union of all Indian states called India. In this partition, and the papers were most graphic, many people slaughtered one another, were murdered and raped, or were separated from their families. If Pakistan were indeed created as a homeland for Muslims, it is hard to understand why far more were left behind in India than were incorporated into the new state of Pakistan, a state created in two halves, one in the east (formerly East Bengal, now Bangladesh) and the other 1,700 kilometres away on the western side of the subcontinent. My husband Yusuf and the Mitha family have said they are not going anywhere and have pledged a loyalty to India and will remain whole of house and property.

The past war has indeed had a profound effect on the people of India and the world in general, as economies have been devastated everywhere. Regardless of Gandhi's actions, which seem to have precipitated Britain's withdrawal, this withdrawal seems to signal Britain's loss of power despite their 'winning the war'. The Brits seem to be leaving India for purely financial reasons.

My husband has taken it upon himself as a lawyer and patriotic Indian to find the truth regarding this partition and has learned the bill was hurriedly drawn up by a British lawyer, Cyril Radcliffe, who had little knowledge of Indian conditions and used out-of-date maps and census materials. Families and communities were cut in two, and the panicked mass migration led to much blood shed and misunderstanding between normally reasonable and tolerant neighbours. This whole event has left me with echoes of what happened in Bohemia. Neighbour turning on neighbour, motivated by fear and false tales deliberately spread to create misplaced hatred and prejudice. I thought I had left this terrible behaviour behind. History does indeed seem to repeat itself. For me, the partition and the withdrawal of British rule has sharply reinforced the fact that the European is no longer as welcome in India.

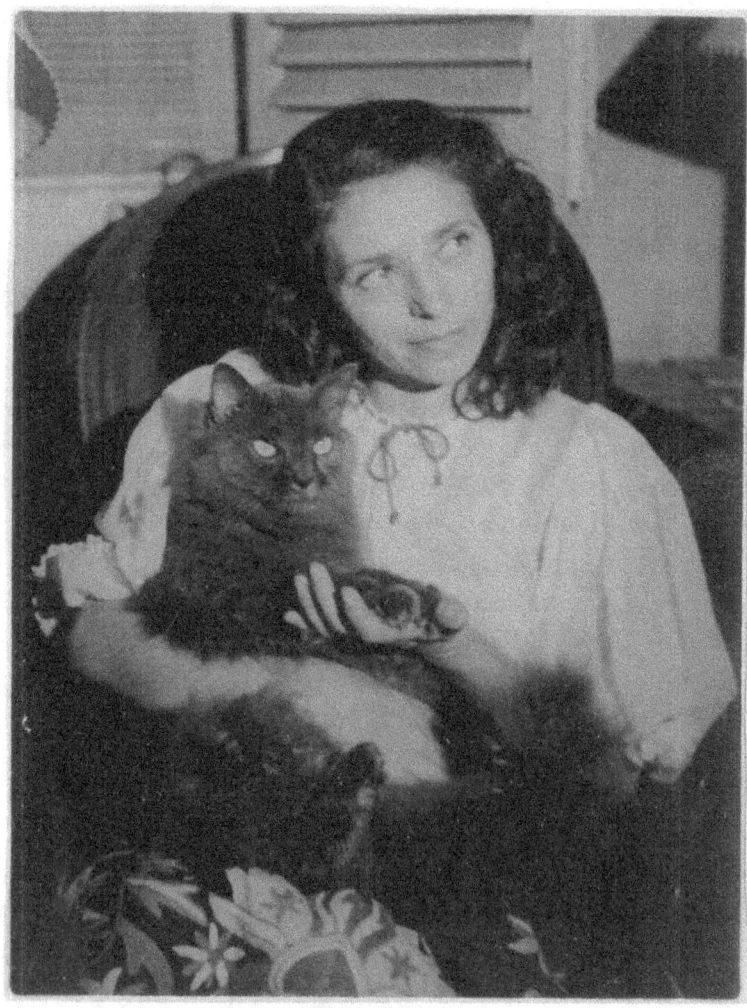

Magda, Bombay, 1948.

Magda: Almost a year later, the papers are still full of terrible stories concerning the partition. They say millions of people were forced to leave their homes and that the number of deaths has still not been ascertained as the numbers have been too high to count. India's first prime minister, Mr. Nehru, has high hopes for the Republic of India. He is famously quoted as saying, "At the stroke of midnight hour, when the world sleeps, India will wake up to life and freedom." Perhaps freedom for some but the loss of life and chaos resounds daily on the radio and in the papers, creating unease and fear among many. Gerti and I continue to perform and teach. I have been focusing on the good in our lives, but I am keeping the radio turned off and find myself snuggling up with my cat, Siva, more often then not. We must take our comfort where we may find it.

Pushpanjali A Variety Entertainment at the Excelsior Theatre in Bombay, March 9, 1948. In Aid of Bai Maneckbai Naoroji Gamadia Girls' School. Pupils of the Hanova sisters were on the bill.

Gertrud: Well, once again we are performing for a worthy cause. This time in support of the Bai Maneckbai Naoroji Gamadia Girl's School. The pupils from our dance school performed Rhythmical Fantasy in Slavonic style, a classical waltz by Brahms. I very much enjoyed the other dance offerings on the programme. Particularly Bansriwalla performed by Kumar Jaykar. This dance quoting from the programme notes: "Depicted the God Krishna pirouetting to the strains of a melody wafted across the air. A Gopi is singing a song. She chides Krisha playfully, for making eyes at her." This dance made me think of times long past. Of when I was being courted and swept up in new feelings of love. I remember the woman I was then. I was enamoured, flattered, and finally ready to be cherished by a husband. But I was never ready to put aside my dreams of the dance. And I haven't .

The other piece, Indian Ballet, performed by the school's pupils, had this to say in the programme notes. "Education prepares the girl for the climax of her career, marriage. The building of the home must be her care, the wifely burden-her responsibility." Well, thank goodness I value myself as a person and not for my ability to do housework or be a wife. While the dancing in this piece was quite good, the message is not one I agree with.

Freedom for women has not come to India and does not seem on the horizon any time soon. The path of the female in India is to obey her father and husband. This is frustrating for Magda and I, as we are treated respectfully as women of social standing but with condescension as women, who 'don't understand a man's world of politics and finances'. I wonder if Europe has retained the flair and panache of the 1920s, where a woman could drink, smoke, and be counted on to speak intelligently in a decent conversation? In Europe, the push for women's suffrage, the right to vote, of course, was a huge achievement. For women to have some say in political decisions that affect our daily lives was important. In India this is left to the men exclusively. Women, who are not overcome by poverty, do not work or have a career. The Hanova sisters are certainly an anomaly for many. We are viewed as eccentric because we are artists, which seems to excuse our 'unbecoming' behaviour. Indian families seem only to wish for sons. Our dear Papa loves that he had two girls and said, "Be the captain of your own ship and not just a crew member." Ha! Ha!

Programme cover from a performance by K.K. Shetty, December 1948.

Our Love Affair with Dance

Magda and Gertrud also studied Indian dance with the famous Indian dancer K.K. Shetty, founder and director of The Bharathiya Kala Mandal. They attended a performance by Shetty in early December of 1948. The sisters said they greatly admired Shetty because of his deep comprehension of the universality of dance for India and the world. I include a few quotes by Shetty from the programme notes to illustrate his profound understanding of the dance as an art form.

He states, "Art is the great saviour of the Indian civilization to-day and still more in the future. Art is the very essence of the spirit of India. Art transcends all languages because it is language itself."

> The Institution has for its aim the revival of the Art of Indian Classical Dance and Music as practised in India. The further aim of the school is to make these arts a respected and desired profession and to make the dance play again an important part in the life of the people.
>
> If in the dancer dwells the dedicated spirit, all forms of the dance can be channels for the message of its spirituality, for there is an influence that comes through Beauty which can change the world from coarseness, from vulgarity, from cruelty, to an observance of the highest ideals of culture and compassion.
>
> In the Dance, Divine dancer
> Freedom finds its image
> And dreams their forms
> Its cadence weaves the threads of things
> And unwinds them for ages
> Charms the atoms' rebellions into beauty
> Gives rhythm to symphony of stars
> Thrills life with pain churns up existence into
> Surging Joys and Sorrows.
>
> The movement whose body is the world
> Whose speech the sum of all languages,
> Whose jewels are the moon and the stars
> To that pure Siva I bow.

Magda (in the foreground) and Gertrud (across the table) at a Taj Mahal Hotel Gala, December 1948.

Gertrud: The recent gala we attended will enable funding for the dance arts and additionally the poor and unfortunate who have lost their homes and property due to partition. Being at the Taj Mahal Hotel reminded me of my trip to Agra with Yusuf to see the actual Taj Mahal Mausoleum. I must say, I have enjoyed travelling in India over the years to see the famous sites, despite the uncomfortable heat. But the trip to the Taj Mahal in Agra was well worth taking. The buildings and gardens were so impressive. Imagine, the deep love the Mughal emperor Shah Jahan had for his beloved wife. She was so cherished, he built her a tomb that took twenty years to complete. Yusuf was so proud to show me the large complex and gardens. Those were happier times. We were still much in love. I sometimes wonder if he would remember me so fondly if I was to go away?

Our Love Affair with Dance

The Hahn sisters' father, Dr. Gustav Hahn was born on June 20, 1869 in Kolovec, Slovenia and died on December 13, 1948 in Bombay, India.

Magda: Our dear Papa has now joined Mutti. His passing was not entirely unexpected but it is still very painful. I will dearly miss his hearty laugh, his loving hugs, the smell of his pipe, and his stories of the Great War. It was terrible for him to have to flee Bohemia and leave all that he had achieved behind. His status as a respected doctor and leader in the town were needlessly taken away. His many longtime friends, no longer friendly or willing to know him. I am still trying to accept what I have heard happened in Europe during the war. Remembering our family's happy past life, I try not to think of Bohemia or what we have lost. Instead I will think of my loving Papa. He was the best father and loved us so. Now this remaining link to our childhood and home in Bohemia is gone. Now, there is only Gerti and I to remember our old home, our old life, our Mutti and Papa.

The Protective Shield of Terpsichore, Wherein Terpsichore Meets Siva

Gustav Hahn 1869–1948.

Gertrud: Our poor Papa has gone… I feel numb from this loss. Where is my grief and sadness? My tears are absent. I feel blank. It seems that while Papa was in the world I could keep up appearances for him. I could smile when I saw him and it was a real smile. I was his beloved first born and so cherished. He never seemed to see my faults, my false pride, or my conceit. He was my most avid audience member and said he admired all that I had accomplished. He told me I reminded him so much of Mutti, her strength, her surety, her conviction about her work. Now, I feel empty.

Magda tries to coax me to the studio and says we must go on. I know she is right. In the dance, I will try to find myself again. With the dance, I will survive our father's demise and dance away my buried grief as our dear Papa told us to, so long ago when Mutti left us. Papa's passing seems a catalyst for change. For that matter, the atmosphere of the country has altered dramatically with partition. And now the war has ended, many ex-pats, especially the Brits, are leaving India. I see numerous Europeans returning to their homelands to seek new lives and identities. We are not yet sure of what we will do. Magda says I must get into the studio and dance. Then we will know. A change is in the air.

Magda and Gertrud spoke many times of the enjoyment of going to the Mitha beach house in the early morning when it was still cool and dancing on the sand when the tide was far out. They said the beach provided a natural dance floor and was particularly invigorating for movement with the fresh sea air. At the beach, they captured many beautiful images in photographs, which visually share the deep joy they experienced while dancing in Bombay.

**Dancing on the beach in Bombay.
Magda and Gertrud far right, with an unknown Hanova dancer.**

Gertrud: I know I often tend to look at life pessimistically. In the German language, 'weltschmerz', meaning world weary, sums up my feelings exactly. How many times has Magda said I should look at things more positively! I tell her, "I have you to do that for me." Feeling joy is just not in my daily nature. And here, I am speaking of real delight, not the kind of fake joy that can be put on a face for the camera, the stage, or to make other people feel all is well with you when it really isn't. Some dancers think they must paste on a cheerful expression, which will lead the audience to experience the enjoyment of that particular dance. But if the performer is feigning their pleasure, I think a discerning audience recognizes this immediately and labels the performance as wooden or 'too sweet'.

However, to contradict myself, I cannot help surrender to the greater call of that something called 'bliss' that wells up in me so unexpectedly in moments when I am dancing. At these times, all negativity is forgotten in the movement and motion. I am at peace with myself and nearer to what the Hindus and Buddhists call 'Nirvana'. I have been released from karmic bondage. I am as a lamp, 'blown out' and emptied of ego. The eastern way of thinking is able to articulate my description of joy quite succinctly. Through the dance, in those moments, I am free to go on with my life, all else is left behind.

I believe we are born with certain personality traits, be it cheerfulness or melancholy. And so I accept myself as I am. I have also observed that some people are gifted at birth with profound talents. The rare individual comes out fully formed, able to mesmerize others with their voice, their painting ability, or their genius as a choreographer. However, when it comes to dancing, I feel we must not worry about being extra ordinary, for all people have a body and are capable of experiencing the gratification of dancing, which as many proclaim is our human right. And here I speak of not dancing to impress an audience but to simply revel in one's own body and to move wherever one is to simply feel the exhilaration of being alive! When I am dancing, my low spirits simply melt away.

Magda and Gertrud dancing on the Bombay beach.

Magda: I am fortunate to have Gerti as my sister. Our bond is blood but our attachment has been cemented by our mutual deep connection to the Muse. We have always been united in our pursuit of the dance arts without jealousy or envy. Our alliance is a dance in which we move in sync and harmony. Gerti is often the lead and I the follower. Travelling in space and time, we circle and spin together, our feet effortlessly creating new pathways. We have our solos, but in our dance we always return to each other. We hold each other tight, arms joined in a warm embrace, and turn around and around, getting dizzy from our passion.

Magda dancing with children from the Hanova Bombay Dance School, 1940s.

Magda: The dancing children inspire me. Their movement is so pure and created in the moment. They have no artifice or falseness about their gestures. Their movement springs out of their youthful enjoyment of the simplicity of running, jumping, skipping, turning, and stretching. In these children, I see movement that is fresh and irreproachable in its unadulterated forms. It gives one pause. A glimpse into an understanding that life may be fleeting but it is in these moments of exultation and motion that we affirm our aliveness. For children this is constant and occurring in steady regularity. As adults, we need to retain this youthful outlook, be more spontaneous, and delighted by each and every move our bodies can make. We need to be at the ready every day to rediscover our bodies as the precious gifts they are.

Magda, Bombay beach photo, 1940s.

Magda on the Bombay beach, 1940s.

The Protective Shield of Terpsichore, Wherein Terpsichore Meets Siva

Magda on the Bombay beach, 1940s.

Magda: The light on the early morning beach is soft and luminescent. The freshness of daybreak soaks into my skin as I bask in the first flush of radiant rays. I wander, dancing down the vast expanse of sand leaving small, indented footprints, which mark my passage. The outgoing tide has left a perfect dance floor to savour. The sand humbly accepts my leaps and frolics as I leave my gentle impressions. Each day I have a miraculous new stage, washed freshly by the waves, to accept my grateful offering to Terpsichore.

Magda on the Bombay beach, 1940s.

Magda, center, with two unknown dance students, Bombay beach, 1940s.

The Protective Shield of Terpsichore, Wherein Terpsichore Meets Siva

Gertrud: I am often the photographer on our early morning pilgrimages to the beach. Magda is always willing to let me capture her image. She says she feels a special euphoria, a communion with the Earth, when on the sand. And I can't argue with that. The cool air and fresh morning atmosphere is invigorating. An aura of possibility hangs over the expanse. A gentle wind blows away any bad feelings I might retain from the previous day. I can start anew on these early excursions as the breeze flows over my body. This air is tender and asks me to let go of the past and look only forward. I get my camera ready.

Magda on the windblown Bombay beach, 1940s.

Magda: There is nothing better than being outdoors on the newly awakened shore, embracing the dawn and the welcome heat and light. As I breathe in the energizing, salty morning air, I move as one with a gentle wind. I take in the great sweep of sand, sea, and sky and feel united with the vastness of the earth, the very cycle of life. The light gusts tease my body with their tender caress and encourage me to flow and turn. I feel the breath of the earth dancing beside me as I revel in the absolute.

Dancing on the Bombay Beach, Gertrud, an unknown friend, and Magda.

Gertrud: So ist das Leben. C'est la vie. This is life. The time has come to say goodbye, again, to a place with so many wonderful memories. How can we leave? Well, our season here has ended. That is what I know. What Magda and I both know. We are in complete agreement about this decision. A new life awaits us. Many circumstances have led to this important decision, which I frankly feel was inevitable. Some people will be

The Protective Shield of Terpsichore, Wherein Terpsichore Meets Siva

hurt needless to say, but the time has come to move on. This is our life and it is to be lived fully.

Magda: We have so many wonderful memories of India. In some ways we are sorry to leave, but when the time is right, one must listen and act. So goodbye to Bombay and alas goodbye to the many close ties and relationships we have made over the years. I will miss our many friends and students. We have been gifted with precious experiences in this part of the world but when one hears the call of the Muse beckoning, one must follow. And so back to Europe we go…

Magda on the Bombay beach, 1940s.

Our Love Affair with Dance

7

FOLLOWING THE VOICE OF THE MUSE

London, England: 1949–1957

In 1949, the Hanova sisters both ended their marriages and left India to move to London, England. In the first few years of their residence in London, there is evidence that Gertrud and Magda both taught Rhythmic Movement at the Finsbury Women's Institute. Additionally, the sisters opened a new Hanova Dance School in 1953. They also furthered their dance studies at The Laban Institute with the famous movement theorist Rudolph Laban and with the well-known choreographer and dance education proponent, Sigurd Leeder, at his school.

Magda and Gertrud never went into great depth about their leaving India and divorcing their husbands and I didn't pry too much for details as I realized divorce could be a personal and unpleasant subject. But with Indian Independence in 1947 and the partitioning of British India into India, Pakistan, and Bangladesh, the colonial India that they had initially come to know and enjoy in 1932 had come to an end.

In a paper presented by Vij (2003) on partition he outlines the horror of this period.

> Such was the magnitude of the devastation wrecked by the Partition of undivided India that it was, and is a mammoth task for writers to deal with it. Historians, for one, talked in aggregates: ten million refugees, two million of them dead, seventy-five thousand women raped and so on and so forth. These statistics fail to impart even a fraction of the enormity of the tragedy that was the Partition… Statistics fail to even hint at the trauma of husbands and wives, sons and mothers separated by the Radcliffe line. And the last thing that statistics or historical narratives can ever do is to reflect on identity crises of innocent individuals at a time when identity could be altered by loot and rioting. (p. 1)

As mentioned, Gertrud's husband Yusuf Mitha, was an Ismaili Muslim. Yusuf and his family chose to stay in Bombay and be a part of the new India, as did many Muslims. With all the uproar of partition and the newness of self-governance, life in India probably felt quite unsettled at this time. Gertrud did mention that she divorced her husband quite amicably so that he could remarry and have children, as she did not want children. She laughingly said he did offer to keep her on as a first wife but this did not appeal to her. Magda did not mention her divorce with any details so I didn't dig into what seemed her private memories. The sisters simply said that they no longer wanted to be married and were called to follow the Muse of the Dance back to Europe. Gertrud was forty-six and Magda forty-four in 1949.

I note that the Hanova sisters' lives had already seen many changes in location and circumstances. Seeking new horizons was probably seen as a fresh adventure. But they were always both very positive in their memories of India. The sisters often shared how much they had enjoyed Indian food, the hot, humid climate, Magda more than Gertrud, teaching and performing dance with their Bombay Dance School, and taking classes in Indian dance. Magda and Gertrud, over their sixteen years in residence in India, had as well traveled extensively and embraced the varied cultures of the large subcontinent.

Further, the sisters had strong convictions about how they wanted to live their lives and now the war was over perhaps India was no longer a refuge but felt constricting. Moreover, their father had died, leaving them able to forge on together without any direct family ties, if you don't count their husbands. The Hahn sisters quite often expressed the idea that they were unwilling to compromise their dance goals, especially for men or marriage.

The sisters chose to live in London, England. You might wonder why they did not return to Czechoslovakia. There were several good reasons. After the war in 1945, almost all of the ethnic German population was expelled from Bohemia in a huge anti-German backlash. Czechoslovakia now looked favourably on the Russians who had liberated them from Nazi occupation. Czechoslovakia was still a democracy, although communists were well represented in the Czechoslovakian government. But in 1947, the nation wanted to receive Marshall Aid from America. The USSR forbid the Czechoslovakians from accepting US help. The communists were suddenly not as favoured by the people. After much bloodshed and murder, a communist coup took place in 1948. The emerging totalitarian regime would stay in power for the next forty years.

In 1949, when the sisters left India, Bohemia and the Karlsbad they had known growing up did not exist anymore. Any property their family had owned in Karlsbad had been confiscated by the Nazi regime and then later taken over by the Czechoslovakian communists.

Now that the sisters spoke English, London, a metropolis that promoted the arts, was probably very appealing. Magda and Gertrud both said that they were eager and happy to return to Europe after their long residence in India.

In the early 1950s, reference letters were essential to gain employment in a new place. The following is an excerpt from a glowing letter of reference for Magda from the Alexandra Girl's English Institution in Bombay, which probably enabled her to gain employment with the Finsbury Women's Institute.

> Mrs. Magda Weisskopf (Hanova) has been a Physical Instructress in this school from 1st February 1942 to November 1948. She has taught drill, Gymnastics, Rhythmic Movements and Classical Ballet dancing to all standards of the School. Mrs. Weisskopf has been one of the best teachers I have ever had. She is excellent at her work. Her system combines physical exercise with grace of movement and poise. She has succeeded in making the most clumsy child graceful within a few months. Mrs. Weisskopf has been a good disciplinarian but at the same time pupils have loved their drill classes. I am sorry to lose her services as she is leaving the country, but I heartily recommend her and wish her the best of everything.
>
> Signed: M Benjamin, Principal. Alexandra Girl's English Institution, Ford, Bombay.

The Hanova sisters said they enjoyed life in London as London was a centre for so many rich historical and cultural experiences, such as visiting art galleries, museums, and of course seeing dance performances. In a taped conversation with Gertrud from 1993, she related that London was a hub for dance in the 1950s and she said the sisters saw many wonderful modern dance and ballet performances while living there. They were also able to see Ram Gopal and his New Indian Company in September of 1956 when he performed in London at the Royal Festival Hall.

Our Love Affair with Dance

Announcement of the opening of
The Hanova School in London, June 1, 1953.

Gertrud: I love London and its unique culture. So many expats and old friends were here to welcome us. All looking a bit worn sadly to say. I realize now that our life in India was a life of leisure and abundance. The war hardly seemed to touch us. We certainly did not have the rationing that is still happening to some extent here, or the bombing. The European society in Bombay, I feel ashamed to say, did not seem to suffer unduly at all. In London, by all accounts, life was extremely harsh and uncertain during the war. Magda and I have managed somehow to be in the right place at the right time. I am very pleased that we have recently opened a new Hanova School of Dance in the Bayswater area and have once again attracted a loyal following of students. Wherever we live, the dance will call to disciples of this worthy art form.

Following the Voice of the Muse

The cover of the Hanova School of Modern Physical Culture brochure illustrating 'central control', a staple movement in the Hanova system.

Magda: So quickly, India is becoming a distant memory with the hustle and bustle of this busy London town. But I cannot forget the loss of our loved ones, our dear Papa, our beloved Menaka, or the tearful goodbyes from our loyal dance students of so many years. All will be remembered. However, I look confidently to the future. Gerti and I have each other and of course the dance. We have been quite fortunate to make contact with old friends, who ended up here in London during the war. Such is life, we go on and make the most of it.

Gertrud: Well, now we have moved to Britain, I am embracing the English weather. It is cold and wet, at times dreary and foggy. I am armed with boots, a warm hat, and an umbrella. I love it! I am not a sun worshipper like Magda so it suits me just fine. I have settled in very nicely. We have opened our new school and I find the city very stimulating, the theatres, cinemas, and art galleries in particular. The style of the modern dance we have seen so far is not what I remember or to my taste. The ballet, yes, still the same old, same old. The modern dance, sadly seems to have lost some of its edge. I must see more of the newer companies to give a more informed opinion. We shall see. I still put faith in what we have learned from our European schools. Laban is here and we are studying at his Institute. Luckily, we have found an Indian restaurant near our flat so we can still get our curries, chai, and chapatis. The Indian proprietor was quite surprised when I spoke to him in Marathi and Hindi.

The inside flap of the Hanova School of modern physical culture and dancing brochure, 4 Craven Hill, London.

Magda, with young students at the Hanova London dance studio, 1950s.

Following the Voice of the Muse

In the following excerpt from a Hanova Dance School lecture demonstration in London during the mid 1950s, Gertrud shares her views on the Hanova style of modern dance.

> We, too, use parts of the Ballet, not so much for the actual working out of steps, but as a training so that eventually the whole body can express freely to its utmost limit. For example, plies for strengthening the legs but not for an adagio, where it is a stylized movement.
>
> The style of the Hanova School allows great freedom of expression. Each dancer can build upon it his or her own individual style and yet keep to the original laws of its technique, rather in the way that musical composition is built on scales. It is essential to have an individual style, but this style often passes through various stages before it becomes a style in its own right. Picasso, the painter, proved this. He went through many stages, the blue period, the cave period, for instance, until he evolved his present style, which is so definite that now, in spite of many imitators, one can always recognize his work.

Gertrud at the barre with students, Hanova London studio, 1950s.

The following is another quote from a Hanova Dance School lecture demonstration in London during the 1950s, which illustrates the Hanova understanding of how modern dance may create connections to other art forms:

> Modern dance is an important factor in developing artistic appreciation of every kind. Students learn to observe and recognize beauty or ugliness in their environment, and to be aware of the close relationship one kind of art bears to another. They learn to make use of all that they sense; to be ready to accept the joys and sorrows that are the inevitable lot of the artist; and last, but not least, to form the link between those willing to give and those willing to receive. This should lead to ever increasing understanding in the relationship between the artist and the audience, even though they may differ in their opinions of what is and what is not true Art.

The Hanova London Dance School brochure from the 1950s also aptly reflected the Hanova perspective on the benefits of dancing.

> Health: under proper guidance, Physical Culture stimulates the body to more efficient internal action, invigorates muscles and makes them more flexible. This greatly retards the process of aging. Since aging consists of a gradual, slow (but sometimes rather quick) loss of flexibility which begins in the very first years of life, it is never too late nor too soon to start Physical Culture.

> Grace and Beauty: Grace, poise, beauty of posture, and movement depend on a well-trained body and on perfect command over all its motions. Physical Culture leads to naturally harmonious movement and perfect control, without self-conscious effort.

> Energy: Properly planned physical exercises stimulate bodily and mental energy. After a tiring day, an hour of physical Culture acts as an excellent tonic.

> Satisfaction: The new easy control over all the movements, de-

rived from physical exercise, leads to a fresh feeling of satisfaction and assurance. This can play an important part in removing potential sources of depression and inferiority complexes.

Pleasure: The enormous popularity of sport throughout the world is proof of the great pleasure that can be derived from the purposeful exercise of the muscles. Physical Culture conveys a great sense of general well-being.

A photograph of Rudolph Laban in the 1950s, from the Hanova sisters' collection of memorabilia.

Attending the Laban Institute was a highlight of the Hanova sisters' time in England. By the 1950's, Laban's theories of movement had become well-known in Europe and accepted as a central foundation for most European modern dance and for dance education. The Hanova sisters took this time to thoroughly absorb Laban's ideas in greater depth. They incorporated much of Laban's core beliefs into their own system which dance historian McCaw (2011) outlines:

'Dance' for Laban is largely a metaphor for an activation of those aspects that for him make up a human being. 'Dance', in his view, can and should occur anywhere, everywhere, and it is the experience of dancing itself rather than a performance of dance to a viewer that is key for Laban. (p. 63)

In the Hanova classes, as Laban professed, it was the personal meaning and emotional content of the dancing for the individual in those moments that mattered the most, not the performance or the perfection of the performance. The sisters understood that to be truly fulfilled as a dancer, the dancer required the time and freedom to explore his or her own body before he or she was able to share set choreography with authenticity. Therefore, to culminate a session and to inspire new choreography, an exploration of the self through improvisation was always a component of the Hanova classes.

Taken from Gertrud's notes from a dance lecture from the 1950s, Gertrud discusses the Hanova sisters' views on improvisation:

> Improvisations require full bodily control of movements. Picasso changes a picture by intermingling lines and planes in all directions, over again and again, until a painting emerges, absolute and definite in its composition. The dancer explores lines and planes in the geometrical field of motion. But, whereas the doodling of the painter usually remains unseen in a picture and the main effect lies in the end production, the painting, in the dancer's case the main effect lies in the doodling rather than in the last pose. These improvisations express joy of the dancer's mastery of movement. If this brings pleasure to all those who accept this kind of expression as a reproduction of their own artistic feelings, then the creation has fulfilled its purpose.
>
> The process may appear spontaneous but is built on many previous lessons, where the dance student has learned specific movement elements, such as the use of levels, shapes, dynamics, steps, and patterns and how to execute them proficiently. Then with guidance and support, the student is able to confidently and creatively explore their movement task or ideas alone or with others in memorable expression.

Following the Voice of the Muse

**A photograph of Rudolph Laban from the
Hanova sisters' collection of photographs, 1950s.**

The Hanova sisters' also wholly concurred with Laban's conviction that human beings have an innate capacity and need to move and use their bodies to achieve health and wellbeing. Laban derived his ideas from observing children at play.

> Everybody has seen children jumping around happily. This might be considered as one of the natural forms of dancing. Children may even instinctively feel that their rhythmic jumping or dancing contributes to their bodily and mental well-being and to the development of some of their inner capacities

and powers. This hidden self-education and self-remedy have both been studied and the knowledge acquired hereby forms an essential part of the modern educational dance. (Laban, 1951, 1992, p. 53)

McCaw (2011) in The Laban Sourcebook, captures the essence of Laban's doctrine, which also became a Hanova foundational belief:

Laban said, "We are all dancers: We all carry a dancer in ourselves. Even if we do not know anything about this dancer within us, we have the urge to awaken him (sic) within us. In this sense the budding joy of movement in our time is to be understood…" (McCaw, 2011, p. 15).

While in London, the Hanova sisters also studied with Sigurd Leeder in the early 1950s. Sigurd Leeder (1902–1981) was a German dancer, choreographer, and dance education theorist. He had his own method of teaching expressive dance and promoted Labanotation, which had been developed by Rudolph Laban to record and represent modern dance with symbols.

Leeder had a close collaboration with the German ballet dancer and choreographer Kurt Jooss, who is regarded as the founder of dance theatre or Tanztheater. Both dancers moved to England in 1934 following rising Nazi oppression. Leeder and Jooss established the Leeder-Jooss School of Dance at Dartington Hall in Devon. Leeder developed his method of teaching movement based on the study of eukinetics, which stems from the term Rudolph Laban coined to describe the temporal elements of dance (rhythm, phrasing, and dynamics) and choreutics. The term choreutics, also coined by Laban, from two Greek root words 'khoreia' (dancing in unison) and 'eu' (beautiful and harmonious) is defined as the practical study of harmonized movement.

Leeder moved to London in 1947 and opened his own school. He trained not only dancers but also future dance teachers. He dedicated himself to the advancement and recognition of the signs and language of Labanotation, the transcription of choreographies, and the creating of movement studies for teaching. The Hanova sisters said that they found the Leeder ideology of movement closely aligned to that of Rudolph Laban's in many ways, but Leeder had his own distinct ideas about training and teaching dance teachers.

Following the Voice of the Muse

Unknown students at the Hanova Dance School in London, 1950s.

Unknown students at the Hanova Dance School in London, 1950s. 'Namaste'.

Our Love Affair with Dance

In the ensuing excerpt from a Hanova lecture demonstration in the 1950s, Gertrud shares her thoughts on the value of dancing for everyone.

> The Dance—the Terpsichorean Art—is the highest standard and fulfillment of the beauty of movement. The Hanovas do not believe that everybody who loves dancing must become a professional dancer, but his or her desire to dance should be developed; and quite often the understanding guidance of the teacher can bear fruit. On the other hand, all those who have no inclination to dance, should take some interest in it. For their own benefit, dancing (again with proper guidance) can change awkwardness into harmony of movement and this is of greater importance to happiness than can be imagined. It is much to be regretted that men usually consider dancing a feminine, boring, useless pastime. It is, of course, far from it. For proof, one has to only look at the Spanish and Russian dancers, as examples of fitness, suppleness, and poise.

Unknown students at the Hanova London Dance School with masks, 1950s.

Gertrud's notes also differentiated the Ballet and Contemporary Dance:

> Making the Modern Dance differs from Ballet. Whereas in Ballet the exact execution of the steps is essential, so that the whole corps de Ballet appears as one body, the aim of the group of the Contemporary Dance is not regimentation. With both, naturally, movements are controlled and styled. In Ballet, according to a set pattern of dance movements; in the Contemporary, according to a set pattern of individual movements. What the Modern Stage Dance aims to do is to identify itself with the audience, through originality of movement, of line and plastic formation, with a story or without, rather like a poem or an essay, and through originality of costumes, decor, music, and presentation.

An unknown dance student in 'Oriental' costume at the Hanova London Dance School, 1950s.

Magda: I am still in love with the ballet. I think I always will be. While in London, we have seen so many wonderful ballet performances. Recently, we saw the London Festival Ballet which was formed not too long ago in 1950. There was marvellous dancing by Alicia Markova, who used to be with the Royal Ballet, and the director is Anton Dolin. Of course my favourite to date was seeing the Royal Ballet at the Royal Opera House in Covent Garden. I was thrilled to see Margot Fonteyn dance! She is quite exceptional…

---

20 December 1956 · THE NURSERY WORLD

FOR MOTHERS AND DAUGHTERS
by Janet Hall

THREE tiny figures wearing black tights teetered perilously, their feet in the second ballet position, then dropped a very creditable—if slightly wobbly—curtsey. With a little prompting, they chorused " Good-bye Miss Magda. See you next Wednesday morning," and ran happily out of the studio, leaving their teacher, Miss Magda Hanova, free to talk about her dancing and physical culture sessions for adults and children.

Behind the red-painted front door of number 4 Craven Gardens, this sparkling-eyed Czechoslovakian and her blonde sister, Gertrud, daughters of a doctor, have for two years been teaching pupils of all ages from 3 upwards. Their method combines the best features of many famous systems and has been evolved from their early training in Czechoslovakia, lasting three years, and from experience gained whilst teaching in schools both here and in India. New pupils are first given exercises, then progress to basic classical ballet steps, then to modern ballet movements. In Bombay, the sisters were well known for their " keep-fit " broadcasts.

An interesting experiment which they hope will prove as successful here as it did in India, is the mother-and-daughter classes. They found that many mothers who accompanied their children and sat waiting during classes were eager to take part, and, equally, when mothers came for exercises the children who came with them wanted to imitate their mothers. So began the popular mother-and-daughter sessions which are now being introduced at the Hanova School in Bayswater. Not only do they help to keep Mother trim and supple, and help her to relax, but give added enjoyment to the child.

An early appreciation of rhythm and music is encouraged so that finally even the youngest children are able to express the mood of the music in their dancing. A blackboard stands at one end of the studio and on it children who find it difficult to improvise steps in time to the music are allowed to draw patterns. They then " dance out " the patterns they have drawn in the same way as a dancer interprets the ideas of a choreographer. Music is supplied by one of the sisters at the piano, by gramophone records, or by rhythmic beats on a drum.

An hour's lesson once a week has helped an awkward, angular child to be more graceful, and has given the naturally graceful opportunities for self-expression. Foot exercises help those with a tendency to flat feet. A popular class is that for 7-year-olds on Saturday morning. Expectant mothers whose doctors approve take four lessons in relaxation, each lasting an hour, after the third month of pregnancy, and each month new exercises are introduced which they can practise at home. Several mothers have experienced natural childbirth after these classes. Post-natal exercises, too, are given, to help mothers to regain their figure.

A visitor has the feeling that in the studio behind the red door nothing is more important than the ability to move rhythmically, and—if you are only 3 years old—to drop a perfect curtsey at end of class.

▷▷▷▷▷▷ ★ ◁◁◁◁◁◁

Good press for the Hanova London Dance School in the form of a magazine article titled For Mothers and Daughters from December 20, 1956 in The Nursery World by Janet Hall.

Three tiny figures wearing black tights teetered perilously, their feet in the second ballet position, then dropped a very creditable—if slightly wobbly—curtsy. With a little prompting, they chorused Goodbye Miss Magda. See you next Wednesday morning. And ran happily out of the studio, leaving the teacher, Miss Magda Hanova, free to talk about her dancing and physical culture sessions for adults and children.

Behind the red painted front door of number 4 Craven Hill, this sparkling-eyed Czechoslovakian and her blond sister, Gertrud, daughters of a doctor, have for two years been teaching pupils of all ages from 3 upwards. Their method combines the best features of many famous systems and has been evolved from their early training in Czechoslovakia lasting three years, and from experiences gained whilst teaching schools both here and in India. New pupils are first given exercises, then progress to basic classical ballet steps, then to modern ballet movements. In Bombay, the sisters were well known for their keep-fit broadcast.

An interesting experiment which they hope will prove as successful here as it did in India, is the Mother and Daughter classes. They found that many mothers who accompanied their children and sat waiting during classes were eager to take part, and, equally, when mothers came for exercises the children who came with them wanted to imitate their mothers. So began the popular mother-daughter sessions which are now being introduced at the Hanova School in Bayswater. Not only do they help to keep Mother trim and supple, and help her to relax, but give added enjoyment to the child.

An early appreciation of rhythms and music is encouraged so that finally even the youngest children are able to express the mood of the music in their dancing. A blackboard stands at one end of the studio and on it children who find it difficult to improvise steps in time to the music are allowed to draw patterns. They then "dance out" the patterns they have drawn in the same way as a dancer interprets the ideas of a choreographer. Music is supplied by one of the sisters at the piano, by gramophone records, or by rhythmic beats on a drum.

An hour lesson once a week has helped an awkward, angular child to become more graceful, and has given naturally graceful opportunities for self-expression. Foot exercises help those with a tendency to flat feet. A popular class is that for 7–12 year olds on Saturday morning. Expectant mothers whose doctors approve take four lessons in relaxation, each lasting an hour, after the third month of pregnancy, and each month new exercises are introduced which they can practice at home. Several mothers have experienced natural childbirth after these classes. Post-natal exercises, too, are given, to help mothers to regain their figure.

A visitor has the feeling that in the studio behind the red door nothing is more important than the ability to move rhythmically, and if you are only 3 years old—to drop a perfect curtsy at the end of class.

Mother and son taking classes together at the Hanova School in London, 1950s.

Following the Voice of the Muse

Gertrud enjoying the dance students at the Hanova London Dance School, 1950s.

In another excerpt from a lecture demonstration at the Hanova London Dance School, Gertrud presents the sisters' views on the importance of body control:

> The Hanova sisters, Gertrud and Magda, have built up a school for the study of body control. They are exploiting the different faculties of physical motion and developing the potentialities of its different aspects. This enables the individual to use his or her abilities to the fullest extent, or helps to correct disabilities.
>
> Body control conveys a great sense of general well-being and complete command over the body, which leads to fresh feelings of satisfaction and assurance and brings a rewarding happiness. The Hanova system is both a science and an art. It is based on great personal experience of advanced modern physical precepts and incorporates the most beneficial principles of many famous schools of Europe and India.

Having studied these methods of physical exercise and the dance, and practiced them, the Hanova method has been evolved by careful adapting and blending of these diverse principles to make the modern Hanova School a centre of physical discipline and the art of the dance.

In 1957, Magda, by chance, met some tourists at a party. They were from Vancouver, British Columbia, which she learned is situated on the west coast of Canada. She discovered in conversation, that Vancouver, as far as the visitors knew, did not have any modern dance schools. Magda perhaps impetuously but definitely boldly decided to move to Vancouver to bring the Hanova System to North America. In the fall of 1957, she adventurously left England and traveled to Vancouver, which was indeed fresh and untouched territory for modern dance.

Magda: Our time in London has been fruitful. Attending the Laban Institute and the Leeder School has broadened my understanding of movement theory and reinforced my belief that the dance has a capacity to rejuvenate and revitalize the body, mind, and spirit at any age.

We are no longer performing but instead have put our energies into our dance school. It is sad to say goodbye to the stage, but all dancers come to that time where they must give way to younger and more supple bodies. This can be a difficult time when one still feels the urge to perform. However, putting one's creative energies into teaching and choreography has its own gratification and pleasure.

Gerti is usually the one to take the lead in all our endeavours and up until now I have happily followed. She has been my stalwart companion in the dance during all that has happened in our lives. She is the one who has guided our fortunes and I am grateful. But perhaps now it is my time to be the first to step forward.

I affirm my belief that one should look only ahead and onward with positive feeling so as to create the kind of life one wants and deserves.

8

DANCING INTO NEW HORIZONS

Magda on route to Canada on the Holland Liner, Dalerdyk, September 1957.

Magda: Here I am aboard ship heading into the unknown. But somehow I feel released. I am now free to create a new life. What this will hold I do not know. But I have no fear or worry for I am not alone. I take with me all of my passion and love for the dance and I know this will sustain me.

Air travel was just starting to become common place in the late 1950s. Consequently, Magda began her journey by crossing the Atlantic Ocean on the Holland Liner, Dalerdyk, which took about two weeks. After arriving in Halifax, Nova Scotia, she had a six day train ride across the expanse of Canada before arriving in Vancouver.

I ponder what inspired Magda to leave a doubtlessly flourishing dance scene in the culturally rich city of London to move to the much smaller Canadian city of Vancouver. She mentioned she didn't know anyone in Vancouver and that she had no clear idea of what Canada would be like. But Magda had the confidence to take this step into what most people would feel was uncertain and unfamiliar territory. Armed with her positive attitude, she didn't have any fear of failure or worry about the details of money or habitation.

She was a single and divorced woman. And in the still unliberated world of the 1950s, women did not usually travel or move to new continents alone. Looking back at this period, women were still defined by their husbands and their husband's status. There was no Ms. available yet to put before a woman's name to ward off the nosey or curious as to a woman's marital status, which seemed to dominate a woman's worth. Being called Miss or Mrs. was all that was available and it made a difference to how a woman was treated, especially in the world of business or commerce. Even renting an apartment could be tricky for a Miss. On arriving in Vancouver, Magda introduced herself as Magda Hanova and Miss or Mrs. was added on haphazardly by others who felt the need to label her, particularly in the press.

To understand Magda's daring decision to re-establish herself, one would have to have known her. She was extremely optimistic in nature and seemed to see beyond the everyday worries that other people complained about. She was outgoing, friendly, and interested in other people. She always had a smile on her face and physically exuded health and well-being. Magda was very much her own person and answered to no one, except perhaps to her older sister, Gerti.

Magda's decision to live in Vancouver was perhaps taken on a whim. North America and Vancouver were somewhere new to see, explore, and experience. And if she didn't like Canada, she most likely thought she could always return to England as Gertrud had decided to see how things went for her before making a move herself. Fortunately for myself and hundreds of other Vancouverites, Magda immediately loved Vancouver and quickly established herself doing what she adored, teaching the dance.

Dancing Into New Horizon

Magda leading fellow passengers in exercises and dance movements on the deck of the ship on her journey to Canada, September 1957. On the back of the photograph Magda wrote: "Daily Exercises on Dalerdyk, Beauty in white shorts is Kaptain."

Magda: Here I am. Gloriously free and on a new adventure. I have so much resolute feeling for where this journey will take me. I am in effect becoming an explorer to new uncharted lands and territory. What I will discover is still a mystery. But I will be planting the flag of the Dance Arts in the fresh soil of new acolytes. The Terpsichorean Arts have set sail in my person on a mission to bring all I know and cherish to new vistas.

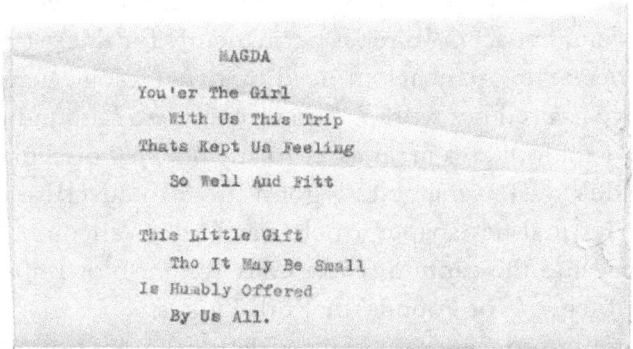

Well-wishers from the ship Magda took from London, England to Canada, gave Magda this poem and a small gift to thank her for all the dance classes she gave aboard ship. The note was signed by all the passengers who took part.

Soon after arriving in Vancouver, Magda immediately sought employment with two letters of reference. The first letter is from a former London student extolling the merits of Magda's teaching.

To Whom It May Concern,

As a lifetime Laban teacher, I felt the need of studying other methods of the Art of Movement and in particular Indian methods. I had the good fortune to be introduced to Mrs. Magda Hanova. She gave me not only a good understanding of the beneficial value of Indian movement but in actual fact helped me greatly to overcome rheumatic pains, disturbances of my circulatory system, and inaccurate breathing. I cannot speak too highly of the assistance Mrs. Hanova has given me. Her patience and the exactness of her explaining each sequence of movement made each lesson a treasured experience. Within four months of only one weekly lesson I was completely freed from pains I had suffered for many years."

Signed: Beatrice Pia Loeb

The second letter of reference from Dr. Walter Spicer of Harley Street in London, dated June 14th, 1957, extols the virtues of Magda's skills as a physiotherapist. There is no record of Magda having credentials or formal training as a physiotherapist, but Dr. Spicer certainly saw results for patients he sent to her for therapy. He said, "I have been in touch with Mrs. Hanova and her school almost permanently for the last two years and a great number of my patients, in need of gynaecological and obstetrical exercises, have praised her work." "I have complete faith in her ability and I am sure that she will be a great asset to any hospital or clinic."

Magda didn't waste time getting good press to advertise her arrival in Vancouver. Her first newspaper article was in the Vancouver Province, in October 1957, and the caption reads 'Gals Weight Not Important: Faults Show Up In Inches, Not Pounds' by Ruth Pinkus.

The feature introduces Miss Magda Hanova, a physical culture expert newly arrived from London, England, who will soon be opening a School of Modern Dance in Vancouver. In the article, Magda explains that diet is not enough to have a good figure. One must also exercise and dance in order to be toned. The article adds:

> The exercises she advocates are a special kind of tense-relax combination that let you go limp all over, after pulling hard not only on individual finger and toe joints. The massage consists of pummelling, pinching, squeezing and kneading your own muscles. But in case you plan to begin tonight, relax. Only a professional can show you how to do it right. Otherwise, says Mrs. Hanova, you'll lose half the value of your efforts by doing it wrong.

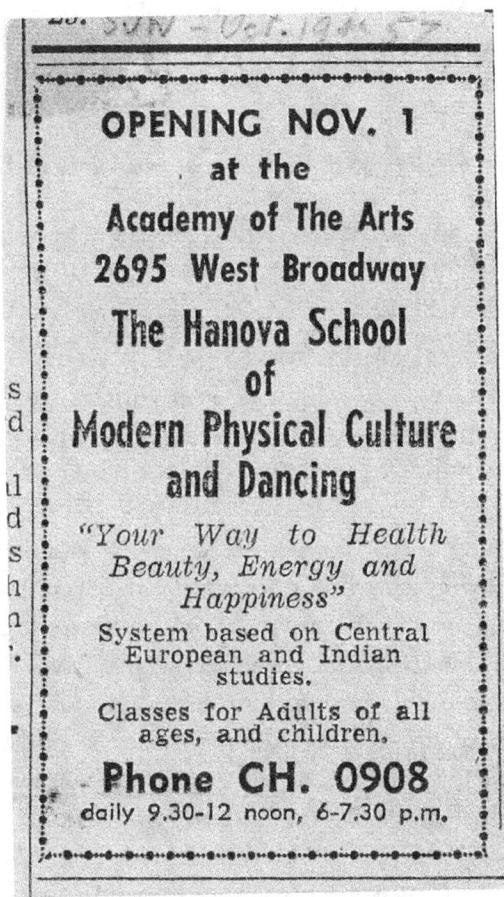

An advertisement for the opening of the Hanova School of Modern Physical Culture and Dancing in Vancouver dated October 19, 1957 in the Vancouver Sun.

Our Love Affair with Dance

After getting settled in an apartment in October, Magda was first hired to teach dance classes at the downtown Vancouver YWCA (Young Women's Christian Association). And while still teaching there, Magda opened the Hanova School of Modern Physical Culture and Dancing, on November 1, 1957 at 2695 West Broadway. Another press clipping from the Province newspaper also advertising the opening of the school proclaims:

> FROM LONDON, ENGLAND, Magda Hanova proudly announces the Opening of THE HANOVA SCHOOL OF MODERN PHYSICAL CULTURE and DANCING (acclaimed one of the leading studies in Great Britain and India) Our system is based on Central European and Indian Studies. A NEW WAY TO HEALTH, BEAUTY, ENERGY, SUCCESS & HAPPINESS.

Classes were offered to children and adults, and to beginners and advanced students, in modern creative dance, ballet technique, improvisations, yoga, and East Indian Dance from 9:30 to 12 noon and from 6 to 7:30 pm.

The first lecture demonstration Magda gave in Vancouver was at the YWCA for the Physical Health and Education Department, on April 17, 1958. She presented Study of Modern Gym, Study of Modern Movements to an Old Tune, and Study of Creative Dance with students from her YWCA classes.

> **Magda:** The Young Women's Christian Association in Vancouver is a haven for women to explore the arts. The programs offered are geared for women who wish to improve their mind and body and expand their artistic selves. My Canadian students are extremely open and interested in increasing the capacities of their whole selves through exercise and the modern creative dance. I am building a devoted following and my converts are embracing all that I share about the Terpsichorean arts. I know that Gerti will love Vancouver! I can tell from her letters that she is now serious about making a move, especially after I have painted such a glowing picture of the city. Finally! I can hardly wait for her to arrive!

Magda with dance students, Stanley Park, Spring 1958.

Magda: This land, this country, how beautiful and welcoming. I have a gorgeous beach and a large city park only a short bus ride away. I love to walk along the sea wall that extends part way around the park. There is a carefree atmosphere here in Vancouver that is quite different than any other town I have lived in. The city is cosmopolitan and everything is very new.

And this newness is not a bad thing. Social disparagements appear to be absent or at least muted when compared to India or Europe. Canada was a colony of Britain and has retained British ways, while somehow managing to achieve a unique identity with the influx of many different types of people from far and wide. This is a place where people from other places can flourish. This is a place where the dance will flourish.

Magda with dance students in Stanley Park, May 1958.

Magda: My dance students love to have our sessions outdoors. We attract so much positive attention and inquiries as to what we are doing. People in Vancouver do not appear to be familiar with yoga, or the Indian dance arts, rhythmic gymnastics, or modern dance. Seeing the enjoyment the members of the class are experiencing is the best advertisement and I have already had many new students sign up after watching the outdoor classes. The park is perfect for exercising and dancing with its wide expanses of grass and fresh sea air. We are embracing the environment with our bodies and souls.

Dancing Into New Horizon

Magda with her cat, Tamu, in the Province newspaper June 27, 1958.

On June 27, 1958, in the Province newspaper, Magda posed for a photograph with her cat, Tamu, which she had recently flown to Vancouver from London. The caption reads:

> Happy Pussy Tamu has joined mistress, Mrs. Magda Hanova, 1106 Gilford, after flying TCA from London, alone. The tortoise shell pussy was left behind with Mrs. Hanova's sister when Mrs. Hanova came here but now the sister is coming here to live. Tamu which is Swahili for "sweet" had to move, too. Mrs. Hanova thought a sea voyage and train trip would be too much for Tamu so bought the puss air passage instead.

Our Love Affair with Dance

The YWCA brochure for 1958. Magda in Vancouver, late 1950s.

Magda taught four classes for the 1958 winter program at the YWCA. In the brochure, Modern Gym, was described as "Exercises and interpretative movements for co-ordination, flexibility and agility accompanied by music." A Posture Class was described as: "Corrective exercises based on the findings of medical examination and individual posture conference." Modern Creative Dance was described as: "Techniques and compositions of modern dance under the leadership of Magda Hanova, from the Hanova School, London, England, Vienna, Austria, and Bombay, India, based on methods of Dalcroze, Wigman, Duncan, etc. Her fourth class was Rhythm and Dance for Teenagers and was described as: "Techniques of Modern Creative Dance under the leadership of Magda Hanova, from the Hanova School in London, England.

In late 1958, Gertrud finally decided to close the Hanova Dance School in London and join Magda in Vancouver. In letters, to persuade her, Magda had painted an attractive picture of Vancouver, describing the city as surrounded by magnificent mountains, beaches, and forests, and most importantly as a haven for artists of all kinds.

After Gertrud's arrival in the Fall, the Hanova sisters taught together at their new dance school on Broadway Street. Additionally, they continued to teach dance at the YWCA and for various school boards in the lower mainland of Vancouver until 1961. The sisters quickly established a following for their dance school through testimonials from their loyal YWCA students, through advertising in the local papers, and with the German and Jewish communities support. Their love of dance and gift for teaching immediately attracted many students who appreciated their innovative and original style. The Hanova sisters, in many conversations, expressed that moving to Vancouver was a wonderful new chapter in their lives. Gertrud and Magda conveyed that they were extremely happy to lead Canadians to a better understanding of the benefits of participating in dance culture.

Magda Hanova poses at the bar with Miss Doris Donaldson and Mrs. Berry McDonnel in The Vancouver Sun, October 25, 1958. The caption reads "Triple Threat to Markova, these three students make like prima ballerinas, enjoying every moment of interpretive dance course at the "Y" and achieve unique variations."

Magda: To dance is to live in the freedom of the body and the best way to really recognize and appreciate the dance is to dance. I am so enjoying teaching in Vancouver. And of course now more than ever because Gerti has arrived. She had some initial reservations about moving to Canada. I think she was uncertain at first as it is so far away from Europe. But now she has seen Vancouver for herself and experienced its beautiful landscapes and diverse population, she is quite happy to be here. I have to say, having her with me again is so comforting. Not that I am unable to get along alone. But now I feel complete. I once again have my close companion and sister near to share my thoughts and feelings. However, some things cannot be said in words and we leave these things to the studio where the dance can express our meaning in more complex and profound ways.

Also from the Vancouver Sun newspaper October 25, 1958, newly arrived from London, Gertrud shows a yoga stretch called the bat. The caption reads, "Three point landing is made by instructor Hanova to the envy of members of her Modern Dance group at YWCA. Modern dance and ballet are two favourite courses for those intent on improving their figures without having to do bend-down-sisters. Dancing is for fun as well as figure."

Gertrud: Well, who would have believed I would be living in North America and immediately embraced by so many wonderful new students. I am so in awe of all Magda has accomplished in such a short time. I am usually the one to forge ahead and be the catalyst for our fortunes but Magda has outdone me this time. I am thrilled to be in such a beautiful place, which is ripe with students, who are positively begging to explore all the things we know and wish to share in the dance.

Magda in a promotional portrait from the late 1950s.

In the YWCA Brochure for the Fall and Winter Programs 1959–60, Magda offered Modern Creative Dance and the unique Ballet for Mother and Child which she had made popular in London, England.

> **Magda:** Teaching at the YWCA has been a wonderful stepping stone to establish ourselves in this new city and garner students who wish to find themselves immersed in the Terpsichorean Arts. I am thrilled to lead this discovery of the Muse.

Our Love Affair with Dance

I am additionally excited to have re-established our Hanova School of Modern Physical Culture and Dancing here in Vancouver at the Academy of the Arts on Broadway Street.

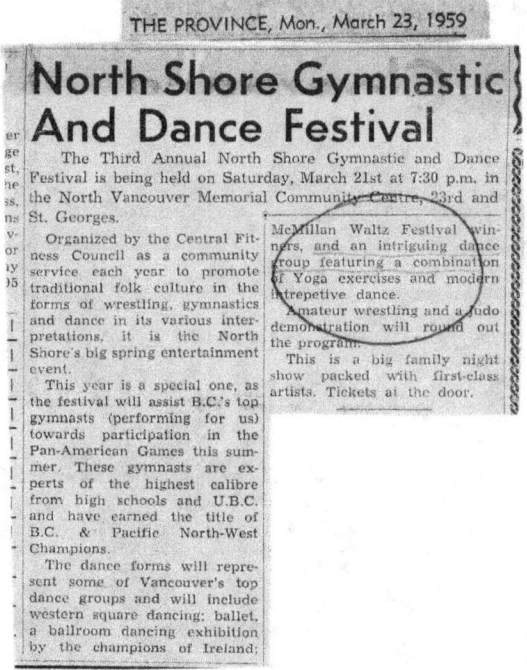

In the Province newspaper March 23, 1959, this article advertises the Third Annual North Shore Gymnastic and Dance Festival in which Hanova students took part. The Hanova School is mentioned as, "an intriguing dance group featuring a combination of Yoga exercises and modern interpretive dance."

Another article from March 1959 from The Citizen newspaper in North Vancouver, with the caption of "Annual Festival Saturday Night/ Gymnastic, Dance Display At Memorial Community Centre", advertises the Hanova sisters' participation.

Organized each year by the Central Fitness Council as a community service to promote the art form of bodily movement in its various interpretations, this year brings to the North Shore the Gertrude and Magda Hanov(er)a School of Modern Dance. The Hanovas studied in India and Central Europe before bringing their forms to BC. Their work shows strong eastern influence and Yoga exercises interwoven into their programs of imaginative dance which primarily is to permit and encourage free expression and interpretation on the part of the dancers.

An unknown Hanova student dancing outside, 1960s.

Gertrud: After arriving in Vancouver, I was immediately impressed with the connections Magda has formed with Vancouver organizations and cultural societies. We have recently presented or collaborated with The Tibetan Society of Vancouver, The German Canadian Cultural Society, and The Vancouver Ballet Society. All have been so welcoming.

At this time in our lives, we are no longer performing but put our energies into initiating others into the art of movement. Relinquishing being the artist seems to be easier for Magda. I have felt it as an unspeakable loss, a deep chasm, tied to aging and a woman's body being no longer what it was. There seems to be an unwritten rule that we are not to speak of this. I stay silent but mourn within, remembering the glory of the stage.

An unknown Hanova student poses in the studio, 1960s.

Through teaching their unique Hanova system, a mosaic of dance styles garnered while living in far away locations, the Hanova sisters attracted hundreds of students in Vancouver in the late 1950s and early 1960s. Their school stood out from other Vancouver dance schools because their pedagogy was so unlike what other dance schools offered.

The students who were drawn to the Hanova School were those who wished to discover 'something more' in the dance which the Hanova Dance School delivered to its dance disciples. The Hanova sisters consistently shared their philosophy that 'the dance' was more than just moving body parts but had transformative powers and underlying qualities that promoted not just physical health but deep and satisfying artistic merits that fed the mind, body, and spirit. Through classes that focused on exercises, kinetics, and creation, the Hanova sisters spread Rudolph Laban's message that dance is for everyone and should be part of humanities striving to experience the full spectrum of life and all it has to offer.

Magda: I am gratified to be presenting our work to the public through the support of The Vancouver Ballet Society. We have similar goals, as we both wish to educate the public about the benefits and joys of the dance. The modern creative dance, however, has different aims or outcomes from the ballet. Modern creative dance is open to all and does not demand a rigid curriculum, a perfect body type, weight, or height. At our school we have created a system that will enable anyone, young or old, male or female, a person in good health or poor health, to reach an individual satisfying level of expression through dancing. Our system opens the dancer to the fullest capacity of their being of which they are capable at that time.

Further, in educating the public, we wish to spread the message that if dance is to be elevated and valued to the same level as other art forms, to be appreciated as is music or visual art, this reverence must start with the education a child receives in the public school. From our observations and inquiries, the Canadian education system does not have a dance component in its physical education program. There are music and art specialist teachers, but the dance specialist seems nonexistent. In Europe, dance has consistently been recognized in the school system as a vital part of a rounded education.

If dance is to be seen as essential in the lives of a culture or society, essential as a crucial function that connects us to our bodies, and improves our physical, mental, and spiritual lives, dance must be seen as a necessity. This can only be achieved through offering dance to all children at school, much as the young child is given an opportunity to draw or paint, sing or play an instrument. Dance and the body, must also be given the opportunity to be valued. The body is often seen as only a vehicle to house our intellect, when in fact it is much more. The body is a unique means of individual expression and animation for artistic purposes.

THE VANCOUVER BALLET SOCIETY

presents

THE HANOVA SCHOOL
OF BODY SCULPTURE AND THE DANCE

PROGRAMME

May 18th, 1960, 8:15 p.m.   Oakridge Auditorium.

1. EXERCISES: Pat Carter   Berry Macdonnel

2. TECHNICAL STUDIES: Pat Carter   Bunty Clements
                                           Lorna Finlayson Karen Hulmose
                                           Nora Johnston   Berry Macdonnel
                                           Penny McMullen Marken Robertson

3. EXPLORATION OF MOVEMENT FORMS WITH PERCUSSION:
                                           Bunty Clements Karen Hulmose
                                           Nora Johnston   Marken Robertson

4. EXPERIMENTING WITH HAND PROPS:

   (a) With Bowl   Pat Carter   Lorna Finlayson
                                           Berry Macdonnel Penny McMullen

   (b) With Leaf   Penny McMullen

   (c) With Wood   Pat Carter

   (d) With Chain   Rolli

   (e) With Masks   Lorna Finlayson

   (f) With Net   Berry Macdonnel

5. THE DANCE:

   (a) Birthday Party   Barbara Frith, Lynda Frith, Vickie Heys

   (b) Improvisations   Barbara Frith, Lynda Frith, Vickie Heys

   (c) East Indian Dance   Berry Macdonnel   Rolli

                          - - - -

            Stage Assistants   -   J. Frith, H. Heys

Presented by the Vancouver Ballet Society, an evening of dance by the Hanova School of Body Sculpture and the Dance at the Oakridge Auditorium on May 18, 1960. Students presented Exercises, Technical Studies, An Exploration of Movement with Percussion, Experimenting with Hand Props, and dances Birthday Party and East Indian Dance, as well as Improvisations.

**In the new studio on Seymour Street,
an unknown student practices a yoga headstand.**

In the West Ender newspaper, August 31, 1960, the Hanova sisters announced that their school was moving to a new studio.

> Already well known in Vancouver, Magda and Gertrud have moved to a new studio at 543 Seymour St. Curriculum at the

Hanova School includes classes for all ages wanting expert guidance in exercising. The Hanova system does not pursue aimless slimming but stresses balanced body proportions, giving poise and elegance. Other branches in studies are "Creative" and "East Indian" dances, intended for students wanting to explore artistic development of movement and experiment in dance composition. Considerable attention is devoted to relationship of exercising and dancing, simulating children to acquire proper body control or develop their own artistry. Students work with great enthusiasm and all who have taken part in Hanova School stage performances have earned praise for artistic and technical balanced presentations.

Hanova students pose at Stanley Park, early 1960s.

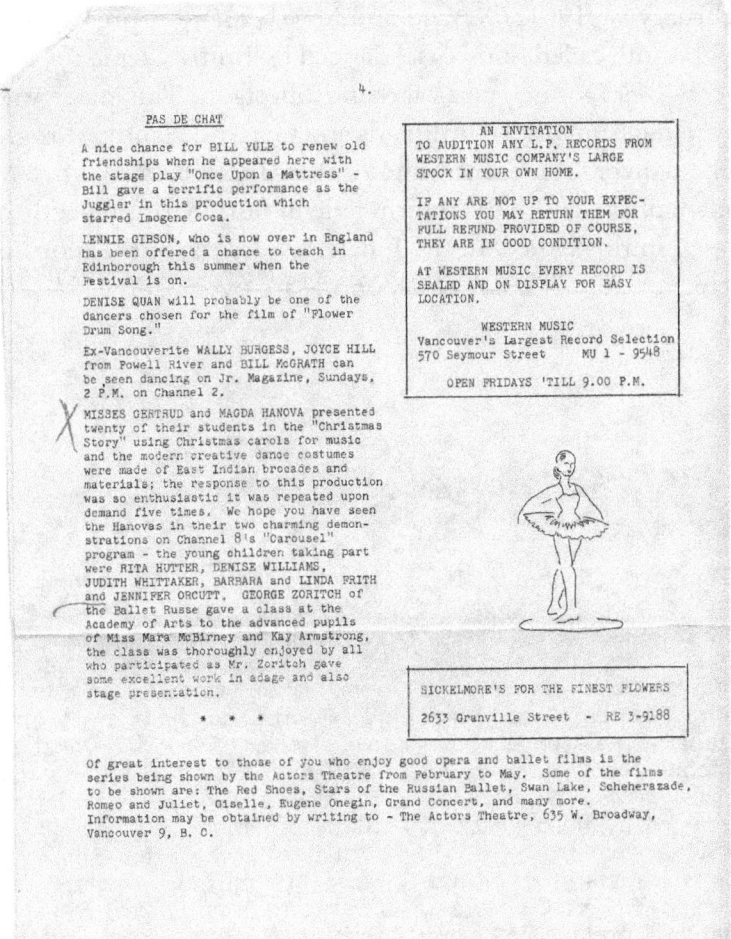

A page from the newsletter published by the authority of the Vancouver Ballet Society called The Ballet-Who dated January 1961, Volume 6, No. 5.

Misses Gertrud and Magda Hanova presented twenty of their students in the "Christmas Story" using Christmas carols for music and the modern creative dance costumes were made of East Indian brocades and materials; the response to this production was so enthusiastic it was repeated upon demand five times. We hope you have seen the Hanovas in their charming demonstrations on Channel 8's "Carousel" program—the young children taking part were Rita Hutter, Denise Williams, Judith Whittaker, Barbara and Linda Frith, and Jennifer Orcutt.

Our Love Affair with Dance

In February of 1961, Gertrud and Magda Hanova presented Creation, for a programme called Showcase, danced by Bunty Clements, Karen Hulmose, Berry MacDonnel, and Marken Robertson. This piece was accompanied by percussion played by Magda and Gertrud Hanova. Program notes state: "The dancers represent "The Ambassadors of a Creative Mind." In all arts, inspiration, and ideas intermingle in both harmony and confusion, as expressed in this dance. In the Finale the desire for the ultimate perfection is achieved and all lesser conceptions are overshadowed."

> **THE PROVINCE, Saturday, February 4, 1961**
>
> Total of 65 young B.C. dancers will take part in eight new ballets on Feb. 16 and 17 when the Vancouver Ballet Society presents its tenth "Showcase" at Queen Elizabeth Theatre.
>
> Included will be a ballet by Gweneth Lloyd, commissioned by the Society. It is "Arabesque".
>
> New ballets will be featured by Robert Calder and Eleanor Fairchild, Joy Camden, Gertrud and Magda Hanova, Kay Armstrong, Mara McBirney and Nickoali Svetlanoff.
>
> The Kay Armstrong ballet was done originally in the East and is now in the repertoire of the National Ballet Society.
>
> Orchestra will be under the direction of Carde Smalley. Tickets for Showcase are on sale at Queen Elizabeth Box Office, Dora Danns, 870 Howe and Sickelmores, 2633 Granville.

An article from the Province, February 4, 1961 advertising Showcase at the Queen Elizabeth Theatre, February 16 and 17, 1961. Presenting choreographers were well known Vancouver dance teachers Grace MacDonald, Gweneth Lloyd, Robert Calder and Eleanor Fairchild, Joy Camden, Kay Armstrong, Mara McBirney, Nickoali Svetlanoff, and Gertrud and Magda Hanova.

Magda: The deeper philosophy and purpose of the modern creative dance, especially here in Canada, requires a much wider platform. In essence, the modern creative dance is an art form which will allow anyone to explore themselves as a dancer. We are working to spread this message.

Dancing Into New Horizon

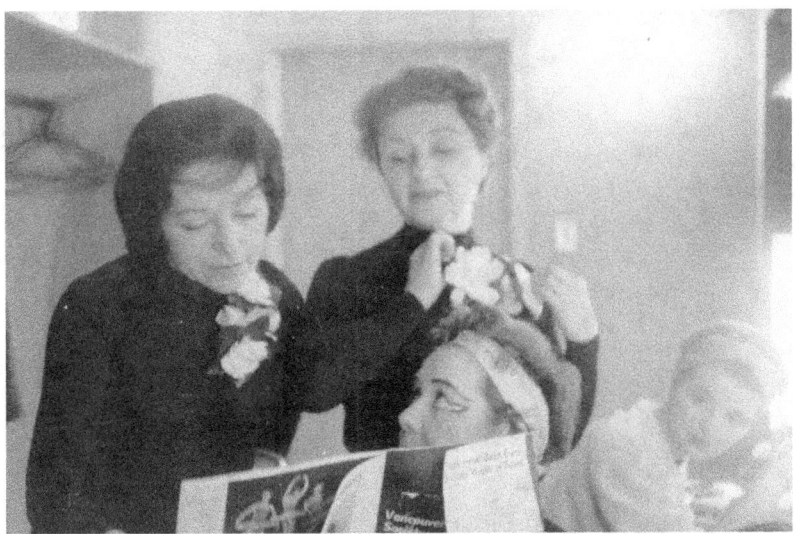

Magda and Gertrud with unknown dancers, preparing back stage for Showcase, February 1961, in which the Hanova sisters presented Creation.

Program cover for Showcase, sponsored by The Vancouver Ballet Society, February 16 and 17, 1961 at the Queen Elizabeth Theatre.

Our Love Affair with Dance

The West Ender newspaper from October 10, 1962 shows
Gertrud and students enjoying the dance outdoors at English Bay.

The caption reads, "Student Group of Hanova School enjoy themselves at English Bay. Gertrud and Magda Hanova, well known through lecture-demonstrations on TV, believe the well-being of the majority of people is benefited by the correct form of exercise, and that study of Creative dance, not restricted to professionals, can be most enjoyable for amateurs too, as the fulfillment of a long favoured ambition."

Gertrud: As we drive by English Bay, the blue expanse fills me up with divine remembrance of lost seascapes and beaches. So

Dancing Into New Horizon

Helga Strassman and Barbara Wall posing at English Bay, 1962.

with delight, Magda and I have found a modest penthouse apartment nearby English Bay and Stanley Park. The landscapes in the park are stunning and perfect backdrops for combining the dance with the natural configurations of the sea, rock, and forest. We are attentive to how the dancer may juxtapose so harmoniously with nature. The photographs we have produced are sensuous images that call to the viewer to experience the contrast of the human body set artfully against formations in the natural world. These visual representations preserve moments of motion, freeze its beauty, so we may ponder the expressive essence of our bodies. We are now enabled to see the body differently, no longer as pedestrian but something more which beckons us to rethink the body as only functional. We may now recognize the similarities of the body and the Earth, both possessing gentle and voluminous curves, continuous motion, sustained pulses and rhythms, and a solid but flowing core.

Our Love Affair with Dance

Helga Straussman posing in a Yoga headstand, Stanley Park, 1962.

Dancing Into New Horizon

Helga Straussman poses at Stanley Park, 1962.

Helga Straussman and Barbara Wall pose at Stanley Park, 1962.

Helga Straussman and Barbara Wall pose on the Stanley Park shore, 1962.

Magda: Moving to Canada has breathed new life into our teaching and we are told that no other dance school in Vancouver offers Dalcroze Eurhythmics, modern creative dance, Indian dance, or yoga. Vancouver has turned out to be a marvellous and welcoming place. Gerti and I have happily made connections with many other dance teachers and organizations that foster our same ideals about the dance arts. The Vancouver Ballet Society has been most supportive.

Of course, there are many ballet schools in Vancouver. The ballet will always be everywhere, as it should. However, the standard and technical achievement is extremely high for the ballet dancer and such a level of perfection very much limits who may and who may not dance. In opposition to the ballet, the modern creative dance is for anyone who wishes to partake. Gerti and I firmly believe as Laban professed that, "Everyone is a dancer." "Dance is for everyone." Vancouverites are drawn to this philosophy and we have established a wonderful group of fellow enthusiasts all over the city.

I ponder our past lives, in our youth Gerti and I both wholly embraced the ballet. I still love its grace and calibre. But for the dancer with nonprofessional aims, the person who wants to reclaim their body in the dance, our methods are much more welcoming and inclusive.

Hanova students enjoying dance classes outdoors.
Written on the back of the photograph, Marpole group, Vancouver, 1963.

Hanova students dancing outdoors.
Written on the back of the photograph, Dunbar group, Vancouver, 1963.

Gertrud at the window of their West End penthouse apartment on Chilco Street with the Hanova cat Tamu, May 1963.

Gertrud: I am looking out the window for Swoopsie. He or she, I can not be sure, is our friendly neighbourhood seagull. She comes regularly to our window sill and gets a bit of bread or fruit. We love to watch her movements. Her bobbing head and neck remind us of the movements of Indian dance. Alas, Tamu is sure to discourage Swoopsie from appearing.

Dancing Into New Horizon

Programme cover for Terpsichore and Siva, May 1963.

In this production, performed at the Queen Elizabeth Playhouse on May 4, 1963 and again on May 18, 1963, The Hanova Studio Group presented a program of Exercises, Technical Studies, and Dances. The main dance story was titled, The Caliph Stork.

The programme notes inform us:

The programme we are presenting consists of Occidental and Oriental dance forms taught at the Hanova Dance Studio.

Our Love Affair with Dance

Terpsichore, the Greek Muse of dance, and Siva, the Indian God of dance, symbolize the two aspects of our programme. The two directors of the Studio, Gertrud and Magda Hanova, have not only a thorough grounding in Modern Western Dance but have also acquired an intimate knowledge of East Indian Dance during a long residence in India.

In the first part, we show how the student of interpretative dance is trained to develop a feeling for movement, rhythm, and space. Beginning with simple exercises to achieve physical control and mental discipline the student is eventually given the basis of self-expression and aesthetic principles but also on personal thought and intuition. The individual dancer becomes part of the group, yet remains an individual. As the result of this form of guidance, dance presentations are the inspiration and expression of both the choreographer and the individual dancer. The second part of the programme is a ballet adapted from a fairy tale by William Hauff, using East Indian dance forms. The limitless possibilities for expression and communication in this form of dance are used to tell the story of The Caliph Stork.

The German Canadian Cultural Society

presents

The Hanova Studio Group

in a DANCE RECITAL in the QUEEN ELIZABETH PLAYHOUSE on MAY 4th, 8:30 p.m.

Terpsichore and Siva

The title indicates the close relation of occidental and oriental Dance - style shown in the Programme.

In the first Part CREATIVE DANCES will be presented.

The second part is "THE TALE OF CALIF STORK" a Dance-theatre in oriental style highlighted by magnificent Indian Costumes.

Tickets available at Vancouver Ticket Centre in the Q.E.T. (MU 3-3255), all Eaton Stores, Fraser Radio, T.V. Centre at 41st Avenue and East Boulevard - $2.00 - $1.50 - $1.00.

Programme cover for Terpsichore and Siva, presented by the German Canadian Cultural Society of Vancouver. The Caliph Stork tells the story of two friends, Casper and Pepper, who find a mysterious magical book filled with secrets. With its help they are able to fly on a magic carpet from Germany to a far away kingdom.

Dancing Into New Horizon

From The Vancouver Sun, Magda in Indian costume poses for an article. The caption reads. "Oriental influence on occidental dance forms will be shown by Magda and sister, Gertrude, in dance recital at Queen Elizabeth Playhouse, May 18, 1963."

Our Love Affair with Dance

Ballet theatre night

"TERPSICHORE AND SIVA" dance theatre night Saturday is being put on by German Canadian Cultural Society. Among those participating are Linda Hall, Evelyn Roth and Berry McDonell pictured with Mrs. H. F. Kastens. It will be performed at the QE Playhouse at 8:30.

From the Vancouver Sun. Photo and caption advertising Ballet Theatre Night. "Terpsichore and Siva" dance theatre night Saturday is being put on by German Canadian Cultural Society. Among those participating are Linda Hall, Evelyn Roth and Berry McDonnel pictured with Mrs. H.F. Kastens. It will be performed at the QE Playhouse at 8:30."

Gertrud: This production reminds me very much of the collaboration called The Golden Gate that was produced with our dear friend Menaka in Bombay so many years ago. In The Golden Gate we were striving to unite Western and Eastern dance forms to create an understanding of the universal nature of the dance. This production is similar in its underlying message but here we have created something entirely new for our Canadian student dancers that reflects their individual personalities and passions.

Dancing Into New Horizon

Evelyn Roth and Berry McDonnel in a pose from Terpsichore and Siva, 1963.
Note: Evelyn Roth (standing) became well known as an artist and
for her Moving Sculpture Company.

Our Love Affair with Dance

Magda: The multicultural nature of Vancouver is both refreshing and stimulating. In Vancouver the unfamiliar or foreign draws an audience as the people here seem to very much enjoy discovering new food, music, and happily for us, dance. We are presenting at the Fall Fair this November and the programme looks to be full of other engaging presentations, which we will be sure to view.

From The Vancouver Sun, November 25, 1963. The Hanova School took part in the International House fall fair. The caption reads, "Exotic entertainment from foreign lands will be part of International House fall fair Saturday at Brock Hall. Berry MacDonnel, manipuri dancer, Ana-Maria Valera, Philippine dancer, and Savithri Shankar, Indian folk singer, left to right, will lend their talents to international scene."

Dancing Into New Horizon

From old programme booklets, there is evidence that the Hanova Dance School also took part in the Annual British Columbia Dance Festivals held at Eric Hamber Secondary School in Vancouver throughout the 1960s.

Gertrud: Our school has entered several pieces in this year's Festival of Dance. But observing the dance works of the other schools has me question the nature of this competition. How can we say one dance is better than another? Some pieces touch one and others don't. Art is subjective. I ask myself what is the dance artist's task? To convey something pleasing in the dance work? Yes. But pleasing to whom? At the Hanova School we endeavour to assist the student to articulate their passions, feelings, beliefs, and inner truth through movement. Bringing this internal life to light as art for an audience is secondary.

From The Province newspaper, April 21, 1965.

Our Love Affair with Dance

The caption reads, "Festival of young dancers, Young dancers from many BC points have converged on Eric Hamber High School in Vancouver for the four-day BC Dance festival which opened Tuesday. Young ballerina Brenda Ashton, 11, of Vancouver, has admirer in Scott Harris, 5, of North Surrey. Below, Linda Frith, 12, of Vancouver practices her interpretive program. Festival has attracted hundreds of entries."

HANOVA WILL PRESENT
Modern Creative Dance
METRO THEATRE CENTER, 1370 S.W. MARINE DRIVE, VANCOUVER 12, B.C.
SUNDAY, MAY 30, 1965, 8.30 p.m.
A DANCE PERFORMANCE CALLED
"Oh, Sailor"
Will be preceded by a short lecture demonstration
Tickets available now: HANOVA STUDIO — PHONES: 685-5016 - 681-8088
Prices: $2.25, $1.50, $1.25, $1.00

Program advertisement from May 30, 1965 for the Metro Theatre performance of "Oh, Sailor".

The presentation of "Oh, Sailor" consisted of first a short lecture demonstration from which I include an excerpt which was voiced by Gertrud and directed by Magda.

> The dancers have been trained to undergo physical discipline through studies in technique and they have been encouraged to create set movements, keeping constantly in view that body and mind must be equally responsive so that creation is under complete physical command. With our guidance as choreographers we have formed and directed these free motivations into sequences of scenes, transforming imitative art into a creative one.

Second, the dance story "Oh, Sailor" was presented by The Hanova Studio Group. From the programme notes I include this description.

The story is itself the story of a sailor who had 'one too many'.

In this slightly dozy state he stumbles along the beach and his mind gets rather mixed up. He can no longer make out what is real and what is an illusion. From dawn till dawn again, many strange things happen. It is not only that people appear on the beach but also the Greek God Poseidon, mermaids, and many more mystical figures of the sea. At midnight a ghost-ship arises from the bottom of the sea and ghosts chase each other around. When the sun at last rises again, he wonders whether all he saw was an apparition or what was it? That question will be answered in "Oh, Sailor!"

Recreating a dance from "Oh, Sailor" on the Vancouver shore, 1965. Berry MacDonnel, Bunty Clements, and Sonja Christjansen.

Gertrud: "Oh, Sailor" was a unique performance. So many original pieces were choreographed to the amusing story line. We garnered inspiration from our beach walks, our local seagulls, and our students contributed their individual ideas and movements to each scene. Each dancer had a special role created for them. This production was quite successful in highlighting the individual dancer's abilities and personalities. Berry was an exceptional 'sailor'. Dancing as if inebriated was challenging, but she made her role humorous without over acting and her movements retained grace and fluidity. She was able to make the audience sympathetic to the sailor's perils and imperfections.

At the Seymour Street studio, an unknown Hanova student at the barre, 1960s.

The last public performance of 1965 was a studio performance on November 26th and 27th. The programme included a demonstration of body sculpture exercises in which each student demonstrated a yoga exercise, technical studies, which included a demonstration of Laban's movement qualities, and guided improvisations, which included percussion instruments, and impressions and expressions of tragedy and comedy. Creative dance compositions included the students own choices of theme and choreography. Titles of the pieces were The Tree, Construction, Clotho, Awakening, The Beach at Night, The Snail, The Necklace, and Old Elephant. The last part of this studio performance were excerpts from "Oh, Sailor".

And so we arrive at the point in time in which I started as a student at the Hanova studio. The sisters' artistic and inspiring life stories have been told, except for the last chapter of their lives.

9

COMING FULL CIRCLE WITH TERPSICHORE

Gertrud and Magda hosting a gathering for their students on the roof of their Penthouse apartment, 1990.

The Hanova sisters, from 1957 on, once again, created new lives for themselves in Vancouver, never looking back. Throughout their time in Canada, the sisters frequently visited Europe in the summer months but on returning to Vancouver said they were very happy to live in Canada and be Canadians. Magda and Gertrud emphasized that they felt strongly that Canada had been welcoming and generous to them. They enjoyed their West End apartment, English Bay, and living by Stanley Park. The sisters appreciated their students and often had gatherings on the deck of their penthouse apartment. They were hospitable hostesses and an invitation to their gatherings was prized. As the 1990s progressed, teaching dance remained at the centre of Magda and Gertrud's lives. Magda drove them in their Austin Mini to classes until she was 85 and then unfortunately had a minor fender bender and had her license taken away. Then they travelled by public transport or got a ride from a student. The sisters continued to create new choreography with their young and old disciples. The dance at the Hanova School retained its ageless quality concentrating on creating beauty and satisfying the deep artistic and individual needs of each student.

Astrid Fischer-Credo at The Creative Space studio, on 27th and Dunbar, early 1990s.

Astrid Fischer-Credo, Magda and Gertrud, September 23, 1990.

Magda was also an artist and illustrated several books, 1991.

An illustration from 'She and Lucifer' titled
Goodbye Until We Meet Again by Magda Hanova.

Congratulatory flowers for Gertrud and Magda after a studio performance
at The Creative Space on Dunbar and 27th, June 1991.

Coming Full Circle with Terpsichore

**Magda and Gertrud at their West End apartment.
December 23, 1991, Magda's birthday.**

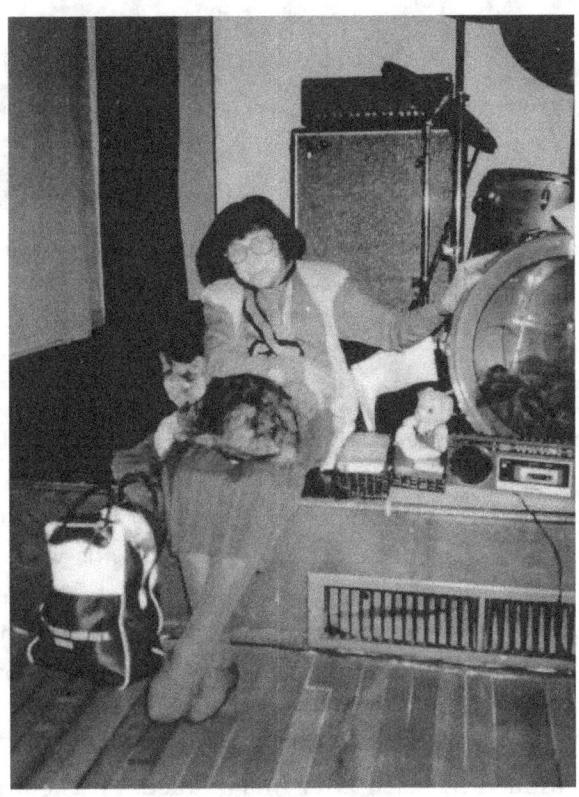

Magda at The Creative Space Studio, early 1992.

Very sadly, Magda, passed away without warning, from a stroke on March 25, 1992. I remember a few months earlier being asked to go to pick up a prescription for her with her identification, which had her birth date on it. That was the first time I knew exactly how old the sisters were. They had both been very private about their ages. I saw that Magda was born in 1905 which made her 87. From what they had related, I knew Gertrud was two years older, which made her about 89.

Gertrud at the Creative Space studio demonstrating a yoga pose, 1995. In this picture she is 92 years old.

Gertrud: Magda, has not really left me. She is here and will always be here. There will be no funeral, no memorial, or bidding of adieu. I am leaving everything in her room as it is and will believe she is in her bed asleep, waiting for me to call her to breakfast. Although this is too sad, as Magda was the cook and she was always the one to call me to breakfast every morning. I will have to carry on and I will rely on our memories of a life well lived together. I will be strong and courageous. I will mourn in private.

Gertrud continued to teach after Magda died. She kept a loyal following of senior students and several students that took private classes which included myself. I would pick her up from her West End apartment and drive over to the Dunbar area to the Creative Space studio for my weekly lesson. We became closer friends. Despite her age, Gertrud kept her edge and strong opinions. I noticed she was becoming frailer, but she was still quite capable of teaching. I enjoyed all of the classes over these years. We focused on reviving pieces from the sisters' early repertoire or pieces I had danced many years earlier, as well as creating new choreography.

After Magda died, Gertrud continued to have studio lecture demonstration performances. Her seniors' Wednesday group demonstrated exercise routines, as well as showing 'at the barre' sequences. Gertrud and I presented several innovative exercise dance studies such as Exercises for the Back with music by Mark Knofler, Exercises for the Stomach with music by Janacek, and Etude, a study of kinetics with music by Enya.

Reanimating and recreating pieces from the sisters' past collection of work was gratifying such as Largo (formerly Studie) with music by Handel.

Karen (Wenn) Kurnaedy in Largo, 1990s.

Despite now being in her nineties, Gertrud remained prolific and fresh in her choreographic ideas and we always worked on new choreography at each class. We choreographed I Won't Forget You which was a tribute to Magda set to Debussy's Claire de Lune in 1994. Also Guardian Angel, in which I constructed wings and a medieval dress with a halo, Now and Then a flapper piece with 1920s music and steps at the barre, and Nocturne: A Dance to the Night and the Moon with music by Chopin's Nocturne Op. 48, No. 1 in C Minor in 1995.

Gertrud assists with the costume for Nocturne at the Creative Space Studio.

There was always a good audience turnout for these performances and Gertrud still enjoyed sharing her vast experiences and knowledge of the dance with her lecture demonstration model before the set programme.

Coming Full Circle with Terpsichore

**Karen (Wenn) Kurnaedy in The Garden. 1990s.
Choreography by Gertrud and Magda Hanova.**

The Garden was a revival of an old work I had danced from 1975. This dance was a blend of Indian dance styles, Manipuri, Bharatanatyam, and Kathakali which the Hanova sisters had studied in India. The music was from an Andre Previn/Ravi Shankar collaboration, entitled East Meets West. The Garden was based on a beautiful poem by the famous Indian poet Rabindranath Tagore (1979, 2005).

> Hidden deep in the heart of things,
> Thou carest for growth and life:
> The seed becomes shoot, the bud a blossom,
> The flower becomes fruit.
> Tired I slept on my idle bed
> in the illusion that the work had an end.
> In the morning I awoke to find
> That my garden was full of flowers.

For this dance, I wore an Indian costume from the Hanova treasure chest of mementos, which included traditional jingling ankle bells. Gertrud told me the skirt had belonged to Menaka, the famous Indian dancer and close friend of the sisters in Bombay. The beautiful skirt was made of many meters of silk fabric which billowed out in a wonderful swirl when I turned or spun. I also wore a colourful top or choli, and a long piece of sari fabric over my head, secured with many pins.

Gertrud: As the dance begins, I listen to the sound of a languid and stirring flute melody entice and draw each gesture from the dancer's body. As she recites the poem, her hands form a seed, which transforms into a bud, then a blossom. She marvels as she creates a glorious lotus flower with fingers and palms.

The dancer then sinks to the floor to convey an exhaustion that emanates from being tired of living and succumbs to sleep. In her rest, the garden rejuvenates her spirits and she awakens, refreshed. She is stopped in this moment to see her garden has bloomed in full to reveal the creations of Brahma, himself.

Now, the music transitions into a much faster tempo and the dancer performs intricate, synchronized foot and hand movements. She simultaneously jumps onto both feet, which prompts the bells to jingle loudly. She quickly turns, squats, and rises, and then travels across the space on toes that fly. The dance is a blur of motion, stamps, and deliberate poses and pauses. The piece ends with a continuous turning, which gradually gains momentum until she is spinning in a flurry of orange silk, her skirt blooming around her as a flower in the garden.

Karen and Gertrud after a performance of Guardian Angel, performed to traditional English Harp, 1995.

Learn, too, how God's own angels keep
Your ways by day,
Your dreams asleep.
Traditional

Gertrud: I am still actively creating. Artistic inspiration cannot be forced, it arises spontaneously, somehow from the depths of a person's inner self. However, what one has to say in the dance can be encouraged or stimulated. I find innovation, a vision of what can be, to come from a combination of the student's imaginative movement and my own experiences. Observing improvisations by the student leads to seeing original steps and stirrings that we can remember and repeat and keep for the composition. My instructions to perform with solid technique and proper execution are always included.

Karen (Wenn) Kurnaedy, at The Creative Space studio, 1990s.

Gertrud: Life goes on with the dance. I continue to choreograph and guide students at the studio. The urge to create is still present. Discovering oneself in the dance is an ever unravelling process. Never done. The dancer, even at my age, always has much to fathom and recognize about oneself, which will inform their dance art. Working closely with my students, I enjoy bringing to light that certain magical something. This will never be finished for me. Designing, shaping, and finding the unity of a work is still exhilarating. Building on a sequence of movements until a whole is conceived has retained its mystery and still holds a remarkable satisfaction. Then comes the analysis of the almost finished work and like a piece of writing there is editing to be done. Does this transition work? Is there a clear beginning, middle, and end? Have I adhered to the principles of the dance? Is there variety, contrast, harmony, and have I created something for the audience that has unity? Here, I mean unity of form, idea, and understanding. Although understanding is subject to much individual interpretation. Nevertheless, I am always working towards creating a work that is a combination of the expression of the dancer's inner world and of the choreographer's vision.

Karen Wenn (Kurnaedy) with Gertrud at the India Gate restaurant in Vancouver. Gertrud always retained her love of Indian food, 1990s.

Gertrud taught dance to devoted students until she was 97. In her last years she continued to live alone in her West End apartment surrounded by the paintings and photographs that spoke of the wonderful life she and Magda had led dancing around the world. Gertrud passed away in 2002 at the age of 99.

Our Love Affair with Dance

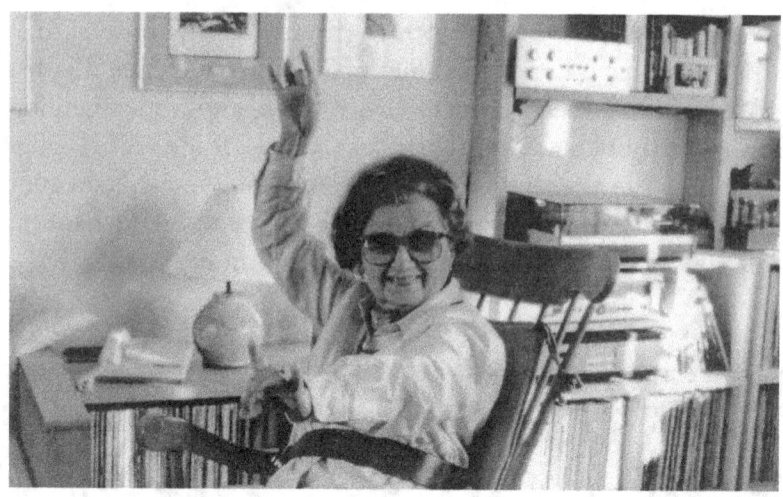

Gertrud at her apartment showing Indian mudras (hand gestures), 1999.

After Gertrud passed away, I taught the Hanova system of modern dance in my community of Port Coquitlam through Continuing Education. During my teaching career in the public school, I also continuously taught dance using the Hanova system and gradually expanded and increased the role of dance in my daily classroom experiences, knowing with deep conviction that children need to move and explore with their bodies frequently. I connected the need to move and dance to my own experiences as a child at the Hanova Dance School and realized I was sharing a fundamental element of our humanity that is often overlooked in our Canadian school system and culture. In my teaching practice, dance was a way to foster the presence of joy and bring forth the vitality all children seem to possess.

I will always be grateful that it was my destiny to meet and study with Magda and Gertrud Hahn. They were significant mentors and under their guidance I developed a lifelong appreciation for dance and choreography. I have been deeply inspired by their teaching and friendship.

Throughout the years, I have created dance photographs, which captured the surrounding beauty of British Columbia. Of course, the Hanova sisters were my role models for these outdoor pictures. I will never forget the wall of photos at the top of the stairs at their studio on Seymour Street. I realize now these photographs, so prominently displayed, were a way for the sisters to share and remember the beautiful essence of their past dance experiences.

The camera is sometimes able to capture an image, which represents a true reflection of the dancer's feelings and perceptions while dancing. The dance is after all realized in fleeting moments, seconds of space and time, in which the connections we are making while moving are snatches of radiance. Photographs allow us to recollect and hold close these moments. I have a deep gratitude and appreciation for being entrusted with so many Hanova photographs and memorabilia to commemorate their lives so vividly.

Karen Kurnaedy in I Will Never Forget You. A tribute to Magda Hanova, Victoria, British Columbia mud flats, 1994. Photo by Lynn Onley Bertram.

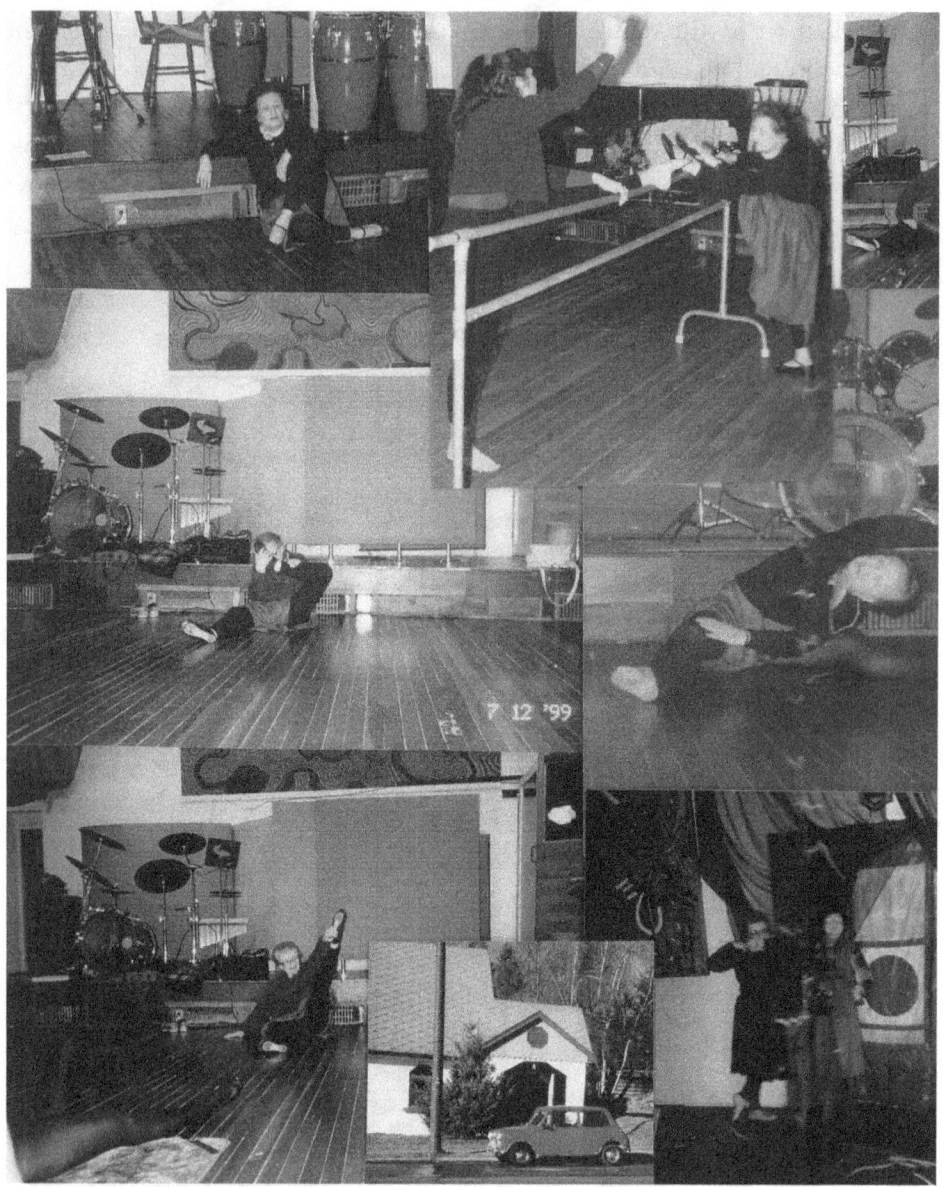

Photo collage from Gertrud's memorial 2002. Credit to Talya Frith.

In this photo collage given out at Gertrud's farewell memorial, Gertrud demonstrates yoga and dance positions at the Creative Space studio in 1999. Even at 97 years old she was still supple and flexible. The Hanova red Austin Mini is also nostalgically pictured in a photo, bottom right.

CONCLUSION

Little writing about the Hanova sisters and their work exists in the public record. However, their presence was not entirely unnoticed, as is evidenced by a short passage about the Hanova sisters from Max Wyman's Notebook in the Vancouver Sun newspaper. Wyman was a well-known arts critic in Vancouver for the Vancouver Sun for over twenty years. This article was written in the spring of 1992 shortly after Magda died. Wyman pays tribute to the Hanova sisters as having been among the first to bring modern dance to Vancouver. He states:

> They were never the kind of women likely to become light-headed with the oxygen of self-generated publicity; so it is no surprise that few people outside a small circle of friends and admirers today know the significance of Magda and Gertrud Hanova in the story of the development of dance in Vancouver. They never had a company to call their own, and the warm glow of limelight shone most brightly on those who came after them. But Magda and Gertrud Hanova can legitimately be claimed as the first to give this city serious exposure to modern dance. The mix of influences that became the particular style that they taught spanned several continents and radically different movement philosophies, establishing them as adventurous precursors of the young choreographic experimenters and seekers of today.

Wyman goes on to relate details of the sisters' lives in Europe and India before discussing their impact on the Vancouver modern dance scene. He continues with:

> In 1961 they competed against Norbert Vesak, the city's only other practitioner of serious modern dance, for a spot on the Vancouver Ballet Society's Showcase programme. They won with a work called Creation—described by adjudicator Arnold

Spohr at the BC Dance festival that summer "as a very interesting work... depth in mood and expression... unique.

Creation, a work performed for the Vancouver Ballet Society's Showcase, 1961.

Wyman (1992) ends his article by remarking that, "The newer trends in modern dance that developed in the 1960s and 1970s largely passed them by. But they always retained their integrity as creative artists."

As I remember the Hanova School, Wyman was right, the Hanova sisters never changed their core dance values and what they believed and to which they remained committed. Trends came and went and still students danced at the Hanova studio discovering modern creative dance, Isadora, Dalcroze Eurhythmics, Rudolph Laban, Mary Wigman, the ballet, Indian dance and yoga. Each student was encouraged in the expression of his or her personal vision of dance, with an underlay of inspiring Hanova principles, to discover the vitality and essence of his or her own dancer within.

The Hanova sisters were rock steady in their belief that dance:

> "The goal of what is referred to as the "Wigman revolt" was clearly not to offer mere dance classes; the goal was to enact a cultural revolution through dance, by which all people could experience a more embodied, expressive, and free life-style." (Sorell, 1969, p. 231)

Further, the work of the Hanova sisters reflected Wigman's understanding that, "Only if the dance is kept, by the artist and by the spectator and lay participator, approachable and universal can it fulfill its promise as a delight and as a vital force in life today" (Sorell, 1969, p. 233). The Hanova sisters in their love for dance and in their quest to encourage all to be dancers are worthy to be remembered as pioneers in the Vancouver modern dance community.

I note that I was one of hundreds of students whom the Hanova sisters influenced and encouraged to dance in Vancouver from 1957 until the year 2000. I find it edifying that when they first moved to Vancouver they were both in their late fifties, but they were not hindered by their age or that they did not know anyone in Vancouver. Failure did not enter into their thinking. They confidently set up a school offering what was then very exotic and unusual dance lessons for the Vancouver of 1957. And students who were hungry for that deeper 'something' in the dance recognized immediately that the Hanova sisters' philosophy and teaching style offered dance that honoured the spirit and the body.

The Hanova dance school was important because although Vancouver had many dance schools, none offered anything like the Hanova sisters' blend of dance experiences, which stemmed from the masters of dance they had studied with in Europe and India. The sisters focused on accessing and addressing their dance student's yearning to discover themselves. Their school provided a community for fellow believers.

In Hanova classes, discussion of the roots and philosophy of modern dance was often visited and the spirit of Isadora Duncan was a tangible presence in the Hanova studio in that a palpable passion for expression was invariably in the air. Their classes were always stimulating and productive. When you left a Hanova lesson, especially after the improvisations at the end, you always felt vital and energized and sorry the class was over. And after the session, in the changing area, cheeks flushed and glowing and feeling slightly out of breath, we would look into each other's eyes and smile. A smile that conveyed wordlessly our mutual pleasure and how much we had enjoyed our dancing experience with the Hanova sisters that day.

Magda, joyfully taught dance students in Vancouver for thirty-five years and Gertrud for forty years. Looking back at the lives they led in Vancouver, the sisters' have left a clear record of two women who utterly committed themselves to their Muse. Their example continues to inspire me. The Hanova sisters' lives stand as a testament that the possibilities for our existence are opened up and multiplied with the dance. The moving body has much to teach us.

To briefly summarize and close, in this book I examined a specific dance history which took place in Vancouver, British Columbia between 1957 and the year 2002, in order to share a retrospective of the work of Magda and Gertrud Hahn, which was ground breaking and innovative for its time. The Hanova sisters bringing their unique modern dance pedagogy to Vancouver brought a new global perspective to an emerging Vancouver dance community in the late 1950s and was formative throughout the 1960s, 1970s, 1980s, and 1990s for many Vancouver dancers.

This work also explored a unique historical perspective of the formation of early 20th century dance in Europe, told through the lives of two dance artists, who lived through extraordinary times and survived many challenges. Through reading about the Hanova sister's formative dance experiences in Bohemia, Vienna, Paris, Berlin, and Dresden, we catch sight of the roots and formation of the modern dance we enjoy today. Further, as the Hanova sisters fled to Bombay, India to avoid persecution and war, we discover a fascinating period in the history and revival of classical Indian dance. Finally, the Hanova sisters, in moving to post war London, England, reveal another aspect of dance history and pedagogy through their study with Rudolph Laban and Sigurd Leeder.

Although the world has changed tremendously since the sisters studied dance as young women, there remain many salient lessons to ponder from their notable pedagogy. The Hanovas' central message, that was learned and echoed from dance theorists and dance masters the world over, is that dance culture is for everyone and the dance will always remain a vibrant and crucial connection to our humanity. The Hanova sisters created their own unique theology of the body. The sisters' dance pedagogy was a vital revelation for dancers who wished to discover themselves through dancing.

Dance was at the heart of the Hanova sisters' lives and their life raft as they traversed the world. Becoming dance artists and dance teachers enabled the Hanova sisters to transcend the traditional roles of marriage and child bearing set out for women. They instead created lives that focused on fulfillment through artistic experiences. The sisters were models of women living lives that matter. What they stood for is timeless and a vital message for today.

How do we measure what the sisters gifted to their many students worldwide over the years? I don't think you can measure inspiration or the sacred sense of being that dancers receive while dancing.

Conclusion

Karen dancing on Hornby Island, 1996.

The dance breaks down the distinctions of body and soul… The body, which in ecstasy is conquered and forgotten and which becomes merely a receptacle for the superhuman power of the soul, and the soul, which achieves happiness and bliss in the accelerated movements of a body freed of its own weight; the need to dance, because an effervescent zest for life forces the limbs from sloth, and the desire to dance, because the dancer gains magic powers, which bring him victory, health, life, a mystic tie binding the tribe when it joins hands in the choral dance, and the unconstrained dance. (Sachs, 1937, pp. 3–4)

Magda Hahn 1905–1992.

Magda: Leaving my Gerti alone is so difficult. She needs me to give her balance, to banish her pessimism. But I know her so well. She has backbone, my sister. She will go on with our passion and enjoy what there is in life to enjoy. I realize she will miss me terribly. But passing on to the next stage of my existence must happen. Our time in India taught me this. There is an inevitable cycle of life. We are all bound to creation, preservation, and destruction and cannot escape it. Siva, Lord of the Dance, is the destroyer and regenerator, dancing the cosmic dance of the universe. I have embraced my partnership in this dance and have a veneration for the way life unfolds. I will follow the will of the universe with Terpsichore by my side and take my final steps in the Dance, hoping to be remembered with love and for all that I contributed to making life more beautiful by dancing.

Conclusion

Gertrud Hahn 1903–2002.

Gertrud: I am now ninety-nine, who would have thought. I cannot believe I have survived my dearest sister, Magda, by ten years. There was a birthday party for me recently. I just sat in my chair, eyes down, seeming perhaps unaware of my surroundings or all the people that came to wish me well. Truthfully, I was most pleased that I had managed to get my hair coloured for the event. My long time hair dresser, Henri, graciously came to the apartment so I didn't have to manage the stairs. He is marvellous. Even at my age, I wanted to look my very best.

And now, I shrug my shoulders and give a little thrust of my chin in the European way to suggest I accept my age. So ist das Leben. C'est la vie. Actually, it is an awful thing to be no longer very mobile. To not be able to dance. I know the time will soon come for my last curtain call. I will say Auf Wiedersehen and give a lovely small bow, even a curtsy. But this old me, in this old body, is not how I want to be remembered at all. On the contrary, I wish to be remembered as that young spirited dancer I was in Karlsbad so long ago. She had fire, was bold, and knew no boundaries. Her happiness was being on a stage, dancing with fervour. And if she had the second sight, would she still have done all I have done? Ja, Ja, Ja! No regrets at all. I can still recall the many glorious dancers I have known throughout my life. I, too, just want someone to think of me after I'm gone and say, "I knew her, I will miss her. She was a wonderful dancer! I will remember her…

REFERENCES

Abbey, S. (Ed.) (2002). *Ways of knowing in and through the body: Diverse perspectives on embodiment.* Welland, ON: Soleil Press.

Adler, J. (2002). *Offering from the conscious body: The discipline of authentic movement.* Rochester: Inner Traditions.

Ambrose, K. (1951). *Classical Dances and Costumes of India.* London.

Beardsley, M. (1984). What is going on in dance? In Sheets-Johnstone M. (Ed.) (1984) *Illuminating dance: Philosophical explorations.* Bucknell University Press.

Bode, R. (1922). *Ausdrucksgymnastik.* Munchen: C.H. Beck.

Bergin, T.P. (1975). Introduction to the conversation. In *Why move? A conversation about dance with bella lewitzky.* San Francisco: Chandler & Sharp Publishers, Inc.

Coe, D., Strachan, J. (2002). *Writing dance: Tensions in researching movement or aesthetic experiences.* Qualitative Studies in Education, 15, (5) 497–511, (2002)

Collingwood, R. G., (1938). *The principles of art.* Oxford University Press.

De la Tour, E. (1970). In Haberman, M., Meisel T.G. (Eds.) *Dance: An art in academe.* New York: Teachers College Press.

De Mille, A. (1991). *Martha: The life and work of martha graham. A biography.* New York: Random House.

Duncan, I. (1937, 1970). *The technique of isadora duncan.* A Dance Horizons Republication.

Duncan, I. (1928). The dancer of the future. In *The art of the dance.* New York: Theatre Arts Books. Written c. 1902 and first published 1928.

Duncan, I. (1928). *My life.* London: The Camelot Press Ltd.

Finley, S. (2008). Arts-based research. In Knowles, G. & Cole, A. (Ed.) *The handbook of the arts in qualitative inquiry: Perspectives, methodologies, examples and issues.* NY: Sage.

Florida Center for Instructional Technology, "The Rise of the Nazi Party", *A Teacher's Guide to the Holocaust.* http://fcit.usf.edu/holocaust/. 8 November 2019.

Fraleigh, S.H., (1987). *Dance and the lived body: A descriptive aesthetics.* University of Pittsburgh Press.

Fraleigh, S. H. (1998). *A vulnerable glance: Seeing dance through phenomenology.* In Carter, A. (Ed.) Routledge Dance Studies Reader. UK: Routledge.

Fraleigh, S. (1998). *Good intentions and dancing moments: Agency, freedom, and self knowledge in dance.* Emery cognition project with the Mellon Foundation, Colloquium on the Self, Emery University, Atlanta, Georgia, 5 May. 1989.

Fraleigh, S. H. (2004). *Dancing identity: Metaphysics in motion.* University of Pittsburgh Press.

Gandhi, M. (1964). The collected works of mahatma gandhi. Volume XII, April 1913 to December 1914. The Publications Division, Ministry of Information and Broadcasting, Government of India. *Collected Works of Mahatma Gandhi* at gandhiheritageportal.org.

Graham, M. (1991). *Blood memory.* New York: Doubleday.

Hackney, P. (2002). *Making connections: Total body integration through bartenieff fundamentals.* Great Britain: Routledge.

Halprin, A. (1969). Intuition and improvisation. In M.Van Tuyl (Ed.), *Anthology of impulse: annual of contemporary dance.* New York: Dance Horizons Incorporated.

Halprin, A. (1995). *Moving towards life: Five decades of transformational dance.* Wesleyan University Press.

Halprin, A. (2000). *Dance as a healing art: Returning to health with movement and imagery.* USA: LifeRhythm Energy Field.

Hartley, L. (1989, 1995). *Wisdom of the body moving: An introduction to body-mind centering.* Berkeley, California: North Atlantic Books.

Hawkins, A.M. (1964). *Creating through dance.* Prentice-Hall, Inc.

Hawkins, E. (1992). *The body is a clear place and other statements on dance.* Pennington, NJ: Princeton Book Company, Publisher.

H'Doubler, M. (1940). *Dance: A creative art experience.* The University of Wisconsin Press.

Hesse, H. (2008). *Poems: Selected and translated by j. wright.* Farrer, Straus and Giroux Paperbacks.

Holm, H. (1951, 1992). The mary wigman I know. In Sorell, W. (Ed.) *Dance has many faces.* a cappella books.

Homans, J. (2010). *Apollos' angels: A history of ballet.* New York: Random House Trade Paperbacks.

Howe, D. (2000). Mary wigman: One artist's definition of dance. In L.Y. Overby & J.H. Humphrey (Eds.) *Dance: Current selected research, Volume*

4. New York: AMS Press.

Humphrey, D. (1951, 1992). Dance drama. In Sorell, W. (Ed.) *Dance has many faces*. a cappella books.

Irwin, R. (2007). Plumbing the depths of being fully alive. In Liora Bresler (Ed.), *International handbook on research in arts education*. Dordrecht: Springer.

Irwin, R., de Cosson, A. (Eds.) (2009). *a/r/tography rendering self through arts-based living inquiry*. Vancouver, Canada: Pacific Educational Press.

Jacques-Dalcroze, E. (1924). The technique of moving plastic. *The Musical Quarterly*, Volume X, Issue1, 1January 1924, Pages 21–38, https://doi.org/10.1093/mq/X.1.21

Jacques-Dalcroze, E. (1925). Eurhythmics and art. In *Eurhythmics Art & Education*. (1930). London: Chatto & Windus.

Jacques-Dalcroze, E. (1930). *Eurhythmics art & education*. London: Chatto & Windus.

Jarvis, J. (2005) The wigman school. *Dance Collection Danse*. http://www.dcd.ca/exhibitions/jarvis/wigmanschool.html

Jsenfels, P., Herion, I. (1927). *Getanzte harmonien*. Stuttgart: Verlegt Bei Dieck & Co.

Joshi, D. (1989). Madame menaka. New Delhi: *Sangeet Natak Akademi*. Sar.sagepub.com/cgi/reprint/27/1/25.pdf

Joshi, K. (2012). Giants who awakened indian dance. *Culture Magazine*, April/May/June 2012.

Khokar, A.M. (2011). The role and contribution of pioneering gurus and foreigners in the revival of classical Indian dances (1900s–50s). *The Dance History Column*. www.narthaki.com

Krueger, M. "Nudity in Germany: Here's the Naked Truth". *CNN Travel*, https://www.cnn.com/travel/article/naked-germany/index.html. 1 December 2018.

Kuruvachira, J. (2004). *Religious experience: Buddhist, christian, and hindu: A critical study of ninian smart's philosophical interpretation of the numinous and mystical*. New Delhi: Intercultural Publications.

Laban, R. (1976). *Modern educational dance*. London: McDonald & Evans.

Laban, R. (1975). Ullman, L. (translator) *Life for dance: The autobiography of rudolph laban*. Princeton Book Co.

Laban, R. (1951, 1992). Educational and therapeutic value of the dance. In Sorell, W. (Ed.) *Dance has many faces*. a cappella books.

Leavy, P. (2009). *Method meets art: Art-based research practice*. The Guildford

Press.

Lee, J. (1994). *Writing from the body: For writers, artists, and dreamers who long to free their voice.* New York; St. Martin's Press.

Lewitsky, B. (1975). (Interview by Yvonne McClung). In *Why move? A conversation about dance with bella lewitzky.* San Francisco: Chandler & Sharp Publishers, Inc.

Manning, Susan (1993) *Ecstasy and the demon: Feminism and nationalism in the dances of mary wigman.* Berkley: University of California Press.

Margolis, J. (1984). The autographic nature of dance. In Sheets-Johnstone, M. (Ed.) (1984) *Illuminating dance: Philosophical explorations.* Bucknell University Press.

Martin, J. (1963). *John martin's book of the dance.* New York: Tudor Publishing Company.

Maslow, A. (1964). *Religions, values, and peak-experiences.* Ohio State University Press.

McCaw, D. (Ed.) (2011). *The laban sourcebook.* Routledge Taylor & Francis Group.

Meerloo, J. (1962). *Dance craze and sacred dance.* London: Peter Owen.

Newhall, M. (2009). *Mary wigman.* Routledge Taylor & Francis Group.

Newlove, J., Dalby, J., (2004). *Laban for all.* London: Nick Hern Books, Ltd.

Oesterley, W. (1923). *The sacred dance: A study in comparative folklore.* Cambridge at the University Press.

Palmer, P. (1993). *To know as we are known: Education as a spiritual journey.* San Francisco: Harpercollins.

Palmer, P. (2000). *Let your life speak: Listening for the voice of vocation.* San Francisco: Jossey-Bass Publishers.

Partsch-Bergsohn, I. (1994). *Modern dance in germany and the united states: Crosscurrents and influences.* Harwood Academic Publishers.

Partsch-Bergsohn, I., Bergsohn, H. (2003). *The makers of modern dance in germany: Rudolph laban, mary wigman, kurt joos.* Highstown, N.J. Princeton Book Co.

Randall, T. M. (2005). Hanya holm, community, and dance as "genuine folk culture". *Congress on research in dance.* Spring 2005 Conference.

Redfern, B. (1965). *Introducing laban art of movement.* MacDonald & Evens Ltd.

Ross, J. (2000b). *Moving lessons: Margaret h'doubler and the beginning of dance in American Education.* Madison, WI: University of Wisconsin Press.

Ross, J. (2007). *Anna halprin: Experience as dance*. The Regents of the University of California.
Russell, J. (1968). *Modern dance in education*. New York: Frederick A. Praegon.
Sachs, C. (1937). *World history of the dance*. New York: W.W. Norton & Company, Inc.
Sheets, M. (1966). *The phenomenology of dance*. The University of Wisconsin Press.
Sheets-Johnstone, M. (Ed.) (1984). *Illuminating dance: Philosophical explorations*. Associated University Presses.
Sheets-Johnstone, M. (Ed.) (1992). *Giving the body its due*. Albany: State University of New York Press.
Sheets-Johnstone, M. (1999). *The primacy of movement*. Amsterdam/Philadelphia: John Benjamins Publishing Company.
Snowber, C. (1997). Writing and the body. *Educational Insights, 4(1)*, on-line http://www.csci.educ.ubc.ca/publication/insights
Snowber, C.N. & Giard, M. (Spring 2003). Daring to dance our life. *Educational Insights* on-line http://www.csci.educ.ubc.ca/publication/insights.
Snowber, C. (2007). The soul moves: Dance spirituality in educative practice. In *International Handbook of Research in Arts Education*. Springer.
Snowber, C. (2009). The eros of listening: Dancing into presence. In *Landscapes of aesthetic education*. Cambridge Scholars Publishing.
Sorell, W. (1969). *Hanya holm: The biography of an artist*. Wesleyan University Press.
Sorell, W. (1975). *The mary wigman book: Her writings edited and translated by walter sorell*. Middletown, CT: Wesleyan University Press.
Sorell, W. (Ed.) (1992). *The dance has many faces*. A cappella books.
St. Denis, R. (1992). Religious manifestations in the dance. In Sorell, W. (Ed.) *Dance has many faces*. a cappella books.
Stebbins, G. (1885, 1902). *The delsarte system of expression*. Published by E.S. Werner, New York.
Sultanova, R. (2011). *From shamanism to sufism: Women, islam, and culture in central asia*. I. B. Taurus & Co. Ltd.
Tagore, R. (1979, 2005). *Farewell my friend/the garden*. Jaico Publishing House.
Tagore, R. "Dance My Heart." *Tagoreweb*, https://www.tagoreweb.in/Verses/one-hundred-poems-of-kabir-202/dance-my-heart-3885, 16 April 2019.

"The Roaring Twenties." *Wikipedia*, Wikimedia Foundation, (9 September 2019) https://en.wikipedia.org/wiki/Roaring_Twenties.

Toepfer, K. (1997). *Empire of ecstasy: Nudity and movement in german body culture 1910–1935*. Berkeley: University of California Press.

"Unitarian Universalists," *Wikipedia*, Wikimedia Foundation, (17 August 2019). https://en.wikipedia.org/wiki/Unitarian_Universalism.

Venkatachalan, G. (1947). *Dance in india*. Bombay: Nalanda Publications.

Vertinsky, P. (2004). Schooling the dance: From swastika to movement education in the british school. *Journal Of Sport History*. Fall 2004.

Vigier, R. (1994). *Gestures of genius: Women, dance and the body*. Stratford, Ontario: The Mercury Press.

Vij, S. (2003). *Borders and boundaries in partition literature*. A paper presented on 12 September 2003. BA English I, St. Stephenís College, University of Delhi. http://www.sacw.net/partition/SVij092003.html

Wigman, M. (1966). *The language of dance*. Wesleyan University Press: Middletown, Connecticut.

Winearls, J. (1958). *Modern dance: the jooss-leeder method*. London: Adam and Charles Black.

Winton-Henry, C. (2009). *Dance - The sacred art: The joy of movement as a spiritual practice*. Skylight Paths.

Wyman, M. (1992). Max wyman's notebook: *Vancouver Sun newspaper*, April, 1992.

Worth, L., Poynor, H. (2004). *Anna halprin*. Routledge, Taylor & Francis Group.

References

Photo credit: Kalli Paakspuu.

Photo credit: Rhea Verge.

ABOUT THE AUTHOR

Karen McKinlay Kurnaedy lives in Port Coquitlam, British Columbia. She is a dancer, writer, and educator. She began her dance training in the 1960s at The Hanova School of Modern Studies in Body Sculpture and the Classical Dance, the first modern dance school in Vancouver, where she was forever imbued with the spirit of Duncan, Dalcroze, Laban, Wigman, and Menaka.

Karen's work as a writer includes publishing several essays, articles, and books about dance and dance education. Karen received her Bachelor of Education with distinction from the University of Alberta and also earned a Master of Arts and a Doctorate in Philosophy from Simon Fraser University. Her teaching experience includes thirty years in the Coquitlam School District, as well as being a Faculty Associate and instructing in the Graduate Diploma program at Simon Fraser University. Her interests lie in fostering an appreciation for all of the arts and promoting dance, dance education, and dance history.